D1231371

What differences do welfare state variations make for women? How do women and men fare in different welfare states? In the first truly comparative book on this topic, Diane Sainsbury answers these questions by analyzing the situation in countries whose welfare state policies differ in significant ways: the United States, Britain, Sweden, and the Netherlands. Building on feminist criticisms of mainstream research, Professor Sainsbury reconceptualizes the crucial dimensions of welfare state variation and identifies those relevant to gender. She uses this framework to determine the extent to which legislation reflects and perpetuates the gendered division of labor in the family and society, as well as what types of policy alter gender relations in social provision. The application of the framework calls attention to the importance of distinguishing between women's entitlements as wives and as mothers, in contrast to previous analysis which has generally conflated women's social rights based on wifely and motherly labor. It also underlines the need to examine the social rights of both women and men in order to move toward greater equality.

Diane Sainsbury tracks policy changes from the late 1960s to the present day and evaluates the impact of gender equality reforms to show which reforms work and which do not. She increases our understanding of how policy mechanisms, especially the bases of entitlement, exclude or incorporate women, and offers constructive proposals for securing greater equality of the sexes.

Gender, equality, and welfare states

Gender, equality, and welfare states

Diane Sainsbury

University of Stockholm

Published by the Press Syndicate of the University of Cambridge
The Pitt Building, Trumpington Street, Cambridge CB2 1RP
40 West 20th Street, New York, NY 10011-4211, USA
10 Stamford Road, Oakleigh, Melbourne 3166, Australia

First published 1996

Printed in Great Britain at the University Press, Cambridge

A catalogue record for this book is available from the British Library

Library of Congress cataloguing in publication data

ISBN 0 521 56277 5 hardback
ISBN 0 521 56579 0 paperback

SE

To Robert Brewster

Contents

List of figures

List of tables

Acknowledgments

This book grew out of a paper "Welfare state variations, women and equality," written for a workshop on Equality Principles and Gender Politics at the 1989 Joint Sessions of the European Consortium of Political Research (ECPR). In the process of writing the paper and discovering crucial cross-national differences in the impact of welfare state policies on women and men, I realized that this topic merited a book. Accordingly, I initially wish to thank the two organizers of the workshop – Elizabeth Meehan and Selma Sevenhuijsen – and the other participants, especially Jet Bussemaker. After the workshop she sent me materials on Dutch women which strengthened my conviction that the inclusion of the Netherlands in my choice of countries was extremely fortunate. Also vital in the early stages of the project and throughout its development has been the support of Maud Eduards and Anne Marie Berggren, who believed in the importance of this research.

Many associates and students have commented on various sections of the manuscript, and their comments have been invaluable. In particular, two forums played a key role in shaping and testing my ideas. The first was an ECPR workshop on Welfare States and Gender in 1993. The second was the Crossing Borders conference in Stockholm in 1994, organized by Barbara Hobson, which was truly a memorable event. I also owe a major debt of gratitude to Dutch colleagues for filling in the gaps in my knowledge of social policy in the Netherlands, and especially to: Marry Neiphuis-Nell at the Netherlands Social and Cultural Planning Office; Siv Gustafsson, Hettie Pott-Buter, and Susan van Velzen, members of the Gender and Comparative Economics Seminar at the University of Amsterdam; and Jantine Oldersma and Riki Holtmaat at the University of Leiden. The publisher's two referees offered several useful suggestions.

I am deeply grateful for the financial assistance that made implementation of the project possible. Grants from the Swedish Council for Research in the Humanities and Social Sciences (HSFR) and from the Swedish Council for Planning and Coordination of Research (FRN) provided generous support to initiate the project. A Nordic mobility grant in 1992 allowed me to visit the London School of Economics and Political Science where I did most of the research on retrenchment in Britain. Gordon Smith, John Madeley, and Jane Lewis were extremely helpful during my stay, and at a later stage Hilary Land was a source of thoughtful advice. A fellowship at the Swedish Collegium for Advanced Study in Social Sciences (SCASSS) in Uppsala during the spring of 1995 provided the ideal environment to complete the book, and my thanks go to the directors of SCASSS – Björn Wittrock, Bo Gustafsson, and Wlodzimierz Rabinowicz – and the helpful staff. Most of all, however, I thank my significant other, Robert Brewster, to whom this book is dedicated.

Introduction

Until the mid-1970s conceptions and studies of the welfare state largely revolved around a generic notion with little emphasis on types of welfare state. However, within the span of a few years, three works (Titmuss 1974, Mishra 1977, Furniss and Tilton 1977) containing the first efforts at constructing typologies of welfare provision initiated a trend of underlining the importance of welfare state variations. Although exceptions exist, comparative studies of welfare states and social policies have scarcely touched upon the issue of the consequences of different welfare states and social policies for women. As in many areas of social inquiry, the gender dimension has been conspicuously missing in mainstream typologies of welfare states and comparative analyses. These studies tell us little about the impact of the welfare state on women and men or the differences in impact, and they have largely ignored the disparities in welfare provision between the sexes.

On the other hand, feminist scholarship adopting a critical perspective has dealt extensively with women and social policy and underscored gender inequalities in the public provision of welfare (e.g. Lewis 1983, Baldock and Cass 1983, Ungerson 1985, Nelson 1984, Glendinning and Millar 1987, 1992, Gordon 1990). However, these studies have been set in the specific context of one country and have inadvertently reinforced a generic view of both the state and the welfare state. This tendency was also strengthened by a major current in feminist theory which views the state as an epiphenomenon of patriarchy, thus ruling out both significant variations between specific states and the possibility of variations that might be beneficial to women. Furthermore, the specific contexts of these policy studies were overwhelmingly the – English speaking countries. The concentration on the experiences of these countries led to the assumption that they were representative, and feminists dealing with other countries often adopted these assumptions in their analyses.

Gradually, however, feminists began to consider the implications of different state formations for women and to draw on the experiences of a variety of countries (Sassoon 1987, Hernes 1987, Dominelli 1991, Langan and Ostner 1991, Lewis and Ostner 1991, 1995, Lewis 1992a, Sainsbury 1994. Cf. Randall 1982, Ruggie 1984). Similarly, comparativists have started to refer to the family, women, and gender (e.g. Esping-Andersen 1990, Schmidt 1993, Ginsburg 1992, Kolberg 1991). Despite these signs of convergence between mainstream research on welfare state variations and feminist analysis, there is a dearth of systematic comparisons to illuminate the possible implications of different welfare states for women. Thus an underlying theoretical aim of this study is, first, to confront these two bodies of literature in their analyses of the welfare state in an effort to reveal the shortcomings of each and, second, to combine their insights in order to transcend their limitations.

The main empirical concern of this book is to examine the impact of welfare states on women by focusing on variations. Put in the simplest of terms the question is: what differences do welfare state variations make for women? In exploring this question it is important to examine countries that represent a broad array of variations – and especially to move beyond comparisons of the English-speaking countries. Accordingly, the analysis here deals with the United States, the United Kingdom, Sweden and the Netherlands whose welfare states, as we shall see, differ in significant ways.

It is important to include countries which have similarities as well as differences in order to identify the source of inequalities. The UK and the Scandinavian countries, for example, are often bracketed together because of their greater emphasis on universalism and social citizenship compared to the welfare states on the continent. Universalism and social citizenship are manifested in unified programs covering the entire population, with considerable funding through taxation. On the other hand, Mary Ruggie in her book *The State and Working Women* challenges the image of commonality between the British and Swedish welfare states with respect to how women fare. In her analysis, she focuses on state–society relationships as the crucial factor in determining positive outcomes for women. In addition to this difference and other possible variations between the two welfare states, however, it is necessary to unpack the notions of universalism and social citizenship and to compare what they mean in theory and practice in the two countries. This task is all the more necessary since these concepts are intimately associated with the post-World War II British welfare state, and our understanding of them is heavily influenced by British experience and welfare state thinking.

The selection of the Netherlands has been primarily predicated by the desire to include a welfare state of the continental variety. In addition, the "pillarization" of Dutch society – its organization into separate segments based on religious or political beliefs – although in the process of eroding, and the pivotal role of a Catholic party as consistently a party of government, set the Netherlands apart from the other countries. At the same time it is also viewed as sharing features of the Scandinavian welfare states, especially in having an ambitious level of welfare provision, as evidenced in heavy social expenditure. In analyses using a variety of quantitative indicators, the Netherlands and Scandinavia generally rank among the top countries (Wilensky 1975, 1976, Castles 1978, Heidenheimer et al. 1983, 1990, Therborn 1989, Esping-Andersen 1990). Intuitively, one might think that large-scale public involvement in welfare provision would automatically benefit women more than minimal intercessions. Yet as this book unfolds, it will become clear that this is not necessarily the case.

On several counts, the United States deviates significantly from the other three countries. Major social policy programs, such as sickness benefits, national medical insurance covering the entire population, and family allowances are non-existent, and social spending lags behind that of many nations. Further contrasts include the stronger role of the market in social provision through private insurance and employer sponsored schemes, along with the diversity of programs and benefit levels produced by a federal system.

Before proceeding to outline the broad contours of this book, two additional comments are in order. First, the comparative thrust of the analysis here differs from the more conventional approach of country by country descriptions. Instead the focal point is welfare state variations, and the comparisons are organized around dimensions of variation. Second, in assessing cross-national policy variations and their effects, one common procedure has been the "profile" approach based on model or typical recipients (Bolderson 1988). This approach emphasizes the nature of legislative provisions and examines their effects for model or hypothetical recipients, such as the average single or married production worker (OECD 1984b, Palme 1990a, b, Wennemo 1994, Korpi and Palme, forthcoming) or family types (Heclo and Cockburn 1974, Heidenheimer et al. 1975, Adams and Winston 1980, Kahn and Kamerman 1983, Bradshaw et al. 1993). Although useful in demonstrating the possible differing consequences of dissimilar policy constructions, this approach is marred in two ways. By utilizing model recipients with assumed characteristics rather than real beneficiaries, the approach produces an analysis of how social programs could or should operate but not necessarily how they actually function (see Shaver and Bradshaw 1993). An additional difficulty is that the hypothetical characteristics of the model beneficiaries may not be very representative of recipient populations, and in comparative research these characteristics can vary a great deal across countries and over time.[1] To avoid these difficulties, the analysis in this book as far as possible is based on real recipients and the actual distribution of benefits. It primarily employs data from official national statistics, special surveys both national and international, for example the Luxemburg Income Study, and international compilations of statistics from the OECD and the European Communities.

The structure of the book

The first chapter of this book provides the reader with an overview of the main features of social provision in the four countries. It maps out the major similarities and differences between the four welfare states and clarifies their distinctive aspects. The key dimensions of variation used to analyze the four countries are borrowed from the mainstream literature on types of welfare state and models of social policy. However, since most of this literature on welfare state variations has paid little attention to gender, chapter 1 offers few insights as to dissimilar outcomes for women and men or what sorts of variations are important for women.

Chapter 2 seeks to rectify this defect of mainstream analysis of welfare states. It begins by examining the contributions of feminist scholarship on the welfare state and suggests an alternative framework of analysis which is gender relevant. As in chapter 1 the emphasis is on dimensions of variations but in this instance they are gleaned from feminist literature. Drawing upon feminist criticisms of mainstream research, a number of dimensions of variations are identified. As a heuristic device, these dimensions are presented as contrasting ideal types: the male breadwinner and individual models of social policy. Rather than attempt to build the gender dimension into existing mainstream typologies, the strategy behind this framework has been to highlight gender separately. By isolating dimensions of variation related to gender it is possible to examine the interaction between these dimensions and the welfare state variations designated as important by mainstream analysis. The alternative strategy of merging feminist and mainstream perspectives into ideal types or policy regimes makes it more difficult to illuminate the effects of each perspective.

In the next three chapters the focus of analysis shifts to policy variations and their impact on women. An underlying theme tying the chapters together is women's bases of entitlement. An important element of this book's synthesis of mainstream and feminist analysis is to address a broader spectrum of principles of entitlement than either perspective has done, and to discuss the implications for women's and men's social rights. I argue that the bases of entitlement are decisive in determining whether welfare state policies reinforce women's dependency or enhance their autonomy. The criteria for evaluating women's social rights are whether they afford a socially acceptable standard of living independently of family relationships.

Chapter 3 centers on women's social rights as wives – or women's entitlements via their husbands' rights. At issue in this chapter is the extent and manner in which the male breadwinner model has been reflected in the legislation of the four countries. In other words, to what degree has the breadwinner model been a welfare state variation? Chapter 4 concentrates on women's entitlements as mothers and caregivers – and the importance of the principle of care in eroding the principle of maintenance. It documents how benefits based on motherhood and the principle of care can alter the boundary between public and private responsibility setting in motion a new dynamic of interdependence between the private and public spheres. Chapter 5 looks at women's entitlements as workers. During the past three decades women have entered into the labor market in unprecedented numbers. To what extent has their labor market participation been translated into entitlements altering their social rights? In particular, have rights conferred by labor market status enhanced women's autonomy in family relationships?

The next two chapters summarize women's incorporation as beneficiaries of social policies and compare their entitlements to those of men. If the analysis were to focus on women, as in the previous three chapters, we could only comment on the differences between women in the various countries, but not necessarily on dissimilarities in gender inequalities across welfare states. For example, women may fare better in one welfare state than in another but men may also fare better in that particular welfare state so that extent of inequalities between the sexes is similar or even greater than in the other welfare state.

Chapters 6 and 7 examine welfare states as systems of stratification and redistribution. Our central concern is the degree of inequality between women and men in social provision and distributional outcomes. In investigating these issues, Chapter 6 analyzes women's and men's access to social benefits, their utilization rates, and the importance of the bases of entitlement in patterning gender stratification. Chapter 7 turns to gender differences in benefit levels and redistributive outcomes of welfare states. These two chapters also allow us to establish the degree of gender inequalities across the four countries.

The final chapters of the book focus on welfare state restructuring during recent decades, and I use the models of social policy presented earlier to plot change over time. Taking 1970 as a benchmark, chapter 8 discusses gender equality reforms and their effects in altering women's individual entitlements and gender differentiation in social rights. This chapter offers a cross-national balance sheet of the achievements and shortcomings of reforms in order to suggest what works and what doesn't and why. It also indicates the extent to which the individual model of social policy has replaced the breadwinner model in the four countries in the mid-1990s.

Chapter 9 deals with welfare state retrenchment, comparing policy responses during the 1980s and 1990s. Sections of the analysis in the earlier chapters utilize data from around 1980 – a period which many observers regard as a turning point in welfare state development. Although cuts were introduced during the 1970s, social legislation for the decade as a whole extended entitlements and improved benefits in the four countries. By the early 1980s, however, many governments had called for a major overhaul of social provision in the belief that the welfare state was the problem – not the solution. Chapter 9 considers the nature of retrenchment, the extent of restructuring, and how these policy changes have affected women's and men's entitlements since 1980.

In summary, a theoretical aim, an empirical goal, and a normative purpose have guided the writing of this book. The theoretical aim is to add to our understanding of types of welfare states and to reconceptualize the dimensions of variation used to analyze welfare states by explicitly incorporating gender. This task consists of identifying gender relevant dimensions of variation and analyzing their interaction with welfare state variations designated as important by mainstream research. In effect, this project calls for a synthesis of the insights of feminist and mainstream thinking on welfare states. The empirical goal is to chart the major welfare state variations and to systematically compare policies and their impact on women and men. The prescriptive objective is to increase our knowledge of how policy mechanisms exclude and incorporate women so that constructive proposals can be made in order to secure greater equality between women and men. Central to this objective is a cross-national evaluation of proposed remedies *to shed light on which gender equality reforms work and which do not.*

Part I

Dimensions of variation

1   Mainstream welfare state variations

During the past two decades mainstream scholarship on the welfare state has been characterized by a growing interest in comparing welfare states and social policies in an effort to distinguish between types of welfare state and to identify key dimensions of variation. This chapter addresses the issue of which dimensions of variation have been central to the comparative analysis of welfare states and social policy. Initially it looks at a number of important discussions on welfare state typologies and models of social policy in order to establish how dimensions of variation have been defined, and to flesh out the pros and cons of various approaches. My purpose is to construct a framework for comparison which is subsequently applied to the United States, the United Kingdom, the Netherlands, and Sweden. This comparison provides an initial understanding of the similarities, the range of differences, and the distinctive features of social provision in the four countries. It also sets in sharp relief the limitations of mainstream analysis of welfare state variations, which fails to shed much light on our major questions of investigation: what differences do welfare state variations make for women? And how similar or dissimilar is the impact of welfare state policies on women and men in the four countries?

Welfare state typologies and dimensions of variation

Four approaches have figured prominently in the mainstream discussion on types of welfare state and welfare state variations. The first examines specific countries with the purpose of describing their distinctive features (e.g. Furniss and Tilton 1977, Rainwater et al. 1986, Esping-Andersen and Korpi 1987, Davidson 1989). The second approach highlights major differences through the construction of analytical models based on two contrasting ideal types (Mishra 1977, 1984, Korpi 1980). The third approach utilizes two axes of variation in devising welfare state typologies (Jones 1985, Therborn and Roebroek 1986, Mishra 1990, Pierson 1991). The fourth approach relies on the clustering of attributes in determining welfare state variations (e.g. Kohl 1982) and more recently in distinguishing welfare state regimes (Esping-Andersen 1990, Castles and Mitchell 1990, 1992, 1993, Mitchell 1991, Siaroff 1994).

More specifically, the first approach starts with a particular country or set of countries and seeks to pinpoint the distinctive features of the welfare state/s in question. These distinctive features are then described as a particular type of welfare state, sometimes in general terms. Using this approach, Norman Furniss and Timothy Tilton, for example, outline three types: the positive state, the social security state, and the social welfare state. They construct these types by distinguishing between various forms of state intervention for different purposes. In particular, Furniss and Tilton emphasize the aims and goals of intervention, along with who benefits from a particular form of state intervention.

Several problematical aspects permeate the models, however. The first is that the dimensions of variation underlying the three types remain implicit. Nor is there any assurance that the defining properties of one particular type constitute a variable or dimension of variation pertaining to all types. Conversely, this approach's emphasis on the most salient distinctive features can easily obscure the fact that the same features exist in other welfare states but are less prominent. A final difficulty is the issue of broader applicability. As distinct from the ideal types of the second approach, which are essentially logico-analytical constructs, these models are basically inductive and extracted from the experiences of three specific countries: the United States, the United Kingdom, and Sweden respectively. How useful are they for understanding welfare states in other advanced industrial countries, say, the Netherlands, France, Italy, or Germany? Can the key features of the Dutch welfare state be analyzed with the aid of these models or must a fourth model be devised?

Basic to the second approach of model building is the use of polar ideal types. The distinction between residual and institutional welfare provision has been especially important in the construction of contrasting ideal types, although other distinctions have also been utilized (e.g. Mishra 1984). The residual type assumes that the family and market are the "natural" channels of welfare, and that only when these are malfunctioning should people rely on public welfare structures; and this reliance should be temporary and for emergencies only. By contrast, in the institutional type public welfare structures are an integral part of society, providing an organized system of social services on a regular and legitimate basis to aid individuals and groups to attain satisfying standards of life and health (Wilensky and Lebeaux 1958: 138–40). Building on this distinction, Richard Titmuss sketched the rough outlines of a typology of welfare provision involving three models of social policy: the residual model, the industrial achievement-performance model, and the institutional redistributive model. The major task of the residual welfare model is remedial but temporary aid because of the failure of other channels of welfare provision – the market and the family. In the case of the industrial achievement model the function is to provide a minimum standard of social security, and public provision of welfare largely complements the market economy. As indicated by its name the task of the third model is redistribution; and redistribution focuses on "command-over-resources through time" in order to achieve greater equality (Titmuss 1974: 30–1). Subsequently the residual–institutional distinction has been used to construct contrasting polar models, adding several new dimensions of variation (Mishra 1977, Korpi 1980). Among the dimensions included have been the range of statutory services and benefits, the level of social spending, the extent of coverage, benefit levels, the dominant type of program, the type of financing, the degree of social control, the ideology and agents of provision.

Models based on polar ideal types are useful in clarifying important distinctions, but a weakness of such models is that they limit the framework of analysis to two categories conceived as opposites. There are many instances when it may prove counterproductive or misleading to classify phenomena on the basis of only two categories (Sainsbury 1991, 1993a). For example, the key distinctions informing the models of Furniss and Tilton – the goals and aims of different forms of state intervention advantaging particular groups – are difficult to imagine as polar ideal types without serious oversimplifications. The diversity of the goals and aims of state intervention, the variety of its forms, and the wide range of potential beneficiaries make it necessary to weigh the advantages of formulating clear-cut distinctions against the drawbacks of conceptualizing complex phenomena in dualistic terms.

The third approach constructs typologies on the basis of two underlying axes of variation yielding four types of welfare state. Catherine Jones, for example, devises a typology where one axis consists of the level of spending and the other of the type of social policy (1985: 79–82). The second axis is a continuum with one end corresponding to the industrial achievement-performance of social policy and the other end to the institutional model. In other words, one version of this sort of typology uses roughly the same key concepts as the second approach but ends up with four types of welfare states instead of two (cf. Hadenius 1987). Another version of this sort of typology, suggested by Göran Therborn, introduces a new dimension of variation – policies to combat unemployment or the commitment to full employment. An axis distinguishing the degree of institutionalized full employment policies is combined with an axis of the degree of social security commitment as reflected in public spending (Therborn and

Roebroek 1986, Abrahamson 1991, Pierson 1991, Roebroek 1993). A final variant has combined an axis of the degree of collective responsibility for social security (institutional vs. residual) with an axis of the organization and delivery of services (centralized/state-centered vs. decentralized /pluralist) (Mishra 1990: 113). An advantage of this approach is that it allows for a larger number of types of welfare state than the second approach. However, for my purposes, this possible gain is offset because of the constraints imposed by assuming only two underlying dimensions of variation.

The final approach emphasizing the clustering of attributes has recently focused on the construction of welfare state regimes and policy regimes, and Gøsta Esping-Andersen's regime typology is representative of this approach. Using the quality of social rights as measured by decommodification (eliminating dependence on the market), the pattern of stratification resulting from welfare state policies, and the nature of the state–market nexus, he distinguishes between three regimes: the liberal market regime; the conservative, corporatist regime; and the social democratic regime. Very briefly, the liberal welfare state regime is characterized by heavy reliance on means tested programs, modest social insurance benefits, market solutions in the form of occupational welfare (employer sponsored benefits), and private insurance. In the conservative welfare state regime, social insurance schemes are central but they are differentiated according to class and status. Benefits are designed to maintain the status quo with respect to income distribution, class structure, and societal institutions – the state, the church, and the family. The social democratic regime is typified by universal benefits and services covering the entire population, a weakening of the influence of the market in distribution, and a strong commitment to full employment.

Esping-Andersen's typology captures major welfare state variations but the focus of his discussion is on differences between the regimes which are pure types. His analysis highlights the similarities of countries clustering in the same regime but does not indicate how individual countries deviate from the regime. In other words, he underlines differences between clusters of welfare states but without clarifying differences between individual welfare states.

Equally troublesome, the categorization of particular countries as a type of regime is open to question, and the classification of two of our countries – the Netherlands and the UK – raises serious doubts. On the basis of his cluster analyses, Esping-Andersen classifies the Netherlands as a social democratic regime, but there is considerable ambiguity in the country's scores. Although measures of Dutch policy located it in the strong socialist cluster, the Netherlands also ranked relatively high on measures of liber-

Table 1.1 *Dimensions of variation of the residual and institutional models of social policy*

Dimension	Residual model	Institutional model
Proportion of national income devoted to social purposes	Low	High
Level of benefits	Meager	Adequate
Range of statutory services and benefits	Limited	Extensive
Population covered	Minority	Majority
Dominant type of program	Selective	Universal
Importance of programs preventing needs	Non-existent	Substantial
Commitment to full employment	Secondary	Primary
Type of financing	Contributions/fees	Taxation
Role of private organizations	Large	Small
Ideology of state intervention	Minimal	Optimal
Need based distribution as a value (ideology of distribution)	Marginal	Secondary

Source: Adapted from Mishra 1977: 91, Korpi 1980: 303.

alism and conservatism. Considering the strong elements of universalism in the British welfare state, many observers reject the categorization of the UK as a liberal market regime. Nor are Esping-Andersen's index scores for the UK especially convincing, since they do not put the country in the strong liberal cluster. Even the Netherlands has a higher score on degree of liberalism than the UK (Esping-Andersen 1990: 74). To get at the nature of these anomalies and the actual differences between welfare states, we must revert to the attributes and variations prior to their clustering and conversion into index scores.[1]

Since a major concern of this book is to understand the implications of different types of welfare state for women, a prerequisite is to determine the nature of welfare state variations between the four countries. The decisive criterion in choosing from the existing approaches is that it provides an analytical framework that maximizes the possibilities of investigating and comparing variations. Accordingly I have taken contrasting ideal types based on the residual–institutional distinction as a point of departure. A key asset of this approach is its specification of several crucial dimensions of variation and the possibility of adding others. Table 1.1 combines and sums up these dimensions.

In earlier discussions, these models have been primarily presented to clarify analytical distinctions, and there appears to have been little attempt to apply these models in empirical comparative analysis, although individual dimensions, especially those lending themselves to quantifiable measures – such as social spending as a percentage of the GDP, level of benefits, and coverage of the population – have been utilized. The models have also been loosely applied in descriptions of individual countries (Esping-Andersen and Korpi 1987, Kuhnle and Selle 1989).

Welfare state variations: the USA, the UK, the Netherlands, and Sweden

To determine the welfare state variations of the four countries, this analysis uses the dimensions of variation presented in table 1.1. Its main purpose is to delineate the similarities and differences between the countries, not to classify the countries as either residual or institutional types of welfare states. However, the analysis does clarify the degree of fit and how the countries deviate from the residual and institutional models and Esping-Andersen's three welfare state regimes. The period of comparison focuses on the early 1980s – before the introduction of the major retrenchment measures of that decade.

Proportion of national income devoted to social purposes

The proportion of public resources earmarked for social purposes provides some initial indication of the extent of a country's commitment to the welfare of its citizens.[2] The four countries differ sharply with respect to the share of resources allocated to social purposes. Sweden and the Netherlands ranked as top spenders, devoting around 40 percent of their gross domestic product to welfare expenditures, defined in a broad sense, as made clear in table 1.2, whereas the USA and the UK were located at the other end of the scale utilizing between roughly 20 and 25 percent of their GDP for these purposes.

Level of benefits

Again Sweden and the Netherlands tended to cluster together, providing more adequate benefits than either the UK or the USA. For example, in table 1.2 sickness benefits comprised around 2.5 percent of the GDP in the Sweden and the Netherlands. In Sweden sickness benefits were equivalent to 90 percent of a person's daily wage or salary up to a certain ceiling, and in the Netherlands the figure was 80 percent in the early 1980s (Roebroek and Berben 1987: 682). By contrast, British sickness benefits amounted to roughly a scant 20 percent of the average wage, although supplements

Table 1.2 *Social expenditures as a percentage of the GDP by purpose*[a]

	USA (1980)	UK (1980)	Netherlands (1983)	Sweden (1981)
Total social spending	21.7	26.6	40.4	40.2
Purpose				
Pensions	8.5	8.9	13.3	11.8
Health and medical care	4.1	5.2	6.5	8.7
Sickness benefits	na	0.3	2.7	2.5
Unemployment/employment policy	0.6	1.5	4.9	2.0
Social assistance	2.8	1.0	2.2	0.2
Family policy	na	1.7	2.3	4.4
Education	5.7	5.5	7.2	7.1
Housing	na	2.5	1.3	3.5

Notes:
[a] For definitions of the expenditures included in the various categories, see table 1.3.

The figures for the UK, the Netherlands and Sweden in this table are compiled and in some cases recalculated from data in the institutional synopses and tables in Flora, 1987 (i.e. Parry 1987, Roebroek and Berben 1987 and Olsson 1987). Recalculations have been necessary to achieve greater comparability. For example, in the chapter on Sweden invalidity pensions have been included under pensions, whereas in the chapters on the Netherlands and the UK they are included under health and sickness benefits. Furthermore, the Swedish chapter reports the same expenditures under different functions or purposes, e.g. housing allowances for the elderly are included under pensions and housing, but not in the above table (here they are placed under housing). Despite these efforts, inequivalencies no doubt remain and the figures should be regarded as approximate.

The data presented here diverge substantially from other contemporary comparative analyses based on OECD and ILO statistics. Among the important differences are spending on family policy and social assistance. For example, a study by O'Higgins (1988) suggests a higher level of spending for the Netherlands (2.1 percent of the GDP) and similar levels for the UK and Sweden (1.6 percent). However, his analysis is limited to transfers, whereas this table includes expenditures on services. In Sweden spending on public day care exceeds that for transfers, and thus largely accounts for the difference. With respect to the second major divergence, Gordon's (1988) analysis of social assistance presents higher figures for Sweden in this area (5.2 percent of the GDP in 1979–80 based on ILO statistics and 2.9 percent in 1980 based on OECD data) which reflect broader definitions of public assistance.

Sources: For the USA, OECD 1985a: 85, *Statistical Abstract of the United States* 1989; for the UK, Parry 1987, *Social Trends* 1982: 59, 1986: 132, DHSS 1981: 232; for the Netherlands, Roebroek and Berben 1987, *Statistical Yearbook* 1984: 356–7, 1985: 117; and for Sweden, Olsson 1987, *Statistisk årsbok* 1982/83: 384–7, *Kommunernas finanser* 1981, SCB 1983b.

Table 1.3 *Components of social expenditure in table 1.2*

Pensions	Expenditures on old age, early retirement, disability and survivors benefits and services for the elderly. In contrast to OECD includes public employees' pensions.
Health and medical care	Expenditure on hospitals and clinics, medical, dental, and paramedical practitioners, public health, medical equipment, drugs and medicine, and other health related products, research and development
Sickness benefits	Expenditure on temporary sickness benefits or injury benefits
Unemployment benefits labor market policy	Expenditure on unemployment insurance and assistance and benefits to compensate for loss of income due to unemployment. Also includes expenditure on employment services, training programs, labor mobility allowances, sheltered employment schemes, etc.
Social assistance	Expenditure on major means tested programs
Family policy	Cash benefits such as family allowance, maternity or parental benefits, and one parent benefits. Also includes benefits in kind such as school meals and public day care
Education	Current expenditure for educational system and related services plus student financial support
Housing	Expenditure on housing subsidies and rent allowances but not tax expenditures
Total social spending	The total of the eight categories listed above

could double the percentage (Parry 1987: 365). In the USA there is no public provision of sickness benefits for short-term illness. For pensions, family benefits, unemployment compensation, and disability benefits the picture is much the same. Further evidence of the inadequacy of benefits is exhibited in the poverty rates among various groups of social policy beneficiaries, such as pensioners and single mothers in the USA and the UK (Smeeding et al. 1990: 67).

Range of statutory benefits and services

On this dimension the United States and Sweden appear as polar opposites. The US social policy system is generally less complete than those of other welfare states. Most obvious is the lack of sickness benefits, a national health insurance covering the entire population, the absence of family policy measures, such as general family allowances or maternity allowances, and a parsimonious public housing policy. To some extent the major gaps in social protection show up in Table 1.2, which presents the percentage of the GDP allocated to total social expenditures and spending by purpose. On the other hand, Sweden stands out in terms of the variety of policy areas to which substantial resources were allocated, and Swedish spending on health services, family policy, and housing outstripped that of the other countries.

Nevertheless it is on this dimension that a clear-cut pattern between the countries starts to become blurred. At first glance, the Netherlands, largely because of its higher levels of spending, seems the most likely candidate for second place on this dimension, too. In one respect, however, the pattern of British spending challenges such a conclusion. The UK put a good deal more resources into public housing than the Netherlands.

One problem here concerns the conceptualization of this dimension of variation. By including both cash transfers and services, this dimension conceals a crucial difference between welfare states. They differ considerably with respect to their reliance on transfers and the priority given to provision of services, as reflected in public consumption expenditures (excluding defense). In the Netherlands more resources have been devoted to transfer expenditures, whereas in Sweden and the UK public consumption figures indicate that provision of services has been favored (Kohl 1982: 312). In fact, confining the comparison to public consumption as a percentage of the GDP, we find Sweden at the top of the list, and the Netherlands near the bottom, and clearly below the OECD average in the early 1980s (Lybeck 1984: 61. Cf. OECD 1989: 38).

Coverage of the population

In all the countries the long-term trend has been toward a wider coverage of the population. Despite this trend, sizable variations in coverage characterize the four countries. In part, these variations are a reflection of the range of benefits and services as well as the extent to which policies are targeted to special groups. However, even looking at programs common to all four countries – such as income maintenance – we find substantial differences. In most countries income maintenance programs (pensions, sickness benefits, and unemployment benefits) cover the labor force, and estimates of coverage are percentages of the labor force (cf. Heidenheimer 1982: 295, Heidenheimer et al. 1983: 219, Zarf 1986: 128). A less common estimate is coverage in terms of the entire population, yet this sort of measure points up a major welfare state variation. In Sweden the basic pension, disability benefits, parental benefits, and an unemployment cash allowance have covered groups outside the labor force, although benefits are set at a lower level than those of the workforce except in the case of the basic old age and disability pension.

Dominant type of program

It is no easy task trying to fit the programs in the four countries into the categories of "selective" versus "universal" for two very different reasons: the complexity of reality and the ambiguities built into the categories. First, the sheer diversity of the programs, which have incrementally evolved since the turn of the century, does not lend itself to classification into two broad categories. Second, the categories themselves are not as clear cut as they may appear at first glance.

On the one hand, "selective" is a notoriously wide category. It may be interpreted as targeted measures or as measures not covering the entire population. Accordingly, this category can include as diverse programs as means tested measures and social insurance programs limited to employees. On the other hand, "universal" programs are equally fraught with ambiguities, and at least four different meanings – not always distinguished from one another – are associated with universalism. They are: compulsory legislation rather than voluntary arrangements; entitlement applying to the entire population irrespective of the individual's financial needs or income; "equal" benefits or in principle "equal" access to services; and a uniform and integrated scheme of benefits rather than diverse programs tailored to specific groups (Sainsbury 1988: 339).

In any event, universal non-contributory programs are conspicuous by their near absence in the United States. Only in the areas of primary and secondary education does a universalist approach exist. Otherwise programs are either targeted to the needy or they are earnings related, as in the case of social insurance legislation. Public services – hospitals, housing, and employment programs – frequently cater to welfare clientele groups.

The dominant type of program in the Netherlands has been selective in the sense that many programs were tied to occupation, sector of employment, branch of industry and/or enterprise. Furthermore, in the past (until the mid-1960s) compulsory programs were often limited to groups under a certain income – and this was still the case for employee health insurance providing medical benefits in the mid-1990s. Family allowances – typically and historically a universal program in the UK and Scandinavia – followed the continental pattern and were differentiated until consolidated by legislation in 1980. Previously one set of provisions existed for wage earners, another for the self-employed, a third for public employees, and a fourth for residents (Roebroek and Berben 1987: 690–2). In many areas the trend has been toward consolidation and uniform programs covering all residents. Or, as the trend has been aptly described, the Beveridge approach (programs aimed at the entire population and administered by state institutions) has supplanted the earlier reliance on a Bismarckian solution (programs for wage earners to replace loss of income, financed by employees and employers and administered by corporatist bodies) (Roebroek 1989: 148–9, Cox 1993). However, fragmentation and complexity still exist. These fragmented and particularistic programs are hardly in accord with the ideal of uniform benefits inherent in universalism. Despite this, the Dutch welfare state has approximated the universal ideal in terms of coverage of the population and standardization of benefit levels.

In comparison with the Netherlands, the UK through its national insurance scheme has had a more unified system of social security benefits, which applies to the entire labor force and their dependants. Payment of these benefits is, however, contingent upon past contributions. Furthermore, a unique characteristic of most programs has been the provision of flat rate benefits. Non-contributory universal programs are primarily limited to family allowances (now child benefit), some benefits for the disabled, and the national health service. Selective measures in the sense of means tested programs have also been characterized by a unified national administration, and in the early 1980s they constituted a relatively small portion of income maintenance programs (in terms of spending around 13 percent) (Parry 1987: 359). Assistance programs are aimed at individuals and families without adequate resources or insurance benefits.

In several respects, the universalist thrust is stronger in Swedish social policy. First, citizenship or residence is the basis of entitlement to numerous benefits, and universal non-contributory benefits are more prevalent than in the UK. Second, a unified system applies to a wide range of benefits. For example, Sweden is one of the few countries with a uniform compulsory state program of occupational pensions which covers the entire labor force (until 1982 the self-employed could opt out, however). Third, public services are widespread and based on the principle of equal access. The universalism of the Swedish welfare state has distinguished it from that of the other countries. Nonetheless, universalism has been complemented by selective measures and extensive earnings related programs, and universal programs with respect to cash transfers were less dominant in the 1980s than they had been two decades previously (Nasenius and Veit-Wilson 1985: 146, Olsson 1986: 7–12).

Importance of programs preventing need

Table 1.2 also discloses a striking contrast between Sweden and the other three countries with respect to spending on social assistance – on "welfare" in the narrow sense of the word. In this area Sweden spent an infinitesimal amount of its GDP – 0.2 percent – whereas spending on social assistance ranged from 1.2 percent to 2.8 percent of GDP for the other three countries. (Spending in the Netherlands and the UK is actually larger since social assistance paid to unemployed persons without insurance benefits or those who have exhausted them has been included under unemployment.) In large measure, the low level of spending in the Swedish case is because programs in other policy areas provide benefits and reduce the necessity of resorting to public assistance. For example, income tested housing allowances are available to ensure that low income groups have access to high quality housing. Perhaps the best illustration of programs preventing need are in the area of employment policy (see Esping-Andersen and Korpi 1987: 56–7).

Commitment to full employment

Although governments in the countries have professed full employment as an aspiration, there are striking differences in their efforts to secure this goal. On this dimension of variation Sweden is set apart by assigning priority to active manpower policy – training, job placement services, and job creation schemes – rather than passive measures like unemployment compensation. The priority given to active measures has been coined as the work approach or the work principle (*arbetslinje*) (Heclo 1974, Sainsbury 1993b). In accordance with this principle, only around one-fourth of Swedish appropriations in this policy area was spent on unemployment benefits and three-fourths were devoted to active manpower measures in 1980. The spending pattern was the reverse for the other countries, and by virtue of its high expenditures on unemployment compensation the Netherlands appears as the polar opposite of Sweden (see table 1.2). The USA, owing to its negligible manpower measures and meager unemployment benefits, stands out in contrast to Sweden and the Netherlands (Flora 1987: 17, 685–8, 725. Cf. Therborn 1989: 233 and OECD 1989: 42, 103, Janoski 1990: 3).

The impact of Sweden's work approach can be observed in its low unemployment rates and growing labor participation rates during the 1970s and 1980s. Without active manpower measures the rate of unemployment would have been nearly 6 percent instead of 2.5 percent during the 1973 economic slump (Johannesson and Schmid 1980: 401–2) and around 9 percent instead of 4 percent at the height of the recession in the early 1980s (Therborn 1989: 228–35). Low unemployment rates have been accompanied by a steady increase in the labor force as a proportion of the population. In 1980 the Swedish labor market participation rate was nearly 80 percent, compared to the British rate of 70 percent, the US rate of 67 percent, and the Dutch rate of 54 percent (OECD 1984a: 15).[3] Again the Netherlands and Sweden appear as polar opposites. Swedish policies have facilitated entry into the labor market, whereas Dutch policies – not merely unemployment compensation but also disability benefits and the lack of training programs for the regular workforce – have not encouraged people to enter the labor market and have allowed them to exit.

Type of financing

Of the four countries the Netherlands has relied most heavily on the social insurance model which entails contributions and fees. Funding of income maintenance programs is overwhelmingly through contributions by employees and employers. Even family allowances have been based on the insurance principle. Similarly, health services have been largely financed as "fees for services" through an extensive medical insurance system, and private expenditures figured more prominently in Dutch health care than in Sweden and the UK, although less than in the USA (Jones 1985: 147, 150). Contributions by insured persons constitute the lion's share of social security receipts, and contributions are earnings related. Government funding of social security programs through taxation has been primarily limited to social assistance, extended employment benefits, housing subsidies and allowances, exceptional medical expenses, and most recently family allowances (Roebroek and Berben 1987: 688, 905, 703, SZW 1990: 46).

At the other extreme is Sweden, where the contributions of insured persons, as a share of social security receipts, fell during the 1960s and 1970s, amounting to a mere 1 percent in the early 1980s. By contrast, the employers' share increased over the years, jumping sharply in the early 1960s and again in the mid-1970s (Olsson 1987: 53). Uniquely, at least in relation to our other countries, employers funded non-contributory programs, such as the basic pension, national dental insurance, and the labor market allowance, which were available to persons without unemployment insurance and even to persons without labor force status. Funding by employers did not take the form of contributions earmarked for employees but was more in the form of a general payroll tax. Looking at total social expenditure, taxes accounted for nearly 85 percent of the revenue.

Both the UK and the USA were hybrids as far as financing is concerned. Taking the British case first, the national insurance scheme was funded primarily by the contributions of employers and employees with a small part (20 percent) coming from government subsidies in the early 1980s (Parry 1987: 359). Non-contributory benefits are financed through taxation. Taken as a whole, slightly over half of income maintenance expenditures were financed by contributions. However, social spending was overwhelmingly financed by taxation. Contributions only amounted to approximately

25 percent of total social expenditure, whereas in the Netherlands contributions comprised nearly 50 percent. In the US case, social insurance is also essentially financed through the contributions of employees and employers. Funding through the contributions plays a greater role than in the UK because US social insurance constitutes a larger proportion of social expenditures.

The role of private organizations

One of the fundamental differences between welfare states is what has been called "stateness" (Flora 1986b: xvii), that is, the degree of state involvement in welfare provision. To some extent, the role of private organizations can be seen as an inverse measure of stateness. According to Peter Flora, the major implication of stateness is that involvement of the state circumscribes or delimits the arenas of activity for private organizations. An inherent difficulty in this conceptualization, however, is its global and residual nature; it leaves open all manner of diversity.

In attempting to sort out this diversity, we need to distinguish, first, between welfare provision as social benefits and as services, and second, between types of private organization – economic enterprises (to which Flora does not allude in his discussion), religious institutions, ethnic associations, and voluntary organizations or networks. On the basis of these distinctions we can identify basic patterns or tendencies. Looking initially at the provision of benefits and private organizations, three variants are especially important. The first is the extent to which enterprises provide benefits for their employees in the form of occupational welfare. The second variant, which might be termed corporatist welfare, is where the organizations of employers and employees are jointly engaged in the determination and administration of benefits. The third is altruistic welfare where charitable and voluntary organizations are prime agents in the dispersal of benefits or provision of services.

Occupational welfare is most pervasive in the USA. In areas where the US public system of social protection is incomplete or non-existent, employers and enterprises often provide benefits in connection with employment and as a means of attracting desirable labor. One telling illustration and contrast with Europe is the lack of legislated paid vacations. Instead, individual employers and enterprises decide vacation benefits. Similarly, sickness and medical benefits are frequently fringe benefits related to employment. The end result is fragmentation, partial coverage, and enormous inequalities in the provision of benefits – with occupational welfare tending to conform to the pattern of market distribution. Coverage is most widespread among professionals, executives, and administrators and least among workers in such sectors as farming and services (*Statistical Abstract* 1988: 396–7), and the level of fringe benefits is often graduated so as to replicate the pay scale and place a premium on seniority.

Nonetheless, occupational welfare co-exists with public provision in all four countries, and over the years occupational benefits have steadily grown. All countries have experienced a proliferation of benefits in kind, such as the use of a company car or equipment, partially or wholly subsidized meals, accommodation, recreation facilities, discounts, transport subsidies, services provided by company doctors, etc. The profusion and growth of these benefits should cause us to be wary of stating a simple inverse relationship between state provision and occupational welfare.

Of our four welfare states, two – the Netherlands and Sweden – are frequently classified as prime examples of "neo-corporatism" or "democratic corporatism" (Wilensky 1976, 1982, Schmitter 1981, Katzenstein 1985). This categorization rests on the degree to which the organizations of employees and employers are represented in the broad processes of policy formulation and implementation. But what role do these organizations play in the provision and administration of social benefits? That is, what is the extent of corporatist welfare in these two countries? Despite shared associations with neo-corporatism, the patterns of corporatist welfare in the two countries have diverged drastically, with state institutions generally playing a dominant role in Sweden. At first glance, this may seem highly paradoxical in view of the much greater strength of union organizations in Sweden compared to the Netherlands.[4]

In the Netherlands corporatist welfare arrangements were found in the areas of occupational pension schemes, the administration of basic pensions, unemployment and sickness insurance, and family allowances. These benefits have been administered by one of two sets of corporatist hierarchies of organizations comprised of employer and employee representatives: the Labor Councils (*Raden van Arbeid*), organized on a regional basis, responsible for basic pensions and family allowances; and the Industrial Insurance Boards (*Bedrijfsverenigingen*), organized according to branches of industry, deal with sickness, disability, and unemployment benefits and the recently introduced supplementary benefit. At the apex of both hierarchies has been the Social Insurance Council, on which the state, employers, and employees have been represented.[5]

The involvement of Swedish unions and employers' organizations in the administration of social benefits is negligible in comparison with their Dutch counterparts. Instead, public bureaucracies administer social benefits. The major exception has been unemployment insurance benefits. However, unemployment insurance has been organized solely by the unions and heavily subsidized by the state – and does not qualify as a corporatist arrangement defined as bodies with joint representation of employers and employees. Corporatist structures and arrangements have been essentially more important in other policy areas such as employment and labor market policy, industrial policy, labor legislation, and the policy process more generally.

Turning to altruistic welfare and the role of voluntary agencies and non-profit organizations, we find that they have generally been more active in the provision of services than benefits. However, in the Netherlands medical benefits, under the Health Insurance Act, are administered by health insurance funds, which are non-profit organizations. In addition, Dutch non-profit organizations have played a vital role in housing (Lundqvist 1992).

With respect to services, the UK and Sweden revealed similarities in the marginal role of private provision in education and the health services. In both countries private provision covered 10 percent or less of the relevant population in these two fields (for the UK see Parry 1986: 162). In Sweden this pattern has applied to a wider variety of services, such as employment services and training programs, day care, and other social services. The two countries are also similar in the extent to which state institutions have been responsible for the administration and delivery of services. They differ, however, with respect to the role of local authorities. In contrast to the more centralized pattern in the UK, both local and regional government in Sweden have an independent power of taxation and these levels of government are active in providing public assistance, health care, education, social services, and housing.

The Netherlands and the USA represent the other end of the scale but also completely different variants. In both countries state provision in education and health is not as extensive, although the state plays a substantial role in funding. In fact, the Netherlands constitutes virtually an inverted image of Sweden and the UK inasmuch as only about 10 percent of all health, education, and social welfare services is provided directly by local or regional government (Kramer 1981: 19, cf. James 1987: 399). Instead, education and health services, social services, day care, etc., are largely organized on a denominational basis reflecting the religious divisions or pillarization of Dutch society. More specifically, organizations often originally located in one of the pillars have been major providers of education, health care, housing, and social services. Collectively, these organizations are referred to as *particulier initiatief*, which is generally translated as "private enterprise" (Brenton 1982: 61). In certain respects, "private enterprise" is a misnomer. A cardinal feature of the organizations is that they are non-profit making. Further, although their legal status is private, they *de facto* assume quasi-public status, by virtue of heavy funding from the state and their tasks as providers of legislated benefits and services.

In the USA market solutions have figured more prominently in the provision of services – education, health, employment, day care, and personal social services. Voluntary agencies have traditionally been and are still involved in running personal social services, but since the 1960s the practice of purchasing services accelerated, increasing the element of public funding. In addition, because of the leeway provided by limits of state action, the voluntary element is strong and the ethnic and religious mosaic of US society is in part projected onto the delivery of services.

In sum, looking at this dimension of variation across the four countries, the role of private organizations stands out in the Dutch and US cases. In the Netherlands we encounter an intricate pattern of cross-cutting segmentation in the provision of benefits and services with state administration confined mainly to social assistance. Corporatist structures are heavily involved in the provision of benefits, while denominational and non-profit organizations, often with a strong element of voluntary work, are active in services.[6] Simultaneously, state legislation applying to a wide range of benefits and certain services has ensured coverage of most of the population, uniformity in benefits, and a supervisory framework. In this way, private organizations have been integrated into the public provision of welfare. By contrast, the role of private organizations in providing benefits and services in the USA has been more autonomous and supplemental to state provision, and in many instances it has been the only form of benefits and services. Nor has the profit making capacity of private organizations been shunned.

Ideology of state intervention and distribution based on needs

The philosophy and values underlying the welfare state form a crucial dimension of variation. In fact, some authors (e.g. Furniss and Tilton 1977, Ashford 1986) argue that values constitute one of the most decisive distinctions among welfare states. This dimension, as formulated in table 1.1, focuses on conceptions of the state and principles of distribution.

In the USA several factors – the lack of a feudal past with a centralized state encompassing the church and crown, a revolutionary break with the UK, the enthusiastic and enduring embrace of liberalism, and the settler experience – created a unique environment with respect to the formation of the state and attitudes toward it. These influences worked to produce a fragmented state structure and the prevailing conception that the proper sphere of state action is limited and that individuals are primarily responsible for their own welfare.

In the Netherlands social doctrines embedded in Catholicism and Protestantism have shaped conceptions of the legitimate purview of the state. Catholics have enshrined the principle of "subsidiarity," essentially a hierarchical principle of intervention where the state intercedes only when smaller and lower bodies have failed, while Protestants subscribed to the doctrine of "sphere sovereignty" which holds the sovereignty of God over the family, state, church, and society, each of which has its own sphere of influence (Kramer 1981: 20–1, Roebroek 1989: 148; cf. Therborn 1989: 206–8). These beliefs have assigned a special role to church authorities and individual responsibility. On the other hand, the hierarchical view of authority inherent in subsidiarity has placed the state above divisional interests; it has been envisioned as a higher agent in harmonizing the conflicting interests of groups with the aim of maintaining their autonomy (cf. Wilensky 1982: 353). This formula has been applied to the religious communities themselves and to aspects of social provision. The organic view of society in Dutch religious teachings has also emphasized solidarity, and the state has increasingly become a vehicle for achieving solidarity. The state's responsibility to safeguard a social minimum is reflected in a constitutional guarantee and the notion of the caring state (*Verzorgingsstaat*) (Hupe 1993).

British notions of state responsibility in welfare provision have been broader than those in the USA and the Netherlands. More generally, the state has been viewed as a vehicle for combating social evils and providing a minimum standard of life for all. Nevertheless, major currents of economic liberalism have set important limits on state intervention in terms of proper forms of action in at least two decisive ways. First, although liberal dictates on the separation of state and the economy have been eroded through state intervention, they prevail to the extent that intervention is confined to compensating for market deficiencies rather than modifying or abolishing them (cf. Ruggie 1984: chapter 1). Second, economic liberalism prevails in the concern attached to individual incentives in the provision of social benefits.

Three aspects of Swedish conceptions of the state have facilitated the expansion of state responsibility in welfare provision. The first is basically an instrumentalist view, that is, that the state is an instrument for achieving collective purposes and the common good. The second is a communitarian notion of the state. Solidarity has infused views of the state, and in Social Democratic thought, as distinct from liberal thinking, the ideas of the state and society interlock (Tingsten 1973: 345). Simultaneously universalist social policies have tended to nurture these images of the state, since these benefits and services have been available to everyone. The third aspect, shaped by a spirit of social trust, is that the state has been less perceived as an instrument of repression than in many other societies (see Allardt 1986, Kuhnle and Selle 1989).

The strength of an ideology of distribution based on need also varies in the four countries. In the USA such an ideology has been overshadowed by a creed stressing that rewards should be allocated on the basis of individual initiative and achievements. However, alleviation of misery and need, along with social protection, have been motivating forces behind welfare legislation. In the UK and the Netherlands distribution based on need has been inextricably related to provision of a minimum standard. It is typical of the UK, however, that the discussion of basic needs has been heavily influenced by studies on poverty. Equally important, the doctrine of "less eligibility" – the principle that the resources of recipients of welfare should be less than the lowest income of the working poor – has colored the British definition of an adequate standard. These two influences have resulted in a narrow conception of basic needs and an emphasis on a bare minimum. This emphasis reflects a concern that social benefits might corrode individual incentives and disrupt the functioning of the market. By contrast, the Dutch define a socially adequate standard in more generous terms. Religious humanitarian values have stressed the elimination of human misery as a prerequisite for enabling individuals to live Christian lives; poverty has been viewed as robbing persons of their fundamental dignity as human beings – and preventing the needy from being able to live according to the laws of God (see Roebroek 1989: 148). Nor has the conception of needs been limited to material needs. These views have undermined market considerations and, unlike in the UK, have brought the social minimum in line with the minimum wage (cf. Therborn 1989: 212–13). In Sweden the fulfillment of basic needs has been increasingly viewed as a right of citizenship. This linkage with citizenship has also broadened the definition of basic needs inasmuch as citizenship consists not only of participation in politics but also the sharing of social goods.[7] Notions of an adequate minimum have been successively upgraded, and in the 1950s the idea of an equal standard throughout one's lifetime or a guaranteed standard replaced a minimum standard conceived as a safety net. Furthermore, distribution based on needs has been fused with an ideology of equality which underlines not only equal opportunities but equality in outcomes. Last, solidarity is often invoked as an underlying principle of social policies in Sweden and the Netherlands but it is notably missing in the British and US political vocabularies. Solidarity has been of major importance in justifying distribution on the basis of needs rather than the market.

In conclusion, although conceptions of the state and distribution based on need are crucial variations, a fundamental issue is whether the ideological dimensions suggested by the contrasting ideal models based on the residual–institutional distinction are sufficient to capture the important ideological differences between the welfare states considered here. In contrast with the previous dimension, which was excessively broad, this dimension appears too narrow for exploring the relevant variations between welfare states.

Welfare states: types and distinctive features

This comparison discloses substantial variations in the role of the state in welfare provision, the coverage of the population, the range of statutory provision of benefits and services, the level of benefits, dominant type of program, the nature of funding, the role of private organizations, and the ideological underpinnings of public provision. However, it is extremely difficult and hardly meaningful to classify the four welfare states in terms of the residual versus the institutional type. True, in terms of the contrasting types, the USA comes closest to approximating the residual model – and Sweden the institutional model. Nevertheless, both countries deviate in important ways from the defining characteristics of each of the models. Furthermore, the UK, and especially the Netherlands, are difficult to accommodate within this scheme.

Our analysis also raises the question of whether the Netherlands and Sweden should be classified as representatives of the same welfare state regime, and in particular the appropriateness of categorizing the Netherlands as a social democratic welfare state regime. On several dimensions the Netherlands and Sweden are polar opposites – state involvement in the delivery of services versus private but non-profit provision, active employment policies versus compensatory unemployment measures, and reliance on the insurance model and fees versus funding through taxation.

Analyzing the welfare state variations across the four countries allows us to determine to what extent the countries conform with or deviate from specific types of welfare state and welfare state regimes. It also helps to identify the amalgam of variations which are distinctive to each of the four countries. By way of conclusion, let us sum up the principal variations of the four welfare states, thereby delineating the distinctive features of each.

The United States: the incomplete welfare state

A residual and an institutional conception of social welfare co-exist uneasily in the USA, resulting in a two-tier system of public provision of welfare. One tier consists of insurance benefits, or in popular parlance "social security," and these programs enjoy overwhelming public support. During the past decades their funding has steadily grown from roughly

35 percent of social expenditures in 1960 to around 50 percent in 1985 (*Statistical Abstract of the United States* 1988: 334). The second tier, commonly referred to as "welfare," consists of non-contributory programs directed to the poor – or more precisely to categories of the poor – on a means tested basis. Expenditure for these programs has also grown, but the increase is relatively modest compared to that of social security benefits. Nor are these targeted programs widely supported by the public.

Besides the two tiers of public provision, a third tier of private or occupational welfare assumes special prominence in the USA. During the postwar period large sections of the labor force have become eligible for occupational benefits, such as sick pay, disability benefits, medical and dental insurance, and pensions (Stevens 1988). Because several of these benefits lack statutory equivalents, they are more important in the USA than in the other countries. The importance of private welfare is evidenced by the fact that non-public spending amounted to nearly one-third of welfare expenditures in 1980 (calculated from Kerns 1992: 59).

In sum, a basic feature of the US welfare state is the lack of a fully developed system of statutory social protection. Underpinning the limited nature of the welfare state is a philosophy of economic individualism, self-help, and a preference for market solutions involving a minimum of state intervention. As we have seen, US social legislation is characterized by major gaps, especially in the areas of sickness benefits, health insurance, maternity and family policy, public housing, and social services. In all these areas, market solutions, fragmentation, diversity, and incomplete coverage prevail. Diversity and fragmentation are reinforced by federal institutions, a heavy reliance on voluntary agencies, sometimes of a religious or ethnic complexion, and the large role of occupational welfare. The result has been benefit levels that vary by factors of 4: 1 among states and localities (Heidenheimer 1982: 286). The incompleteness of the US welfare state also extends to the area of public assistance. The USA lacks statutory provision which applies to the entire population. Instead, nationally legislated programs provide assistance to vulnerable groups: the elderly, the blind, the disabled, and families with dependent children. The distinction between the "deserving" and "undeserving poor" survives as a centerpiece of the incomplete welfare state.

The Netherlands: the segmented welfare state based on transfers

Social policy in the Netherlands has been characterized by a high degree of segmentation with respect to benefits and services. Social insurance benefits fall into two categories. National or citizen insurance schemes have been superimposed upon an older Bismarckian type of insurance covering employees. Medical insurance also has a dual structure. While health insurance retained the earlier Bismarckian principle of compulsory insurance for only lower income groups, a special scheme against exceptional medical costs covered the entire population. National insurance schemes and employee insurance schemes also have entirely different ideological underpinnings. The principle of solidarity is often cited as a justification of the national insurance schemes (and social assistance), because all insured persons share the burden of contributions according to their ability to pay, but benefits providing a flat rate minimum are available to all. The principle of equivalence applies to the employee insurance schemes, and it prescribes that benefits should be equivalent to contributions.

The segmented nature of the Dutch welfare state has also been reflected in the administration of benefits and services. In contrast to the other countries, a complex network of corporatist bodies representing employees and employers – and at the apex including also government representatives – has been responsible for the administration of most benefits. Historically the pillarized society influenced the provision of services and poor relief. Services such as education, health, and personal services have been mainly organized and run on a confessional basis.

An outstanding feature of the Dutch welfare state is the extent to which benefits consist of transfer payments (26 percent of GDP in 1983). The bulk of these benefits are based on contributions, and the insurance principle is widely applied. It is also striking that transfers represented a high level of spending in terms of both social insurance benefits and welfare grants (OECD 1989: 39–41). Of the four countries, public assistance absorbed the largest proportion of the GDP, despite generous insurance benefits. This paradox probably reflects two circumstances: first, the centrality of benefits attached to one's job, and second, the Dutch emphasis on an adequate social minimum for the entire population. In the Netherlands the social minimum has been defined as equivalent to the net minimum wage, and in the early 1980s the minimum wage was much closer (roughly 75 percent) to the average wage than in most countries (OECD 1989: 68–70). This fairly ambitious definition of a social minimum, linked to the minimum wage, also has been an unusual feature of the Dutch welfare state (see van Amelsvoort 1984).

The UK: the guaranteed uniform minimum welfare state

Several distinctive characteristics of the postwar British welfare state have been associated with the ideas of William Beveridge and universal principles. The cornerstones of universalism have been uniform social insurance and assistance programs, along with the health service. For the most part, the combination of national insurance and social assistance has resulted in universal coverage of the population and a guaranteed minimum standard. The scope of the British welfare state has been ambitious in terms of its uniform programs of cash benefits and its breadth of services in kind in health, education, personal social services, and housing. In these respects, the UK approximates the institutional model and Esping-Andersen's social democratic welfare state regime.

Social policies have been less ambitious and diverge from the institutional model in two important ways. First, benefit levels can hardly be viewed as generous, and the low replacement rate of benefits has been shaped by the principle of a uniform national minimum. This principle has also been manifested in flat rate benefits, which have been one of the hallmarks of the British universal welfare state. Compared to the other welfare states, earnings related benefits have occupied a modest position in British income maintenance programs.[8] Uniformity in benefits has also meant roughly the same level of benefits regardless of type (Rainwater et al. 1986: 160) and strict observance of the rule against receipt of several benefits simultaneously. In the early 1980s, for example, most cash benefits for a married couple ranged between slightly less than 30 percent and 40 percent of the average earnings of industrial male workers (Parry 1986: 188), and the replacement rate of the major public pension was the lowest of the four countries (Palme 1990a: 112). Moreover, the levels of insurance benefits and social assistance were similar, so that insurance benefits were only slightly above the poverty line, which is conventionally defined as an income beneath the threshold for social assistance (Parry 1986: 188–9, 1987: 372). In fact, the benefits of pensioners receiving assistance were generally higher than those with only a state retirement pension under the national insurance scheme. The low level of insurance benefits, in part, stemmed from Beveridge's original formula of flat rate benefits for flat rate contributions and the importance assigned to meeting contribution requirements. The second divergence from the institutional model is that the coverage of benefits in kind has not always been universal. With the exception of medical and dental services, benefits in kind have generally been targeted to low income groups and the socially deprived (Ruggie 1984: 199–210, Heidenheimer et al. 1983: 92–3). In short, Beveridge's brand of universalism did not leave much room for generous benefits whose entitlement was solely based on citizenship or residence.

Sweden: the comprehensive welfare state

Among the typical features of the Swedish welfare state has been its comprehensiveness with regard to the range of publicly provided benefits and services, the coverage of the population, and the high levels of benefits (Heckscher 1984: 79–80, Furniss and Tilton 1977, chapter 6, Allardt 1986: 114). One effect of this comprehensive scope has been to diminish the impact of market forces on distribution, resulting in less dependency upon one's market position and a decommodification of wants and needs (Esping-Andersen and Korpi 1987: 40–1). Instead medical services, education at all levels, day care, family services, and transport have largely assumed the character of public goods. The centrality of public services in the Swedish welfare state has led to its characterization as the "social service state" (Siim 1987: 3).

An additional distinguishing characteristic has been a strong emphasis on entitlement to benefits and services based on citizenship or residence (Elmér 1975: 252–8, Esping-Andersen and Korpi, 1987). However, flat rate benefits whose eligibility is based on citizenship have gradually been complemented but not replaced by earnings related schemes whose entitlement derives from labor market status. The funding of benefits also reflects the idea of social citizenship rather than the insurance principle. Taxation has constituted the main source of revenues and contributions by the insured and fees have been minimal. An additional characteristic is a commitment to equality and solidarity as social policy goals (Esping-Andersen and Korpi 1987). What is distinctive is that the commitment to equality is not limited to equal opportunities but extends to equality of result. Solidarity is manifested in inclusive policies as a means of integrating the entire population (see Davidson 1989).

The Swedish welfare state is further distinguished by an institutionalized commitment to full employment through active labor market measures. A full employment policy has been the core of a larger preventive strategy – the development of policies and programs to prevent rather than alleviate need. The combination of programs to prevent need and entitlement based on citizenship has drastically reduced the role of means tested benefits and altered the quality of social rights.

Having clarified the nature of welfare state variations and the way in which the countries differ, we are left with our initial question. Out of the array of variations described, which have the most important implications for women? How do the differences in social provision of the four countries affect women and result in dissimilar outcomes for women and men? The lack of an answer, even the beginnings of an answer, also raises the issue of the utility of mainstream models and typologies in the analysis of welfare states and gender. It is to these questions we turn in the next chapter.

2 Gendering dimensions of welfare states

Mainstream typologies of welfare states fail to provide much indication of what sort of variations might be important to women, and the dimensions of variation discussed in chapter 1 offer few clues. Inherent in much mainstream thinking no doubt is the assumption that the impact of welfare states is roughly the same for men and women. A further obstacle to considering differential benefits according to sex appears to have been underlying assumptions about the superiority of the institutional model and the social democratic welfare state regime. Protagonists of the institutional model seem to have thought that massive state intervention in welfare provision would automatically benefit most people, including women. One of the most telling examples of this sort of reasoning is Esping-Andersen's categorization of the Netherlands as a social democratic welfare state regime. Similarly, the definition of the fundamental goals of the institutional model as redistribution and equality easily reinforces the supposition of similar welfare outcomes for both sexes. In any event, certain variations, unrelated to the amount of state involvement, work either to the advantage or disadvantage of women. The small amount of information on women in the mainstream literature also causes one to wonder how suitable mainstream models and typologies are for analyzing welfare states and gender. Can these models and typologies be used or must we formulate new ones?

To answer these questions and to devise a framework of analysis for the next chapters of this book I have adopted a two pronged strategy. The first consists of examining feminist scholarship and its critique of mainstream literature in search of gender relevant dimensions of variation. Drawing on this literature, I identify several dimensions and outline two polar ideal types of social policy. This prong of the strategy seeks to set apart the gender relevant dimensions from those of the mainstream school in order to explore eventually the interplay between them.

The second prong aims at a synthesis of the feminist and mainstream perspectives by combining their insights concerning the bases of entitlement. So far mainstream research has focused on a threefold categorization: needs, work performance, and citizenship. Feminists have directed their attention to rights derived from wives' status as dependants within the family and from motherhood. So far there has been little effort in the literature to integrate *all* these bases of entitlement into the analysis and examine their implications for women's and men's social rights.

Feminist perspectives on the welfare state

By applying the prism of gender to social phenomena and making women the focal point of analysis, feminist scholarship has opened up new perspectives and has called attention to deficiencies in a variety of social theories. The emphasis on gender represents a challenge to much social science research because it calls for the explicit inclusion of both sexes in the analysis, whereas previously the unit of analysis was usually either the individual or various collectivities. Although these units of analysis have formally been neutral with respect to the sexes, underlying assumptions about these units frequently took men as their point of departure – as typified by notions such as economic man, or the "worker" as the average industrial male worker, and industrial workers as the core of the working class. In such instances, the inclusion of women in the analysis can create problems since existing assumptions do not necessarily pertain to women; but their inclusion can offer new insights.

In the case of the welfare state, feminist scholarship has made several major contributions. First and foremost, feminists have endeavored to bring gender into the analysis by focusing on women and their relationship to the welfare state. This focus has been necessary since women have been invisible in so much of the mainstream writing on the welfare state, which has concentrated on individuals, households, occupations, classes, or generations. The relationships of women to the welfare state have been conceptualized in a variety of ways. According to one prominent view, women are primarily *objects of policy*. They are "policy takers" or recipients, and their relationships to the welfare state have been primarily analyzed in terms of dependency and social control. Along similar lines, an important body of literature details how welfare state policies have reinforced the position of married women as dependants of their husbands.

Other analytical perspectives, adopting the categories of "claims" (Peattie and Rein 1983) and "statuses" (Hernes 1984) as focal points, have transformed women into claimants and actors, as well as pointing to the complexities and multiplicity in women–state relationships. In conceptualizing women's relationships to the state, Helga Hernes has concentrated on their status as citizens, employees, and clients. Briefly, she discusses women *qua* citizens in terms of influencing issues and holding positions of power, women *qua* employees with the state as a major employer, and women *qua* clients in their role as mothers and a larger proportion of the elderly and sick (1984, 1987). This conceptualization has been supplemented with an additional category, i.e. women as consumers of public services, specifically to differentiate women in this position from that of clients. It is further argued that this is of crucial significance to women, and that "a strong public service sector seems to be one precondition for avoiding becoming solely dependent on the state as clients" (Borchorst and Siim 1987: 146). Finally, studies have examined women's relationships to the welfare state in their capacity as mothers (e.g. Lewis 1980, Borchorst and Siim 1984, Leira 1992, Bock and Thane 1991, Koven and Michel, 1990, 1993).

Second, feminists have examined how social programs and social rights have been gendered. They have analyzed the effects of program rules in advantaging or disadvantaging the sexes in social provision. Central to their analysis is an examination of how formal employment – paid work – results in better welfare state entitlements than informal caring – unpaid work. The traditional division of labor between men as earners and women as carers produces a gendering of social rights and benefit levels.

Recent scholarship has turned to the origins of the welfare state and the patterns of development of social programs catering to male and female beneficiaries. Taking workmen's compensation and mothers' aid as contrasting cases, Barbara Nelson argues that these programs were instrumental in the development of a two tier welfare state in the USA (Nelson 1990, Orloff 1991). In a monumental study Theda Skocpol (1992) seeks to unravel the puzzle of the differing fates of "paternalist" and "maternalist" versions of social policy in the USA during the first two decades of the twentieth century. Why did the USA fail to adopt social insurance schemes benefiting men, but introduce protective labor legislation for women, mothers' pensions, and public clinics for children and infants?

Third, feminists have also demonstrated how key mainstream conceptions and assumptions are gendered in the sense that they are primarily rooted in the experiences of men. That T. H. Marshall's famous discussion of social citizenship – defined as social rights ranging from a social minimum to a full share in the social goods and standards prevailing in the society (1950: 11) – clearly referred to men is apparent from his description of the sequence in the attainment of civil rights, political rights, and social rights (cf. Hernes 1984, Gordon 1990) and his designation of 1918 as the date of the recognition of universal political citizenship. He explicitly states that the adoption of manhood suffrage represented the achievement of universal political rights (1950: 20–1). More importantly, Marshall's conception of social citizenship is laden with patriarchal implications by upholding a division between the public and private spheres. For Marshall, citizenship is a status bestowed on those who are full members of the community and entails equal rights and duties (1950: 28–9). Social rights stem from contributions in the public sphere, and the entitlements of women in the private sphere are via their husbands (see Pateman 1988).

The concept of "decommodification" – one of the key dimensions of variation underlying Esping-Andersen's regime typology – is similarly problematic. Esping-Andersen describes decommodification as occurring "when a person can maintain a livelihood without reliance on the market" (1990: 21–2). The concept is grounded in the idea that labor is a market commodity, and that workers must sell their labor in order to make a living. The true measure of the quality of social rights, according to Esping-Andersen, is decommodification – emancipation from dependence on the market. As many feminists have objected, decommodification scarcely addresses the situation of women who perform unpaid labor in the home, and the conditions for their emancipation (Hobson 1991, Lewis 1992a, Orloff 1993). Esping-Andersen also indiscriminately applies decommodification to both individuals and families; but for women it is vital whether benefits are tied to the individual or the family. When the family is the unit of benefits, the head of the household is usually the recipient (Borchorst 1994). The disconcerting nature of decommodification in its current conceptualization is made clear by Esping-Andersen's empirical analysis. According to his empirical measures, the Netherlands ranked among the leaders in terms of social rights in the early 1980s by virtue of its "superior performance on decommodification" (1990: 53). This ranking is based on men and households but, as we shall see, requires substantial qualification in the case of women (see Bussemaker and van Kersbergen 1994).

Fourth, in contrast to mainstream analysis which has stressed economic processes – especially industrialization – as a crucial determinant in the formation of the welfare state, feminists have emphasized the interrelationships between the family, the state, and the market in structuring the welfare state. Mainstream analysis, especially convergence theory, has viewed the emergence of the welfare state as a functional response to industrialization and the modernization of the economy. Only indirectly has the family been included through the acknowledgment that industrialization produces changes in "primary groups," altering the pattern of needs and making the family and its members more vulnerable (e.g. Wilensky and Lebeaux 1958, Uusitalo 1984).

In the typologies and models of social policy discussed in chapter 1 the place of the family in the provision of welfare has fallen into obscurity. Although the family is a key institution in the residual model, a unilinear logic of development envisioning an inevitable transition from the residual to the institutional model has relegated the family to insignificance. The family is totally ignored in the work performance model and the institutional model. With its emphasis on state provision the institutional model overlooks the role of women in care work and human services. One of the most influential discussions of institutional welfare states (Esping-Andersen and Korpi 1987) completely glosses over the care sector. Despite the authors' emphasis on universal access to public services as a distinctive characteristic of institutionalized welfare states, they only discuss employment services. The institutional model further implies an unlimited expansion of public services which has yet to be realized, and the result is an informal sector where women fill in (Leira 1989, 1992).

Rather belatedly, Esping-Andersen (1990) has acknowledged the importance of interrelationships between the state, market, and family. He claims that these interrelationships constitute a dimension of variation underlying his threefold typology of welfare state regimes (21, 26–8). However, the family is entirely missing in his discussion of the liberal welfare state regime, but state–family relationships do figure in his accounts of the conservative and social democratic welfare state regimes. According to Esping-Andersen, the conservative regime is typified by a lack of day care and family services, the exclusion of non-working wives from social insurance schemes, and the principle of subsidiarity which limits state interference to "when the family's capacity to service its members is exhausted." This contrasts with the social democratic regime where individual independence is enhanced by socializing the costs of the family. Despite these sound observations, there is little evidence of them in the remaining analysis of welfare state regimes. Instead, Esping-Andersen concentrates on the state–market nexus as it affects decommodification, the stratification of benefits – notably without any reference to sex – and the impact of welfare states on employment. In keeping with the mainstream preoccupation with paid market labor, Esping-Andersen analyzes women mainly as workers (1990: chapter 8).

By contrast, feminists have mainly focused on the dynamics and the shifting boundary between the private and public spheres, that is, both their interdependence and separation. While mainstream analysis has equated the public with the state and the private with economic enterprises and the market, feminists often draw the lines differently: the public sphere encompasses the state and civil society and the private sphere is the family. A significant change in state–family relations is the extent to which tasks of reproduction and socialization, formerly activities of the family, have increasingly become functions of the public sector. As aptly put by Helga Hernes, the issue is the degree to which caring tasks and reproduction work, previously done in the home, have gone public (Hernes 1984: 34–5, 1987: 39).

A final contribution has been to raise the issue of the distributional effects of the welfare state with respect to women and men – an area neglected by mainstream analysis which has concentrated on redistribution as it affects classes, occupational groups, generations, or other categories of individuals or households. In a similar vein, feminists have sought to analyze the male/female composition of the poor. Studies of the poor in the USA and elsewhere have called attention to the "feminization of poverty" in the 1980s arising from the increase in families headed by single women – either unmarried or divorced – and the overrepresentation of women among the elderly and especially among the very old. However, as pointed out by feminist historians, a predominance of women and children in poverty is not a new phenomenon (Lewis and Piachaud 1987, Abramovitz 1988, Gunnarsson 1990: 30–1). Besides documenting these aspects, feminists have sought to uncover the mechanisms behind female poverty (see Glendinning and Millar 1987) and distributional patterns.

Despite these contributions, three features of feminist thinking seem to have initially impeded a consideration of the implications of welfare state variations for women and a borrowing from the literature on typologies of welfare provision. First, many feminists have been profoundly suspicious of both the state and the welfare state. From differing perspectives, radical and neo-marxist feminists have viewed the state as a force maintaining a patriarchal society. At bottom, these views share the conception of the state as an instrument of repression, as illustrated by the following quotation: "social welfare policies amount to no less than the State organization of domestic life. Women encounter State repression within the very bosom of the family" (Wilson 1977: 9). Similarly, the welfare state has been viewed as reproducing the traditional social division of labor between the sexes. The notion that the prime function of the welfare state is social control has also colored much of feminist writing on the welfare state.

A wholly negative view was called into question as too simplistic, and this perspective was subsequently replaced by an ambivalent position which either recognized the state as a non-determined entity or that certain state policies had positive effects for women. For example, Helga Hernes alternatively describes the Scandinavian state form as a "tutelary state for women" because of its corporatist nature and as a "women-friendly state" or a potentially women-friendly state (1987: 15, 135–7). Similarly, Carole Pateman acknowledges that even in the patriarchal welfare state certain measures have promoted women's independence (Pateman 1988).

The current trend, however, has been toward a more thorough consideration of the ways in which policy interventions can advance women's concerns through altering the gendered division of labor and reducing inequality between the sexes. The emancipatory potential of welfare state policies has been increasingly emphasized and related to the goals of women's autonomy *vis-à-vis* the family and the economy (Eduards 1988, 1990, Bussemaker 1991, Orloff 1993, O'Connor 1993). This endeavor has also been spurred by the desire to empty Esping-Andersen's conception of decommodification of its male bias. Ann Orloff has argued that decommodification as a measure of the quality of social rights needs to be complemented by two additional dimensions: *"access to paid work"*; and *"the capacity to form and maintain an autonomous household"* (italics original) (1993: 318–19). The capacity to form and maintain an autonomous household underscores women's freedom to enter and exit from marriage and cohabitation. As Ruth Lister notes, however, this formulation glosses over the ability to achieve financial autonomy within marriage (1994b: 33). Drawing a parallel with decommodification, she suggests "defamilialization" as a criterion for evaluating social rights. Lister defines defamilialization as "the degree to which individual adults can uphold a socially acceptable standard of living, independently of family relationships, either through paid work or social security provision" (1994a: 37 and 1994b: 32).

Second, the feminist project has had the noble aim of ending women's oppression, and its stance has been to provide a critique of society. A potential danger is the possibility of a mirror image which, despite a critical posture, accepts certain original underlying assumptions. In emphasizing the victimization and powerlessness of women, feminists run the risk of underestimating women as agents of change and their influence. Similarly, in a brilliant critique of liberal political tradition, Pateman challenges the idea that concepts such as the individual and citizenship are universal (1988, 1992). She argues that these concepts have solely pertained to men and their extension to women can only make women into lesser men. However, her discussion is rooted in T. H. Marshall's assumptions of social citizenship where rights are accorded as a result of fulfillment of the duty to work (1950: 78).

In some cases, feminists propose to jettison concepts because of the way male scholarship has gendered them. Comparative analysis can offer a means of reclaiming concepts that have been gendered in a specific way by exposing the ethnocentric limitations underlying their central assumptions. For example, comparativists have pointed out the country specific nature of Marshall's description of the sequence in the development of civil rights, political rights, and social rights. His gendered analysis of citizenship has yet to be put to the test of a cross-national scrutiny.

Third, perhaps because of the ubiquity of male domination, feminist theories have often been cast in a universal idiom, and this seems to be particularly the case in feminist thinking on the state and the welfare state. In earlier scholarship there was a general neglect of the importance of national contexts as a variable; yet ironically specific national contexts have had a major effect on theorizing. On the one hand, analysis has been dominated by the experiences of a few countries, most of which are in the English speaking world. As a result, national traits and particularisms have been portrayed as generalities and universal givens. Certain attributes have been conceived as intrinsic features of the welfare state rather than possible variations of welfare states. On the other hand, since so few rigorous comparisons have been made, a basic problem is that we really do not know what the differences and similarities are between various welfare states with respect to their impact on women and men, and this ignorance tends to reinforce a generic approach based on theorizing founded upon the experience of individual countries.

In summary, the feminist perspective has acted as a counterpoint to several assumptions underpinning the models presented in chapter 1. This perspective suggests an alternative view and points to a number of limitations inherent in the models presented earlier. First, several feminists have stressed the interplay between the public and the private and the necessity of viewing welfare provision in terms of a public–private mix (Hernes 1987, Leira 1992). They have criticized the public–private split assumed by the models and their concentration on market–state relations at the expense of the interrelationships between the family, state, and market. Feminists call for an examination of both paid work and unpaid work inside and outside the home. Since the focus of the models has been on the extent of state responsibility in welfare provision, they are poorly equipped to deal with other welfare providers or "sectors" of provision. Second, feminists have emphasized the necessity of examining how the public sector in providing employment and services affects the situation of women. However, the models pay little attention to the distinction between benefits as cash transfers and benefits in kind in the form of services. In fact, in Ramesh Mishra's version (1977) the two are combined as a single dimension of variation. On the whole, mainstream analyses have highlighted social insurance benefits and income maintenance policies, while downplaying services. Third, feminists have underlined the importance of ideology in shaping welfare policies but they have cast light on a completely different set of values than the residual and institutional models. Rather than ideologies of state intervention or distribution, feminists have made familial and gender ideologies pivotal to the analysis of the welfare state. Fourth, feminists have sought to redefine the emancipatory potential of welfare state policies so that they also accommodate women.

Gender relevant dimensions of variations

One intriguing question is whether mainstream models and typologies are adequate for analyzing welfare state variations and gender. Is the dearth of information about women and welfare states in the mainstream literature simply the result of a lack of interest in gender and a failure to apply mainstream constructs to the sexes? Or are mainstream models and typologies ill designed to deal with gender? I believe that applying the mainstream models and typologies to an analysis of women and men would produce valuable insights, but that the models are fundamentally lacking.

In large measure, the feminist critique has indicated what is problematic. To eliminate the problematic aspects of mainstream constructs it is necessary to reconceptualize gendered concepts and assumptions so that they are applicable to both women and men. Feminist criticisms also suggest how mainstream models and typologies are lacking. The essential points in these criticisms can be formulated as gender relevant dimensions of variation. For the most part, feminists have tended to formulate their criticisms as generalizations relevant to all welfare states or as intrinsic features of the welfare state. Instead I propose to recast these generalizations as possible welfare state variations – as gender relevant dimensions of variation.

Implicit in the feminist critique are a number of dimensions of variation. They consist of the type of familial ideology; its influence on social policy in terms of the unit of benefits and contributions and the nature of entitlement; its influence in other policy areas reinforcing the actual division of labor within the family; the boundary between the public and private spheres; and the degree to which women's caring work is paid or unpaid.

As a heuristic exercise these dimensions are presented as contrasting ideal types: the male breadwinner and the individual models of social policy. The dimensions of the models are the variables that I am interested in comparing cross-nationally in an empirical analysis of policy constructions and women's and men's social rights. However, I do not assume that the ideal types will be replicated in reality or that variations across countries necessarily follow the logic of the models. Ideal types posit the co-occurrence of several defining attributes. By contrast, empirical analysis makes no such assumptions and is investigative. Accordingly the purpose of this analysis is to ascertain to what extent the four countries vary in terms of the dimensions in table 2.1.

In the male breadwinner model, the familial ideology celebrates marriage and a strict division of labor between husband and wife. The husband is the head of the household, and it is his duty to provide for the members of his family – his wife and children – through full-time employment. The duties of the wife are to make a good home and provide care for her husband and children. This division of labor is codified in family law, social and labor legislation, and the tax system. The unit of benefit is the family, and minimum benefits and pay embody the notion of the family wage. Entitlement is differentiated between husband and wife. Eligibility is based

Table 2.1 *Dimensions of variation of the male breadwinner and the individual models of social policy*

Dimension	Male breadwinner model	Individual model
Familial ideology	Celebration of marriage	No preferred family form
	Strict division of labor	Shared roles
	Husband=earner	Father=earner/carer
	Wife=carer	Mother=earner/carer
Entitlement	Differentiated among spouses	Uniform
Basis of entitlement	Breadwinner	Citizenship or residence
Recipient of benefits	Head of household	Individual
Unit of benefit	Household or family	Individual
Unit of contributions	Household	Individual
Taxation	Joint taxation	Separate taxation
	Deductions for dependants	Equal tax relief
Employment and wage policies	Priority to men	Aimed at both sexes
Sphere of care	Primarily private	Strong state involvement
Caring work	Unpaid	Paid component

on breadwinner status and the principle of maintenance. Most wives' rights to benefits are derived from their status as dependants within the family and their husbands' entitlements. As a result, married women may lack individual entitlement to benefits. In its purest form, the family or household is also the unit of social insurance contributions and taxation. To compensate for the maintenance of his wife and offspring the family provider receives tax relief. The division of labor prescribed by familial ideology also affects wage and labor market policies – assigning priority to men's employment and earnings. The boundary between the private and public sphere is strictly enforced. Caring and reproduction tasks are located in the private sphere, primarily in the home, and this work is unpaid.

The familial ideology of the individual model, unlike the breadwinner model, has no preferred family form and it prescribes shared tasks in the family. Each adult is individually responsible for his or her own maintenance, and the father and mother share the tasks of financial support and care of their children. An essential basis of entitlement is citizenship or residence because it acknowledges that individuals have a variety of useful tasks in life not limited to paid work. It privileges neither earning nor caring and thus accommodates the shared tasks of earner and carer. The unit of benefit, contributions, and taxation is the individual with no deductions or allowances for dependants. Labor market policies are aimed at both sexes. The boundary between the private and public spheres is fluid. Many reproductive tasks are performed in the public sector. Care, even in the home, can be paid work and provide entitlement to social security benefits.

Admittedly this presentation is skeletal, but it seems to me that there are a number of advantages of using this sort of analytic construct at the present stage of gendering welfare state analysis. The dimensions of variations are clearly spelt out. Earlier discussions of the male breadwinner model and the family wage have not always been very explicit on this point. For example, Jane Lewis and Ilona Ostner's typology (1991, 1994) seems to be based on a single underlying dimension – the strength of the male breadwinner model in terms of the traditional division of labor between the sexes and its implications for social entitlements. The resulting typology is "strong," "modified," and "weak" male breadwinner states; and the final category – weak male breadwinner states – is especially problematic. It seems to indicate what a country's policies are not rather than what they are. An additional weakness, recently acknowledged by Lewis and Ostner (1994: 19), is that too many diverse countries can be classified as strong breadwinner states.

Furthermore, and perhaps an explanation of this difficulty, Lewis and Ostner's breadwinner model upon closer inspection consists of several variables or dimensions of variation that are assumed to be correlated. They are married women's entitlements via their husbands' social rights, married women's employment, and the availability of childcare services and generous benefits such as maternity pay. It also needs to be stressed that the ideal types in Table 2.1 are models of social policy, and that their influence on the actual division of labor between the sexes in the family and society is also a matter of empirical inquiry. Lewis and Ostner's typology tends to conflate cause and effect (Hobson 1994).

A further advantage of the models is their potential applicability. In principle the dimensions of variation presented above can be used to analyze the policies of any country over time. A family of nations approach or typologies based on the policies of specific countries (e.g. Langan and Ostner 1991) run the risk of their relevance being limited to those countries. The family of nations approach also downplays differences between countries belonging to the same family, perhaps even preventing the detection of significant variations.

Finally, by isolating dimensions of variations related to gender it is possible to examine the interaction between these dimensions and the welfare state variations designated as important by mainstream analysis. This is more difficult, if not precluded, when the feminist and mainstream perspectives are compounded in single ideal types or policy regimes. For example, a strategy of combining certain elements affecting the provision of welfare for women and men with specific welfare state regimes results in *a priori* configurations, whereas the procedure here is open ended. It makes these relationships amenable to empirical investigation, and it allows us to revise and refine the models.

Bases of entitlement

The second prong in my strategy attempts to integrate insights from both feminist and mainstream research and move beyond the limitations of models based on polar ideal types. A major thesis of this book is that the basis of entitlement constitutes a crucial factor in determining whether social benefits and services contribute to women's autonomy or reinforce their dependence. Let us consider in more detail the basis of entitlement to benefits, since as the coming chapters will make clear, this is one of the most important welfare state variations for women.

The mainstream models utilized in chapter 1 do not squarely address the issue of the bases of entitlement. Furthermore, a major drawback of the analytical construct of polar contrasting types is that it implies only two bases of entitlement. Nor do most of the other typologies and models discussed earlier explicitly make the basis of entitlement a dimension of variation. In fact, upon reflection, the bases or principles of entitlement are conspicuously absent as dimensions of variations in mainstream typologies and models.

However, both Titmuss's three-model typology and Esping-Andersen's welfare state regimes can be interpreted as suggesting that a distinctive criterion of eligibility undergirds each model or regime type. In the residual model and the liberal welfare state regime the basis of entitlement is need caused by inadequate economic and/or personal resources. In the industrial achievement-performance model and conservative corporatist welfare state regime, entitlement derives from labor market status. Eligibility is conferred through work, economic performance, and earnings. To be eligible for benefits a person must be economically active, and frequently contributions and work tests are requirements. Finally, in the institutional redistributive model and the social democratic regime, the criterion is citizenship. Entitlement is viewed as a right stemming from citizenship and increasingly from residence.

As feminists have underlined, these criteria do not exhaust the bases of entitlement in the case of women. Instead, their entitlement has derived from their status as mothers and as wives. More generally parenthood provides a basis of entitlement, but welfare states differ substantially in granting benefits to mothers, fathers, and parents. Historically, a fundamental divide has been whether benefits have been accorded on the basis of the principle of care and awarded to the mother or the principle of maintenance and conferred upon the father. A final basis of entitlement permeates much social legislation with regard to married women, reflecting the traditional notion of the "proper" division of labor between the sexes in the family. From a women's perspective, one of the most important welfare state variations is the extent to which a married woman's entitlement to benefits is via her husband or is influenced by her husband's benefits.

As in the case of mainstream research, feminist scholarship has often concentrated on a limited number of conditions of eligibility. Focusing on the gendered division of labor in the family, Lewis and Ostner's typology builds primarily on two bases of entitlement: as the breadwinner or an earner and as the dependant of a breadwinner. The reasoning which underlies their typology further assumes that the essential variation between welfare states is the extent to which women have been recognized as workers (Lewis and Ostner 1991, 1994, Lewis 1992a). In envisioning a woman-friendly postindustrial welfare state, Nancy Fraser (1994) devises two constructs – a universal breadwinner model promoting women's employment and a caregiver parity model providing care allowances. Because of her normative thrust and the professed undesirability of the male breadwinner model, her discussion skirts women's entitlement as wives. Barbara Hobson, analyzing the situation of solo mothers, considers a wider range of forms of entitlement, and the claim structures of work, need, and parenting (Hobson 1994). But since the analysis is confined to a specific group whose entitlements in some cases are accorded because they are solo mothers, it is unclear to what extent her analysis is directly applicable to mothers and women in general. Finally, although the concept of social citizenship has been central to feminist scholarship during the past decade, it is striking how little entitlements based on citizenship have entered the discussion. Instead, citizenship or residence as a basis of entitlement has been overshadowed by other criteria of eligibility and the notions of the citizen worker and the citizen mother.

By contrast, a major argument of this book is that entitlements based on citizenship or residence are of particular importance to women. This form of entitlement has a special impact on family relationships and a stronger defamilializing potential than other principles of eligibility. Entitlements based on citizenship neutralize the influence of marriage on social rights. Benefits and services are not differentiated between husband and wife, and marital status does not affect entitlements. Also maternal benefits based on citizenship undermine the principle of maintenance and the family wage ideal. Equally important, entitlements based on citizenship and residence make no distinction between paid work and unpaid work, and in this way they undercut the gendering of social rights. Other principles of eligibility transmit the gendered division of labor into social rights. The principle of maintenance and the principle of care stem directly from the traditional division of labor between the sexes. Similarly, entitlements based on labor market status privilege paid work, failing to recognize the value of labor performed outside the market. Entitlements based on need often assist persons without paid work or social rights acquired from labor market participation, and paid work serves to disqualify individuals from this type of entitlement. In short, entitlements based on citizenship and residence can alter gender relations in social provision.

Each of the next three chapters has a specific basis of women's entitlements as its focal point and illustrates the importance of eligibility based on citizenship. Drawing on several of the dimensions of variation in table 2.1, chapter 3 examines women's entitlements as wives based on their dependent status within the family. It also shows how eligibility based on citizenship has weakened the effects of the breadwinner model, whereas entitlements based on need in the form of means tested programs reinstate the family as the unit of benefit to the disadvantage of married women. Chapter 4 looks at women's entitlements as mothers and the interplay between entitlements based on labor market status, need, and citizenship. Of the dimensions of variations in table 2.1 attention is on the sphere of care and the nature of the boundary between the private and public spheres and the dynamics between the two. Chapter 5 deals with women's entitlements as workers and whether these entitlements have defamilializing effects on women's social rights. The analyses of these chapters are subsequently brought together in part III to provide an overall picture of women's entitlements *vis-à-vis* men's.

Part II

Bases of entitlement

3   The male breadwinner model and women's entitlements as wives

Many women have been incorporated into the welfare state through entitlements as wives. While mainstream analysis has totally neglected this basis of entitlement, feminists have underlined its significance – placing it in a larger framework of the gendered division of labor in the family and society. An underlying assumption in earlier feminist theorizing about the welfare state was that the gendered division of labor, as typified by the male breadwinner model or the family wage, had been encoded in the social legislation of the industrial nations, and that public provision of welfare reflected and maintained traditional gender roles. Only as feminists have adopted a comparative perspective have they considered the possibility that the breadwinner model has varied in strength across countries. Yet most discussions present these variations as fairly recent developments, coinciding with women's exodus from the home into the labor market and the postwar growth of public services (Lewis 1992a, 1993, Lewis and Ostner 1991, 1994, Orloff 1993). The original assumption of the male breadwinner model as an intrinsic feature of the welfare state persists in a new guise. Now feminists suggest that the model had a decisive influence in the formative period of welfare states. Early European welfare states, it is held, were designed to fit and reinforce the family wage system, and they were basically "paternalist" (Orloff 1993: 323, Skocpol 1992).

The assumption of the pervasiveness of the breadwinner model, which has underpinned much feminist scholarship, has not been subject to systematic comparison. To rectify the situation, this chapter examines the impact of the male breadwinner model on social provision. To what extent has the gendered division of labor prescribed by the breadwinner model been codified in the legislation of our four countries? And to what extent have women's social rights derived from their status as wives?

The analysis here is primarily set in the late 1960s, but in a few cases policies are traced back in time in order to put variations in a historical context. The latter years of the 1960s have been chosen for two reasons. First, these years are sufficiently in the past, and when combined with digressions back in time, they allow us to probe the assumptions concerning the recentness in the development of cross-national variations. Second, this period offers a useful benchmark in assessing the impact of gender equality reforms introduced during the 1970s and 1980s, which are discussed in chapter 8. Admittedly the 1964 Civil Rights Act, which prohibited discrimination on the basis of sex, was a landmark in US legislation, but it was only in the 1970s that equality between the sexes moved onto the policy agenda and major reforms were enacted in all four countries. An examination of policies and programs at the end of the 1960s also clarifies the nature of the policy legacy in each country and indicates the difficulties it poses to reform.

The influence of the breadwinner model

In comparing the influence of the breadwinner model on the policies of the four countries, we utilize several of the gender relevant dimensions laid out in table 2.1. The comparison reveals an underlying adherence to a traditional familial ideology prescribing a strict division of labor among husband and wife. Despite this, strong divergences in the policy patterns of the four countries emerge. As distinct from the analysis in chapter 1 where the USA and Sweden largely represented opposite types, now the sharpest contrasts are between the Netherlands and Sweden. In the 1960s the Netherlands approximated most closely the breadwinner model, while Sweden least resembled it. The UK and the USA occupied a middle position, but their policies were much more like those of the Netherlands than of Sweden. In these three countries social rights were tied to the principle of maintenance, and tax benefits advantaged the family provider, while Sweden differed in that rights and benefits were also attached to the principle of care. A second difference which further strengthened Swedish women's social rights was the extent of entitlement based on citizenship, and in these cases there were points of convergence with the individual model.

The Netherlands: the family as the norm and the principle of maintenance

In the Netherlands the Catholic principle of subsidiarity and the Protestant doctrine of sphere sovereignty have enshrined the family in its traditional form. Religious teachings have sanctioned state action to protect the family from economic hardships and to aid the family provider in meeting his obligations of support (Borchorst 1994). The principle of maintenance has been firmly entrenched in social provision; and the construction of benefits and contributions has centered on the family as the norm, and gradually a family minimum has evolved.

Initially during the 1960s minimum pension benefits were linked to the minimum wage, and the standard minimum was set for a couple, while single individuals received a smaller amount. Subsequently the social minimum was upgraded and extended to a wider range of benefits in the 1970s. The beneficiary has been the person responsible for maintenance, and benefits have been calculated on the basis of family responsibilities. When fully upgraded, the social minimum was equivalent to the net minimum wage for couples, 90 percent for single parent families, with lower rates for single persons, and young adults living at home. This system contrasts with the UK and the USA where the construction of benefits has been based on the individual, with supplements for dependants.

The unit of contributions to the national insurance schemes was also the household based on family income. Compulsory health insurance automatically covered family members without an income with no additional contributions required (Roebroek and Berben 1987: 689). Because the household was the unit of benefits and contributions, married women lacked individual entitlement to "national" insurance benefits. They were ineligible for the basic old age pension (AOW), and later general disablement benefits (AAW) when they were introduced in the mid-1970s. Nor were married women who were not breadwinners, i.e. earning more than their husband, entitled to extended unemployment benefits (WWV).

The compulsory employee insurance schemes – offering sickness, disability, and unemployment benefits – have also been shaped by the ideal of family protection. Rather than relying on special allowances for dependants, these schemes provided relatively high replacement rates amounting to 80 percent of the daily wage, and supplements topped up benefits if the breadwinner had a minimum wage. Prior to the 1960s the replacement rates of unemployment and sickness insurance were differentiated according to family responsibilities. Women and young men had lower replacement rates than older men (who were assumed to be family providers). Employees were also insured against broadly defined risks. For example, disability insurance protected the breadwinner against loss of work capacity irrespective of its cause and compensated for several degrees of disablement (Kaim-Caudle 1973: 224, 156). Similarly, extended unemployment benefits covered a period of two years of joblessness. The 1960s also witnessed the inclusion of all employees in these insurance schemes through the removal of Bismarckian income restrictions which had excluded those in higher paid positions (Roebroek and Berben 1987).

The principle of maintenance and the notion of the father as guardian and provider for his children influenced family allowances. When originally introduced they were granted to the third and fourth child (ISSR 1970: 47–9), thus supplementing the family wage of those with larger support obligations. Unlike in the UK and Sweden, family allowances have been social insurance transfers and not a non-contributory benefit. As such, they have been paid to the insured person, who was usually the father. The responsibility of maintenance extended to children in early adulthood (to the age of 27) who had limited or no earnings or were permanently ill. Besides receiving an allowance for older children in education, the father was entitled to an allowance if an older child (daughter) either ran or helped in the household when at least three other children were present. The amount of the allowance increased with the number of children, and older children (over 16) and children with special needs entitled the father to larger compensation, reflecting their financial burden to the family (ISSR 1970: 48–9). In contrast to the UK and Sweden, family allowances were indexed, and they were more generous, especially in comparison with the UK. As a proportion of the standard wage the Dutch allowances were roughly twice as high as those in the UK in the late 1960s (Kaim-Caudle 1973: 271–2, 283; cf. Wennemo, 1994). Finally, the father also received child tax exemptions. The combination of family allowances and tax exemptions meant that the Dutch father, regardless of his economic position, was aided in meeting his family responsibilities.

In short, the costs of familyhood were socialized through subsidies in the form of transfers to the family provider. The guarantee of a minimum wage based on the needs of a family with two children, the high replacement rates of employee insurance schemes, and indexed family allowances tailored to large families and reflecting the varying costs of children, gave the breadwinner a substantial buffer of security in supporting the family. These policies – combining a minimum wage with a substantial social wage – produced a situation which seems closer to the ideal of an adequate family wage than the social provision of many other countries.

In cases of family breakdown, state policies have also aided the breadwinner in his maintenance obligations. Upon divorce a basic guideline has been that after child and spouse support the husband should retain the social minimum for a single person (70 percent of the family minimum). If his contributions were insufficient, so that his wife and offspring fell below the social minimum, public assistance has made up the difference (Griffiths 1986: 140–1, Wiebrens 1988: 138–9). This arrangement can be interpreted in terms of a social right of every Dutch citizen to a minimum standard (established by the Social Assistance Act of 1965 and written into the Constitution in 1983) and the widely accepted norms of social provision as embodied in the idea of the caring state. It can also be seen as an extension of state support to the family provider in meeting his maintenance obligations, even in cases of "lasting dislocation" of marriage.[1]

Divorced wives would not seem to be easily accommodated in the social insurance schemes where the family is the unit of benefits and contributions. However, since the national insurance schemes covered all citizens, divorced women without earned income have not been liable to pay contributions, but have still been entitled to an old age pension equivalent to that of a single person. On the other hand, women who were permanently separated (primarily because they could not divorce for religious reasons) received a pension which was half that of a married couple (ISSR 1970: 43) – that is, a pension allowance below the social minimum. Thus social legislation entailed more severe sanctions for a marital breakdown of a couple whose religion held marriage in high esteem and prohibited divorce. During the 1960s judicial separations were much more common than divorces (CBS 1976: 13, 35).

Presumably as compensation for their role in the home and in the absence of a breadwinner, widows fared much better than married women with respect to pensions. Even relatively young widows have not been obliged to earn their own living upon the death of their husbands. Of the four countries, the age of entitlement to a full widow's pension has been lowest in the Netherlands. For a widow without dependent children the age was 40, and if she previously had a widow's pension by virtue of caring for children the age was 35. Nor did a duration of marriage requirement exist, and a divorced woman could receive a widow's pension in the event of the death of an ex-husband with support obligations. The tax system also treated widows more favorably than wives. Upon the death of her husband, a widow's estate tax allowance was double that of a widower (UN 1959: 31).

The breadwinner ideology was also reflected in the tax system and labor legislation. Legislation privileged men as family providers with respect to tax relief, job opportunities, and wages. In the tax system married men were advantaged both in relation to married women and single persons, and in the 1960s single individuals paid much heavier taxes than in the other countries (Oldman and Temple 1960). Prior to the early 1970s taxation of spouses was modeled after the German system with strong elements of splitting (which allows a married couple to divide their joint income into two equal parts for tax purposes) – a legacy of wartime occupation. In general, joint taxation with splitting advantages families with a single earner and in particular those with higher incomes. The modified system of splitting in the Netherlands was weighted in favor of the husband's earnings. Social security taxes also discouraged married women's employment. Because social insurance contributions were assessed on household income and paid by the head of the household, a wife's employment directly affected the take home pay of her husband. The first changes in the tax system to accommodate married women's employment occurred in the early 1960s with the introduction of tax deductions for wives who were family workers or part-time employees (Pott-Buter 1993: 255).

Popular attitudes, legislation, and employers' practices curtailed a wife's possibilities of employment. Prevailing opinion disapproved of married women with children even of school age being employed outside the home in the mid-1960s (SCP 1995: 509). Legislation prohibiting employers from firing a woman for pregnancy, childbirth, or marriage was not introduced until the 1970s (Gustafsson 1994). Similarly, the guidelines of public job placement services which prioritized the employment of family providers were not altered until 1979 in order to comply with the EC directive on equal treatment of the sexes (Pott-Buter 1993: 250). Nor have married women without breadwinner status always been entitled to the minimum wage. Accordingly, it is not very surprising to find that in the mid-1960s only around 10 percent of married women were economically active, and nearly half of them were family workers. In other words, as recently as thirty years ago approximately 5 percent of Dutch married women held jobs outside the family (Pott-Buter 1993: 200–1; cf. *Statistical Yearbook* 1969–70: 284–6), but it is uncertain whether they had rights to employee insurance benefits. The schemes did not cover persons who held a "job of minor importance" from the 1940s to the late 1960s.[2]

Women's place was in the home, and the lack of benefits attached to the principle of care and motherhood in the Netherlands is striking – apart from maternity pay covered by sickness insurance (ZW). Entitlement to these benefits has been based on labor market status as an employee, and originally sickness insurance only compensated the pregnancy of married women (SZW 1982: 31). Because Dutch women's labor market participation rate was one of the lowest in the industrial countries, only a mere fraction of all mothers – around 5 percent – received maternity benefits in the mid-1960s (calculated from *Statistical Yearbook* 1969–70: 26, 315).

In conclusion, because the family was the unit of benefits, married women without breadwinner status were denied social rights in the form of an individual pension, extended unemployment benefits, and eventually general disability benefits. Overall, legislation contained prohibitions and penalties with few rewards for married women entering the labor market, leading to hardly any labor activity outside the family. In the late 1960s the Netherlands was a prime candidate for the archetype of the breadwinner model inasmuch as social rights derived almost entirely from the principle of maintenance, and the recipient of benefits was the head of the household. Only in the absence of the breadwinner did married women acquire social rights as wives. The sole benefit, which could be ascribed to the principle of care but is probably more accurately interpreted as the maintenance obligation of the deceased male breadwinner, was the widow's pension where a wife's duties in the home were assumed to have disadvantaged her re-entry into the labor market.

The UK: discrimination against married women as choice

Several distinctive features of the postwar British welfare state have been associated with the ideas of William Beveridge; and as feminist scholars have documented, the breadwinner ideology was an integral part of Beveridge's thinking (Lewis 1983: 33, 44–6, 67, 90–2; Baldwin and Falkingham 1994). His ideas were especially important because it was the postwar reforms that incorporated all women into the British welfare state.

The breadwinner model left its imprint on postwar reforms – especially the national insurance scheme and the national assistance program – in four ways. First, the national insurance scheme allowed married women to choose not to pay full contributions and instead rely upon their husband's contributions; but in the process they forfeited their claim to benefits in their own right. Because of the unified approach inherent in the national insurance scheme, the married woman's option operated to exclude them from *all* social insurance benefits – except industrial injury benefit and a dependant's pension. Utilization of the option resulted in not only the loss of an individual pension but also other benefits, such as sickness benefit, invalidity benefit, the unemployment benefit, and maternity allowance. Second, married women who remained in the national insurance scheme paid full contributions but received lower benefits than married men and single persons unless they were the main breadwinner (Groves 1983). A third feature of the national insurance scheme – adult dependant allowances – provided an incentive for women to stay in the home, thus reinforcing the traditional division of labor in the family. Unlike Dutch benefits, the system of dependant allowances took into direct account the wife's economic activity. The allowance was paid only for dependants without an income or with earnings less than the allowance. Furthermore, women were not eligible to claim child additions. Fourth, in the case of married couples only the husband could apply for means tested assistance.

In the UK married women on the labor market were not entirely stripped of their rights to a pension and other benefits, as they were in Holland. Instead they were denied equal rights and the married woman's option encouraged them to renounce their rights. The option was widely used, and in the early 1970s three-fourths of married women had opted out of the national insurance scheme (Land 1985: 56–7). Given that the option was really between no rights and minor obligations (i.e. contributions) versus only half rights and full obligations, it is hardly surprising that so many married women made use of the option. On the other hand, Dutch working wives who were not family workers or self-employed could receive employee insurance benefits.

Utilization of the married woman's option made a wife's state retirement pension dependent upon her husband's contribution record. Divorced women were particularly vulnerable, and they were not assured a pension as in the Netherlands. Although divorced women who were not at fault for the marital breakup could count their husband's contribution record during the years of the marriage toward the basic old age pension, this was not sufficient. They also had to pay contributions upon termination of the marriage. In addition, a divorced woman lost the right to a widow's pension in both state and employer schemes (Groves 1983: 48, Abel-Smith 1983: 97–8).

Although not Beveridge's intention,[3] legislation has generally treated widows more favorably – but not as favorably as in the Netherlands. Widows without dependent children were entitled to a full pension from age 50, but benefits could start from age 40 if a woman cared for dependent children. Originally, however, the national insurance scheme included a stiff "marriage duration test" of ten years, subsequently reduced to three years in the mid-1950s and repealed in 1970. Furthermore, the earnings limitation was abolished in the 1960s, making it possible to combine employment with the receipt of insurance benefits. A widow with dependent children received more favorable treatment than other mothers with respect to child benefits. Initially she received a benefit for the first child, and in the 1950s additions for the second and third child were introduced for all national insurance beneficiaries but eventually at a higher rate for widows – one of the few departures from the principle of uniform benefits (Richardson 1984).

Family allowances, in contrast with the Netherlands, were paid to the mother, but the father retained the right of child tax exemptions, which was arguably the most generous form of family support (Land and Parker 1978: 345) in terms of its cost to the public purse. Beveridge's proposal excluded the first child from the family allowance scheme on the grounds that "few men's wages are insufficient to cover at least two adults and one child," while tax exemptions could be claimed for all the children. The family allowance was also subject to tax, and one effect of this arrangement was a redistribution of resources within the family from the wallet to the purse (Kaim-Caudle 1973: 267). The family allowance was originally set at a lower rate than the one Beveridge recommended, and it went for long periods without being upgraded.

While payment of family allowances to mothers represented an initial step toward policies based on the principle of care, British legislation of the

1970s reinforced the notion of the wife's duty to provide care and service in the home without remuneration because she was supported by her husband. Married women were ineligible to receive the invalid care allowance, which had been introduced to compensate people for having to give up employment to care for the infirm. The housewives' non-contributory invalidity pension also imposed more rigorous qualifying conditions than the regular non-contributory pension.

The norm of the traditional family with the husband as the keeper of his wife's income and the financial head of the household also influenced tax legislation. Joint taxation of spouses was obligatory. However, the British working wife received a tax allowance which was identical to a single earner's tax relief. Furthermore, irrespective of whether or not he had a "dependent" wife, the husband received a married man's allowance (Wilkinson 1982), which has been roughly one and a half times the single earner's allowance.

Perhaps because of the married woman's earnings allowance, British women's labor participation rates have been considerably higher than Dutch women's. At the end of the 1960s nearly 50 percent of married women were economically active (Lewis 1992b: 65, Land and Parker 1978: 338). On the whole, the tax system furnished incentives for married women to seek employment, while the structure of insurance benefits pulled in the opposite direction. If a wife used the married woman's option, she received no benefits, and employment meant her husband lost the adult dependant allowance. Men's modest wages and low benefit levels may have obliged women to enter the labor market. In many instances wives' earnings, in supplementing family income, have kept the family out of poverty (Land and Parker 1978: 338, Millar 1987: 163).

At first glance, the UK seems to fit the breadwinner model less well than the Netherlands. British policies deviated in four ways. Payment of family allowances was made to the mother, which can be interpreted as an initial recognition of the principle of care. Second, medical care through the national health service was a citizen benefit unaffected by family status, whereas Dutch married women were covered as family members. Third, British married women received a more generous tax allowance. Fourth, the unit of benefits in the UK was the individual – not the family. As a beneficiary the husband received an adult dependant allowance when his wife was not in paid work, and his wife was entitled to a dependant's pension without extra contributions when she reached retirement age. Since benefits were tied to the individual, the wife's dependant pension was hers. In one respect, the British system was stricter than the Dutch. The husband collected an adult dependant allowance only when the wife had no earnings or her earnings were less than the allowance, whereas benefits were paid to the Dutch household irrespective of the wife's employment status. Nonetheless, underlying similarities in both the UK and the Netherlands were that the husband was the prime recipient of benefits, the wife's benefits were derived from her husband's social rights, and the tax systems treated the husband as family provider generously.

The United States: two tiers of welfare and women's dependency

The minimalist approach to public provision of welfare in the USA might seem to suggest a smaller role for the breadwinner model. Nonetheless, it has exerted a major influence on legislation affecting the two tiers of public provision of welfare and taxation. In the social security tier, married women's claims to benefits have been heavily dependent upon their husband's rights and earnings, while women's claims in the welfare tier have often been based on the absence of a male breadwinner and poverty status.

The breadwinner ideology's most visible impact on the social security tier has been the spouse benefit and survivor benefits of the Old Age, Survivors' and Disability Insurance (OASDI) program. The spouse benefit has corresponded to 50 percent of the insured worker's old age or disability pension, and survivor benefits amounted to 80 percent before 1972. As married women have entered the labor market, they have been covered by social security in their own right. Upon retirement working wives have been able to choose between a spouse benefit or a benefit based on their own earnings – but not both, that is, the spouse benefit plus a benefit based on their own earnings. Married women with social security benefits based on their own earnings which were less than their spouse benefit have had dual entitlement, and they have received a secondary benefit which has made up the difference.

The spouse benefit has generally worked to the advantage of the traditional family with a single breadwinner and to the disadvantage of the two-earner family (Bergmann 1986: 223; cf. Miller 1990: 122; Lopata and Brehm 1986). In many cases when these two types of families have had roughly the same earnings the family with the single breadwinner has received a larger pension and the wife has ended up with more generous survivor benefits (see table 3.1). An inspection of the table illustrates the impact on social security benefits of different earning patterns among spouses in families with the same income in the mid-1960s. In family A with a single earner, both spouses generally came out ahead. Their total retirement benefits and the wife's survivor benefits were higher than the benefits of the other three families. Conversely, family B, where the earnings of the husband and wife were equal, was the most disadvantaged, receiving the lowest retirement and survivor benefits.

Table 3.1 *Average annual lifetime earnings and annual social security retirement and survivor benefits in the USA, 1966 (US$)*

	Family A	Family B	Family C	Family D
Earnings				
Husband	7,000	3,500	4,620	5,250
Wife	0	3,500	2,380	1,750
Total	7,000	7,000	7,000	7,000
Retirement benefits				
Husband	2,016	1,324	1,592	1,728
Wife	1,008	1,324	1,074	925
Total	3,024	2,648	2,666	2,653
Divorced wife	1,008	1,324	1,074	925
		($662)[a]	($796)[a]	($864)[a]
Survivor benefits				
Wife and divorced wife	1,663	1,092	1,314	1,426

Notes:
[a] Benefits if the divorced wife had not been working. Benefits for divorced wives assume that they met the marriage duration test of twenty years.
Source: Calculations are for 1966 based on the 1965 Social Security Act. *Social Security Handbook*, 3rd edn., 1966: 119–40.

The one earner family has been favored not only in terms of benefits but also in terms of costs. In effect, the spouse benefit is a non-contributory benefit, and the one earner family has not had to pay extra social security taxes. By contrast, the earnings of both the husband and wife have been taxed, and they are regarded as separate taxable units. The existence of a ceiling on taxable income for social security taxes further heightened the inequities in the taxation of dual earner and single earner families. If the total earnings of the dual earner couple were greater than the ceiling of taxable income for social security taxes, they paid a larger amount in taxes than the single earner family with the same earnings (Pechman et al. 1968: 81). Furthermore, the total earnings of nearly all women were subject to social security taxes, whereas this was true for only on average around half of male workers in the 1960s (Polinsky 1969: 10). In other words, the traditional family has often enjoyed a larger pension and survivor benefits but paid lower social security taxes.

Aged widows receiving survivor benefits have been treated more generously than younger widows without dependants, but the earliest qualifying age of 60 was much higher than in the other countries, where full benefits were granted at the age of 50. Moreover the US widow who collected benefits at age 60 had her benefits reduced to around 70 percent of what they would have been if she had waited until she was 65. Instead of receiving a survivor benefit of around 80 percent of her deceased husband's benefits she collected slightly less than 60 percent. Besides the problem of reduced benefits, many US widows have experienced difficulties because of the so called "widow gap" – the years when they qualify for neither social security benefits as widows with dependent children nor as aged survivors. At the end of the 1960s around 35 percent of late middle-aged widows who were not eligible for social security benefits lived in poverty, and only 6 percent received public assistance (Thompson 1980: 138).

Perhaps more surprising, at least initially, is the extent of poverty among widows with children in the late 1960s. A widow caring for dependent children was entitled to a survivor benefit equal to 75 percent of the deceased worker's benefit and the children received a similar benefit. Widows with children encountered economic hardship for several reasons. Benefits are earnings related, and death rates have been higher among men with lower incomes. Rules concerning the maximum family benefit also disadvantage families with several children. Benefit levels in the 1960s were relatively low and not indexed. Whatever the reason, the poverty rates among widows with children were even higher than among widows without children – around 45 percent – in the late 1960s (Mallan 1975: 7–9).

Social security regulations were also very harsh on divorced women – and much harsher than in the Netherlands. Divorced women were originally excluded from all benefits, and the first departures from this principle entailed "support" tests. In 1950 divorced widows with dependent children became entitled to survivor benefits if their ex-husband had maintenance responsibilities amounting to one-half of their support. A 1965 social security amendment entitled a divorced woman to a spouse benefit and a survivor benefit under the condition that she had been married for a minimum of twenty years (Abramovitz 1988: 262–3). A divorced home-maker married less than this period still found herself completely outside the system, and her years in the home were a liability in calculating her own social security benefits based on employment after divorce. Even the divorced woman who qualified for a spouse benefit was not much better off, since the adequacy of the spouse benefit as a half benefit presupposes the existence of the retired worker's full benefit. Table 3.1 indicates the meager nature of retirement benefits of divorced wives without employment during marriage. All the spouse benefits in the table were below the 1967 poverty line for a household consisting of a single person, whereas the total retirement benefits for the couples were above the poverty line (Orshansky 1968: 4). Quite clearly, the functioning of the social security system rewarded the married homemaker and punished the divorced homemaker.

In conclusion, the benefits of aged survivors, widows with dependent children, and retired divorced women underline the pivotal nature of the male breadwinner in the social security tier and the increased likelihood of inadequate benefits in the event of his absence. The social security tier has generally failed to provide adequate benefits to persons who were neither the major breadwinner nor married to a breadwinner. In some instances the absence of a breadwinner and ensuing insufficient means have led to entitlement in the welfare tier – but only if one qualified under one of the categories of the deserving poor.

In the welfare tier the male breadwinner model and the principle of maintenance affected the eligibility conditions of women. To be one of the deserving poor, and considered in true need, women had to demonstrate the absence of a male breadwinner in the household. Marriage, remarriages and cohabitation disqualified women from receiving public assistance. The effects were most widespread for single mother families receiving benefits from the Aid to Families with Dependent Children program (AFDC). Its predecessor (ADC) initially provided benefits only to children in the event of the death or permanent absence of the father. The legitimacy of the program stems from the notion of children – or more precisely deserted children – as a category of the deserving poor. It is noteworthy that the defining condition of desert has not been children's poverty but the absence of the male breadwinner. An amendment in 1950 extended benefits to mothers but the importance attributed to the absence of the father resulted in "no man in the house" rules. Likewise state governments have discriminated against AFDC applicants whose children were born out of wedlock. The breadwinner ideology and the principle of maintenance have also influenced AFDC in its concern to establish paternity and to enforce support obligations to recipient children. In the early 1960s federal legislation required the states to establish paternity and collect support payments from these fathers.

The federal income tax system has also favored the traditional family. In 1948 Congress adopted legislation which encoded the principle of community property, and the unit of taxation was changed from the individual to the marital unit (husband and wife) but without mandatory joint taxation, as in the UK. Advantageous tax schedules for couples privileged marriage, and income splitting benefited families with a single provider or with high income inequality among spouses. This system was especially to the advantage of single earner families with high incomes since it counteracted progressivity. Solo parents as heads of household received more tax relief than single taxpayers but less than a married couple with a sole provider. Couples with two earners with similar incomes gained nothing from income splitting (Groves 1963: 72–3). Thus one tax expert quipped, "The two job family may be the true exception to the rule that two people can live more cheaply (per capita) than one" (Groves 1969: 117). Two earner families were further disadvantaged because most of them did not receive any tax concessions for extra household and childcare costs in connection with employment. Tax deductions for childcare were introduced in 1954 but they were limited to single parents and low income working wives. Less than 5 percent of working mothers with children under 12 claimed deductions in the mid-1960s (calculated from SIT 1968: 127–8).

During most of the postwar period the tax system has favored the traditional family on three scores. First, although married couples have been able to choose between individual and joint taxation, the system has actually encouraged joint taxation of spouses. Joint returns have been subject to preferential tax rates, and tax relief has been less beneficial to two earner families in relation to families with a sole provider. Second, the sole earner family has received the same tax exemptions as the two earner family, which virtually amounts to deduction for a dependent spouse. Third, single parent families have not enjoyed the same advantage as a sole provider with a spouse. These three features of the tax system have been aptly described as the two earner marriage penalty; the housewife bonus; and the single parent penalty (Bergmann 1986: 218–20).

Single parent families have been disadvantaged not only because of lower personal exemptions compared to the traditional one earner family but also by the way the breadwinner ideology has affected family support through tax relief for children rather than family allowances. Cash transfers increase the disposable income of families in low and middle income brackets, while tax exemptions provide no help to solo mothers who have low earnings or no earned income.

The breadwinner model was inscribed in the tax and social security systems so as to privilege the traditional family, and in particular such families with high incomes. Despite the disincentives created through disadvantages for the two earner family, it needs to be stressed that the social security system provided incentives for women as individuals. Their social security benefits as workers in all likelihood would be greater than spouse benefit. Married women's labor market participation rate has been much higher than that of their counterparts in the Netherlands and approached that of the UK. In the mid-1960s 35 percent of married women were working outside the home (SIT 1968: 128), and there were relatively few families of the type most heavily penalized by the social security and tax systems – couples with equal or near equal earnings. In 1966 wives, on average, contributed 22.4 percent to family income (SIT 1968: 138), a portion which did not differ very much from that of Dutch or British working wives (see Rainwater 1979, *Statistical Yearbook* 1969–70: 284–6).

In the Netherlands and the UK the breadwinner model had wider repercussions for women because it affected a larger range of social rights, and married women – even those in the labor market – did not share the same rights to statutory social benefits as men or single women. In the USA the repercussions were of a narrower scope, because several of these statutory benefits did not exist. US married women were not stripped of their rights, as in the Netherlands, nor were they encouraged to renounce their rights, as in the UK. In one sense, however, the effects were equally or more severe. In the 1960s the US social security system stood out in its harsh treatment of widows and divorced women.

Sweden: entitlements based on citizenship and the principle of care

The influence of the breadwinner model in the Swedish case has been less pervasive for four reasons. First, entitlement to benefits on the basis of citizenship incorporated married women into major social insurance schemes, providing them with individual entitlement to benefits. Second, married women's entitlements were enhanced by the gradual demise of means tested benefits. Third, legislation has highlighted the needs of children, resulting in supplements for children instead of for wives. Fourth, the principle of care has strengthened women's claims to benefits both as mothers and caregivers rather than as wives.

The breadwinner ideology's influence in social provision was mainly limited to wife supplements in unemployment insurance (1941–64) and the basic pension scheme, survivor annuities of occupational injury insurance, and widow benefits in the public pension schemes. Its influence was stronger on pension contributions and the tax system until reforms in the 1970s, but the principle of care had a moderating effect on taxes. Finally, the strongest impact of the breadwinner model was on wage policy, institutionalized in special women's wages until 1960, and labor market measures gave priority to men's employment through most of the 1960s.

Entitlements based on citizenship date from Sweden's first national old age and disability insurance scheme adopted in 1913, which has been heralded as the first universal pension program legislated in the world (Heclo 1974: 192). Unlike many early pension schemes that covered only wage earners (such as the Netherlands) or only provided pensions to those with a modest income (such as both the Netherlands and the UK), the Swedish 1913 legislation covered all occupational groups and income brackets. What has seldom been noted, however, is that the legislation's claim to universality also rested upon the inclusion of all women as members of the scheme. The importance of this arrangement in the long term was to establish the principle of individual entitlement to a pension regardless of sex, marital status, labor market status, and income.[4]

Nor did compulsory insurance providing sickness benefits (introduced in 1955) restrict coverage to the working population, as in the UK and the Netherlands. Married women at home and single parents at home with children under 16 years old were entitled to minimum cash benefits. In other words, the compulsory insurance system incorporated all women as beneficiaries in their own right – and not as the *raison d'être* of benefit supplements for men as in the UK. This policy construction differed from the earlier state subsidized voluntary scheme which had only provided a minimum cash benefit to members with an income, and married women had been insured as family members entitled to medical benefits. Women's incorporation into the pension and sickness insurance schemes as individuals can be interpreted as a modest recognition that work in the home qualified for entitlement to social benefits.

For benefits based on citizenship to enhance the entitlements of married women, it is equally important that means tested and income tested measures are minimal. Consequently the gradual removal of means testing has strengthened married women's social rights. Among the major landmarks have been the 1946 pension reform that made citizen pensions the main form of old age provision, the introduction of universal child allowances in 1948, the conversion of means tested maternity allowances into flat rate maternity grants in conjunction with the 1955 sickness insurance reform, and the termination of income testing of disability pensions in the early 1960s. For example, prior to the 1960 reform, disability benefits consisted of a basic flat rate allowance awarded to all persons with a certified disability plus an income tested allowance. The general allowance was a basic minimum (one-fifth of full benefits in the early 1950s and around one-tenth at the end of the decade). In the early 1950s married women were mainly recipients of the minimum allowance, while married men were granted full benefits (SOS 1953: 38–9).

It is also striking how few social insurance benefits women have received on the basis of their status as dependent wives, and it is informative to look more closely at those existing in the late 1960s. The sequence of development of wives' benefits in the pension system differs from the other three countries, whereas occupational injury insurance offers a closer parallel. Wives' benefits in the pension system developed late – roughly a generation after the other countries.[5] Instead, the first supplements and "survivor" benefits in the old age and invalidity pension scheme were granted to children – not to wives. A child supplement was introduced in 1918 followed by allowances for fatherless children and orphans in the late 1930s. It was not until the 1946 pension reform that provisions were made for widows and wives, but these benefits were subject to income testing at a time when the elimination of means tested benefits was high on the policy agenda. The

qualifying ages were relatively high (initially 55 for widows without dependent children and 60 for wives), and there were "marriage" tests (Elmér,
1958: 199, 1963: 193–4, 202, 206).

The real breakthrough of widow benefits occurred in the early 1960s. The
income testing of widow pensions was removed, and the qualifying age for
widows without dependent children was lowered in 1960. These changes led
to a sixfold increase in beneficiaries (SOS 1964: 35). More importantly, the
newly adopted state scheme of supplementary occupational pensions
(ATP) included survivor benefits for wives and dependent children. As the
supplementary pension scheme has matured (the first payments were in
1963), an increasing number of women have received benefits by virtue of
their status as wives. To qualify for widow benefits a wife had to have been
married a minimum of five years. Divorced wives and remarried widows
generally lost their claims to benefits. Ironically, because of ATP's strict
adherence to the requirement of legal marriage, cohabiting widows have
not had to relinquish their survivor benefits (Elmér 1971: 211).

Developments in occupational injury insurance followed a different
course. Workmen's compensation enacted in 1901 pre-dated the introduction of national old age and invalidity insurance. One source of inspiration
behind the Workmen's Compensation Act was the 1884 German insurance
scheme. Contrary to the national insurance scheme, the act limited coverage to industrial workers and provided compensation for industrial accidents, including survivor annuities. By the 1960s coverage encompassed all
employees, including domestic, casual, and family workers (with the exception of wives). In contrast to the pension system, marriage was not a
requirement for payment of occupational injury benefits at the end of the
1960s. A divorced wife, a cohabiting woman, and children born out of
wedlock were not disqualified, but the woman's benefits were forfeited
upon marriage (Elmér 1971: 241–50). In summary, a highly contradictory
picture emerges with regard to women's treatment as wives in social insurance schemes, and with respect to pension benefits it contrasted sharply
with their treatment as citizens and as mothers.

Benefits based on the principle of care gained importance with the introduction of population policies in the 1930s to halt a decline in the birthrate.
Maternity grants (*moderskapspenning*) were introduced in 1937 and maternity assistance in kind (*mödrahjälp*) in 1938. These reforms extended coverage so that nearly all mothers received maternity benefits (Elmér 1958: 230,
Abukhanfusa 1987). Advanced maintenance allowances – public child
support payments – to single mothers were also initiated in the late 1930s,
and subsequent reforms have improved the allowances. Universal family
allowances were introduced in 1948 but as distinct from most countries,
including the Netherlands and the UK, the allowance from its inception

covered *all* children – and thus all mothers. The introduction of maternity grants and child allowances also undermined the principle of maintenance. Especially when first enacted, these measures had a major impact on family income and tended to erode claims that a family wage – a higher wage paid to married men because of family responsibilities – was necessary. Finally, the removal of means testing of benefits to mothers, for the most part, came earlier than for benefits to wives.

The breadwinner model influenced pension contributions and the tax system until the 1971 reform introducing individual taxation and contributions. Although state revenues constituted the major source of funding of the basic pension scheme, a contribution fee was levied on each adult Swedish citizen until the mid-1970s. The exact formula for calculating pension contributions varied over the years, but married couples were generally treated more favorably than single individuals. This was especially true during the 1960s inasmuch as the maximum fee was the same for both married couples and single persons. This arrangement entailed a housewife bonus for married couples with a single earner, but it also meant that a wife's earnings were less likely to be penalized (SOS 1953: 9, 1964: 29).

The Swedish tax system, prior to the 1970 decision to eliminate joint taxation of spouses' earnings, combined aspects of the breadwinner model and the principle of care. Married couples, irrespective of the wife's employment status, were entitled to a tax allowance which was double the amount for a single earner. Accordingly, the Swedish single earner couple enjoyed a larger housewife bonus than in the UK but comparable to that in the USA. On the other hand, the Swedish tax system had traditionally allowed relief for families where the wife had her own income from employment (1919–38, 1947–86). The 1952 tax reform entitled working wives with children who were minors to a larger allowance than other working wives. This allowance was successively raised so that on the eve of the 1971 tax reform, a working wife with children received a standard tax allowance, which amounted to nearly twice that of her husband. Finally, tax reforms of the early 1960s benefited single parents by granting them the same conditions of taxation as a married couple – in effect a double tax allowance and the same preferential rate of taxation (Elvander 1972, SOU 1964: 25). In short, despite the generous housewife bonus, the Swedish tax system did not entail a single parent penalty and tax allowances to working mothers often offset a two earner marriage penalty. (However, two job marriages where each spouse had high earnings did confront a marriage penalty because of progressivity in the tax rates.) Also in contrast to the other countries, the tax position of the breadwinner had already been eroded by the loss of exemptions for children with the introduction of general family allowances in the late 1940s. Thus wives – and especially mothers – had more tax advantages and fathers had fewer, compared to their counterparts in the other countries. The favorable tax treatment of mothers – and increases in their tax allowances during the 1950s and 1960s – also signaled growing recognition of women's dual roles as carers and earners.

Lastly, the breadwinner model exerted influence on wage and employment policies through the 1960s, although its strength was in the process of eroding. Special women's wages were commonplace in manufacturing, and in 1960 women's hourly wages were roughly 70 percent of men's. Although the trade unions (LO) had sought to reduce wage differentials since 1951, women's gains were largely negated by wage drift, which increased men's earnings. In 1960 labor and management reached a decision to abolish special wages for women over a five-year period, which eventually led to decreased differences (Qvist 1975: 28–9). The active labor market measures of the late 1950s and 1960s were primarily geared to men who were the participants in training programs and recipients of mobility grants. Training allowances were subject to an income test of a spouse's income (Rainwater et al. 1985) which disadvantaged married women. Perhaps not surprisingly, Swedish married women's rate of employment was roughly on a par with that in the USA and the UK during the 1960s (SCB 1973: 47), although the situation was to change dramatically in the next decade. A major difference, however, was a higher rate of economic activity among women with children, and particularly young children (Rainwater 1979).[6] To sum up, what we find in the 1960s is a gendered division of labor patterning policies through favorable treatment of women as mothers and of men as earners, superimposed upon social provision based on citizenship.

Policy patterns and gender relevant dimensions of variation

To summarize this discussion of policy patterns, let us compare the countries using the dimensions of variation in table 2.1. The celebration of marriage varied across the four countries, and its preferential treatment has been much more apparent in the policies of the Netherlands, the USA, and the UK. Favored treatment took the form of rewarding married couples and penalizing single individuals. Married couples enjoyed wife supplements or benefit levels based on family responsibilities and marital tax relief. In turn, single individuals often paid higher taxes and received lower benefits. Although the housewife bonus was a feature of taxation in all four countries, the Dutch tax system imposed much heavier tax burdens upon single individuals (Oldman and Temple 1960). Similarly the US social security system treated single persons far less generously than couples through lower replacement rates on their earnings (Pechman et al. 1968: 84–6).

Swedish legislation did not exalt marriage to the same extent as the other countries, and certain measures ran counter to a preferential treatment of marriage. Irrespective of their marital status mothers were entitled to benefits, and in some instances solo mothers received extra benefits. By the 1960s single parents received the same tax advantages as married couples, and all women with children received a family allowance. Nor did marriage matter in claiming occupational injury benefits. With respect to these benefits, divorced wives and never married women were not penalized. It is also noteworthy that benefits awarded to women as wives within the pension system were originally quite niggardly.

In all four countries the prevalent familial ideology at the end of the 1960s, as reflected in legislation, applauded a traditional division of labor with the husband as the primary earner and the wife as carer. Swedish policies, however, diverged from those of the other countries in significant ways. First, as a result of social rights based on citizenship, the privileged status of the breadwinner was not translated into social legislation to the same extent as in the other countries. This basis of eligibility resulted in uniform and personal entitlement within marriage. Married women had individual rights to a basic old age pension, disability and sickness benefits, and these rights were unaffected by marital status. By contrast, the basis of entitlement of married women and men in the other countries was highly differentiated. Married women's entitlement was largely derived from their husbands' rights, and they lacked individual entitlement.

Equally important, the traditional division of labor in the family – with the mother as carer – shaped legislation through incorporating the principle of care in a way which did not happen in the other countries. In fact, the Netherlands and Sweden represented polar opposites in terms of benefits attached to fatherhood and motherhood around 1970. Dutch benefits were almost entirely attached to the principle of maintenance; even family allowances and child delivery were covered through the father's insurance. The Swedish reforms of the 1930s introduced maternity benefits paid to nearly all mothers. Similarly child allowances were paid to all mothers – even unwed mothers – and advanced maintenance allowances aided single mothers. The Swedish tax system also granted women workers with children – and especially solo mothers – considerable tax relief.

The Netherlands, the UK, and the USA cluster together with respect to the breadwinner ideology and its effects on social provision, although the policy constructions differed. The Dutch have structured benefits around the family as the normal unit. Instead of relying on supplements for family members, benefits and wages themselves should be adequate to meet the needs of the average family. Accordingly, minimum benefits for single individuals have been calculated as a portion of the standard family benefits. This policy construction deprived married women of individual entitlements as long as the family was intact. As widows, however, they enjoyed ample pensions under lenient eligibility conditions. By contrast, mothers who were not wives were originally barred from maternity benefits and family allowances (Roebroek and Berben 1987: 692).

In the UK and the USA the *individual* was the unit of benefit but the principle of maintenance resulted in supplements to cover the additional costs of family members – often both the wife and children. In the UK the husband was entitled to the supplements with the exception of the dependant's pension, whereas in the USA benefits were generally conferred upon the wife. The UK adult dependant's allowance has been fairly generous in relative but not absolute terms. The allowance has provided 60 percent of the benefit of a single person. The US spouse benefit amounted to 50 percent of the husband's benefit and in absolute terms has been quite generous, and the survivor benefits were even more generous, totaling 80 percent of the husband's benefit. For these benefits the unit of contribution has been the family, since they have not entailed extra contributions or social security taxes. Nonetheless, the individual as the unit of benefit has meant that wives whose entitlements are based on their husbands' insurance have received a pension of their own. Ironically, because of this arrangement, wives' economic dependency has been less among pensioners than among other married couples (Sørensen and McLanahan 1987).

The male breadwinner model was also reflected in labor legislation, and again policies in Sweden and the Netherlands exemplified the extreme positions. Already by the late 1930s the first Swedish measures had been taken to prohibit employers from firing women as a result of engagement, marriage, or pregnancy. In the 1960s legislation protected a woman from dismissal for childbirth if she had been working one year for the same employer. Job protection in the event of marriage or engagement extended to all jobs irrespective of length of employment. In the Netherlands legislation did not forbid employers from firing women workers because of marriage and pregnancy until 1970s.

In conclusion, applying gender relevant dimensions results in a clustering of countries which is quite different from the clusters produced by mainstream typologies. Using mainstream models the Netherlands and Sweden have often been bracketed together as ambitious and comprehensive welfare states scoring high on decommodification (eliminating dependence on the market), while the USA and the UK have been categorized as both less ambitious and less decommodifying. However, along several gender relevant dimensions of variation the policies of the Netherlands and Sweden represented polar extremes. Dutch policies were the most "familialized," with benefits and contributions revolving around the family, whereas Swedish women's entitlements were the most "individualized." Benefits in the Netherlands were tied to the principle of maintenance and fatherhood, while the principle of care and motherhood underpinned several Swedish benefits. The policies of the two countries also differed diametrically in their treatment of working wives and working mothers.

Mainstream scholarship has also grouped together Sweden and the UK as similar types of welfare state because of their universalist approach to social provision and emphasis on social citizenship. This classification overlooks differences in women's social rights and how women have been incorporated into the welfare state. Universalism in the UK has referred to coverage of the working population including the family dependants of workers, whereas in Sweden coverage has encompassed all citizens and eventually all residents. The British brand of social citizenship has been molded by the liberal tradition, where rights are based on obligations. Social rights in the national insurance scheme are contingent upon fulfilled obligations – the duty of work and payment of contributions. By contrast, a radical ideal has imbued many Swedish social rights. Each individual as a human being and all members of the community possess social rights. These dissimilar philosophical foundations have enormous repercussions for women's social rights. In short, the differences in women's and men's social rights in Sweden *vis-à-vis* the other three countries, and the sharp contrasts between Dutch and Swedish policies, underline the incomplete nature of mainstream typologies and the importance of incorporating gender in order to capture major welfare state variations.

Limitations of the breadwinner model

As this chapter has unfolded, it has also become increasingly apparent that the Swedish case does not square with assumptions concerning the pervasive early influence of the breadwinner model on social insurance schemes, producing "paternal" welfare states. At several critical junctures, Swedish decision makers opted for policy constructions which deviated from the Bismarckian social insurance model. Of the early social insurance schemes only workmen's compensation was patterned after Bismarckian legislation by narrowing beneficiaries to industrial workers. Instead old age and disability insurance covered all citizens. Nor did the 1930s' population policies adopt an insurance model but instead provided state grants to nearly all mothers. The 1935 pension reform further departed from insurance principles by reducing the importance of contributions and making public revenues the main source of funding, and the 1946 pension reform broke the link between state funding and means testing. The 1955 sickness insurance reform also provided cash benefits to nearly all citizens. These policy constructions had far-reaching repercussions for the social rights of women in general and married women in particular as citizens and mothers and in the process dwarfed their entitlements as wives.

A central point emerging from this chapter has been the importance of entitlements based on citizenship and the principle of care in undermining the influence of the breadwinner ideology and the principle of maintenance in social provision. This has been clearest in Swedish policies. The same phenomena, although less pronounced, are evident in the UK and the Netherlands and point to the defamilializing potential of these forms of entitlement in a cross-national perspective. In the UK the family allowance paid to the mother and medical benefits based on citizenship through the national health service were unaffected by marital status, and in this respect lessened women's dependency in marriage since divorce did not deprive them of these benefits. Similarly, Dutch widow and old age pensions covered all citizens, and divorced women were not outside these benefit systems, as they often were in the UK and the USA. In other words, entitlements based on citizenship have defamilializing effects, irrespective of the national context.

The preceding analysis also suggests the need to revise the breadwinner model in two respects. First, although the breadwinner model strongly influenced the policies of the Netherlands, the UK, and the USA, the differences in policy constructions between the Netherlands with the family as the unit of benefit and obligations, and the other two countries with benefits and obligations tied to the individual, suggest two variants of the breadwinner model. The fact that benefits have been attached to the individual has had important consequences for married women. Even if their entitlement was based on their husbands' rights, pensions have been paid to women, providing them with a source of income which Dutch wives did not receive.

Second, Swedish policies in the 1960s deviated from the breadwinner model but did not fit the individual model either. Swedish women did have more individual social rights but several of these entitlements were rooted in a traditional familial ideology and a strongly gendered division of labor which is the antithesis of the individual model. To accommodate the Swedish case we can conceive of a traditional family model of social policy encompassing two types: the breadwinner variant, and the separate gender roles variant. Both variants share a familial ideology which prescribes a strict division of labor between husband and wife, and entitlement is differentiated. In the breadwinner model the principle of maintenance prevails and married women's social rights are via their husbands. In the separate roles variant there are two bases of entitlement – the principle of maintenance underpinning men's social rights and the principle of care enhancing women's social rights.

More important for the following analysis are the implications of the Swedish case for the male breadwinner model. Although the male bread-winner model is useful in analyzing social provision in the Netherlands, the UK, and the USA, it does a much poorer job in accommodating the Swedish configuration of policies. A major shortcoming of the breadwinner model is its concentration on the husband as the principal beneficiary and the main source of women's social entitlements. The model fails to distinguish between women's entitlement as wives and as mothers. Swedish policies suggest the necessity to rethink the male breadwinner model and to consider a female caregiver model focusing on motherhood and the principle of care as a basis of entitlement as a crucial welfare state variation.

4   Women's entitlements as mothers and caregivers

Women's social entitlements as mothers and caregivers have seldom been the focus of analysis in the literature on contemporary welfare states. Mainstream welfare state typologies and models of social policy have devoted little attention to family policy, and they have attached even less weight to maternal benefits. Although comparative policy analyses have dealt with family and maternity benefits, they have been divorced from a larger context of welfare state variations and theorizing about types of welfare state. Interest in maternal policies has experienced an upswing in feminist scholarship, but most of this work traces the origins of social policy, placing women's entitlements as mothers in a historical setting.

Feminist discussions of women's present day entitlements have instead largely revolved around the breadwinner model and social rights derived from status as a dependant in the family. These analyses have either highlighted women's entitlements as wives or equated wifely and motherly labor. When women's entitlements as wives and mothers are compounded, a fundamental difference in the construction of family benefits is easily missed: whether benefits are tied to the principle of care with the mother as the recipient or to the principle of maintenance, conferring rights to the father. This difference, for example, cuts across Lewis and Ostner's typology of breadwinner states. Both the Netherlands and the UK are categorized as strong breadwinner states; but, as we have seen, the principle of maintenance underpinned Dutch benefits, while family benefits in the UK have entailed a recognition of the principle of care.

The problematic nature of the male breadwinner model is not limited to how it has been applied. Its inadequacy in analyzing women's social rights is obvious in the case of single mothers (Lewis and Ostner 1991, 1994, Hobson 1994). Their entitlements are at odds with the model, challenging the very essence of the breadwinner ideology – its celebration of marriage and a strict division of labor between the sexes, and in some instances the centrality of the principle of maintenance. Furthermore, as Barbara Hobson (1994) has shown, the degree to which social benefits provide mother only families with an adequate standard of living varies across countries classified as strong breadwinner states, such as Germany, the Netherlands, and the UK.

The point of departure of this chapter is that women's entitlements as mothers constitute an important welfare state variation that needs to be distinguished from their entitlements as wives. It is also necessary to make a distinction between social rights derived solely from motherhood and entitlements based on additional qualifying conditions, such as need and labor market status. A central argument here is that benefits based on motherhood and received by *all* mothers have the potential to undermine the principle of maintenance. Maternal benefits may also have a defamilial-izing capacity in providing a decent standard of living independent of family relationships. Viewed in these terms, the female caregiver model does not necessarily merely perpetuate the traditional gendered division of labor. Policies based on the principle of care that alter the boundary between the private and public spheres can serve as a stepping stone in the development toward the individual model of social policy.

Besides examining the extent and nature of entitlements based on moth-erhood this chapter also deals with the effects of these entitlements at the micro level – for individual mothers – and the macro level – societal notions of the range of proper activities in the private and public spheres. What is the emancipatory potential of social entitlements for individual mothers? To what degree has care in the home become "paid work" compensated by social benefits in our four countries? And to what extent has care and repro-ductive work been transferred from the private sphere to the public sphere?

In mapping out the extent to which women as mothers are entitled to social benefits and public services, this chapter initially looks at mothers who head families and assesses the quality of their social rights. Although these mothers have been in the limelight in policy discussions, it is impor-tant not to confine the analysis to them. To understand women's entitle-ments as mothers we must examine the social rights of mothers in general. Accordingly, the discussion moves onto all mothers, looking first at bene-fits most basic to motherhood – those in connection with childbirth and the care of infants. Finally we turn to the provision of care outside the home and other services.

Solo mothers' entitlements: a challenge to the male breadwinner model?

The entitlements of solo mothers are of special interest for several reasons. Theoretically, solo mothers pose a challenge to the breadwinner model. As single parents, they must often fulfill dual roles as earners and caregivers. If solo mothers actually perform these twin tasks, they approximate the division of labor of the individual model of social policy rather than the highly gendered division of tasks in the family as prescribed by the breadwinner ideology. On the other hand, the ways that the male breadwinner model and female caregiver model are encoded in legislation affect both solo mothers' ability to fulfill these roles and the quality of their social rights. Solo mothers are also of theoretical interest because they, more dramatically than women in general, expose basic contradictions and limitations in Esping-Andersen's reasoning on decommodification.

In particular I want to assess the emancipatory potential of solo mothers' social rights. The mainstream literature has viewed the emancipatory potential of social entitlements as eliminating class inequalities (Marshall 1950) or more recently as decommodification – independence from market forces (Esping-Andersen 1990). Esping-Andersen argues that the decisive criterion in determining the decommodifying potential of policies is whether they provide a genuine work–welfare choice, allowing individuals and families to uphold a socially acceptable standard of living independent of market participation (1990: 23, 37, 50, 54). The emancipatory vision of feminists has stressed women's financial independence and autonomy in family relationships, and that "defamilialization" offers a yardstick for evaluating women's social rights (Lister 1994a, 1994b). This criterion is important in determining the extent to which solo mothers' social entitlements challenge the breadwinner model. The term "defamilialization" has two unfortunate consequences. As a parallel to decommodification it perpetuates a clumsy vocabulary. More importantly, the term conjures up associations of weakening or abolishing the family; but what is at stake is remaking the patterns of family relationships and bestowing social rights upon family members.

In comparing the social entitlements of solo mothers I use two criteria: their decommodifying and defamilializing effects. These effects can be gauged through the degree that social policies enable solo mothers and their children to enjoy a socially acceptable standard of living independent of the market and of family relationships. At a minimum, a socially acceptable standard of living can be specified as a livelihood above the poverty line, and a widely used poverty line is defined as 50 percent of the median disposable income adjusted for family size. Parity in the economic well-being of single and two parent families furnishes an additional way to establish the existence of such a standard.

Social policies to aid mother only families are a common denominator in the four countries. The policies of the USA, the UK, and the Netherlands, however, cluster together in that assistance programs are the main form of social provision available to these mothers. Admittedly widows have received insurance benefits but their share of mother only

Table 4.1 *Mother only families, labor force participation, and poverty status around 1980*[a]

	Mother only families as a % of all families	Solo mothers % in the workforce	Married mothers % in the workforce	Solo mothers % on welfare	Lone parents' pre-transfer poverty rate	Lone parents' post-transfer poverty rate	Two parent families' post-transfer poverty rate
Netherlands	9 (1985)	24 (1985)	28 (1985)	63 (1983)	73 (1983)	6 (1983)	7 (1983)
UK	11	49	52	45	54	19	5
USA	18	68	54	53	53	46	12
Sweden	18	87	76	18	33	5	2

Note:
[a] The poverty line is 50 percent of the median income adjusted for family size, which differs from the "official" poverty lines of various countries. The data for the USA, the UK, and Sweden are for 1979–81 and for the Netherlands 1983–5.

Sources: Mitchell 1991: 68, SCP 1988b: 54,17, Gustafsson 1990: 155,152, SCB 1981: 203, GHS 1983: 113, EOC 1988: 44, Kamerman 1984: 257, Reischauer 1989: 15.

families has dwindled over the past three decades. At the beginning of the 1980s assistance benefits constituted the main source of income of between 45 to 55 percent of single mothers in these three countries. Two crucial differences between the assistance schemes of the countries are benefit levels and the degree of uniformity in benefits. These differences affect the capacity of these programs to provide a socially acceptable standard of living, and the extent that solo mothers are lifted out of poverty has varied enormously across the countries (table 4.1).

The Swedish policy matrix is significantly different. Although social assistance has been available to solo mothers, and a disproportionate number of single mothers received such allowances in the early 1980s, social assistance has rarely been the major source of income for solo mothers. Instead earnings, together with universal and selective benefits and services, have comprised the basis of the well-being of mother only families in Sweden.

The Netherlands: solo mothers and the social minimum

Dutch family policy, as we have seen, has provided generous transfers which were almost exclusively the prerogative of the married man as the head of the family and family provider. Because so many benefits were granted to the father and the norm of the maternal care has been so strongly ingrained, mothers often lacked both entitlement to insurance benefits and employment. Unlike married mothers, however, the solo mother as the head of the household has been entitled to a family minimum in her own right – 90 percent of the social minimum of a married couple. On the other hand, like married mothers, the caregiver norm has influenced the situation of solo mothers.

The impact of the norm is visible in the employment pattern of Dutch mothers who have had a low labor market participation rate; the employment rate of solo mothers was even slightly lower than that of married mothers in the early 1980s (table 4.1). Only about 25 percent of solo mothers had paid employment as their major source of livelihood despite several incentives, especially compared with married women. When employed, the solo mother as primary earner was not excluded from certain benefits, as married mothers were, and she also received special tax relief. These measures making employment more attractive have been counterbalanced by powerful disincentives, however. Of special importance, the norm of the mother as caregiver has operated to exempt solo mothers from the requirement of availability for work in order to qualify for the social minimum. The strength of the norm also shows up in mothers' attitudes to combining children and work. In the mid-1980s nearly half of mothers of young children did not want to work, and a larger number believed that the absence of the mother from her children was harmful for the children or the mother (SCP 1993a: 35–6). Second, although a special earnings disregard has existed for solo mothers, the disregards have been for "secondary employment" (SZW 1982: 87), and full-time earnings could reduce means tested benefits. Third, the average disposable income of female headed families appears to have been roughly the same regardless of whether the mother was working or not (Wiebrens 1988: 147, *Statistisch jaarboek* 1992: 292, Hobson 1994).

Under these circumstances it is perhaps not surprising that social transfers constituted the main source of income for about three-fourths of solo mothers, and that they were heavily reliant on public assistance (ABW), especially if they were divorced and unmarried mothers (60 percent of divorced and unmarried mothers) (Wiebrens 1988: 148; SCP 1988b: 56). Mother only families have been dependent upon assistance for fairly long spells (Wiebrens 1988: 151), and in 1980 around 45 percent of the mothers on assistance had been receiving benefits for more than three years (SCP 1993b: 146–7). Solo mothers have also made use of housing allowances and several public services – legal aid, family counseling, day care centers – to a much greater extent than two parent families (SCP 1988b: 60, 63, 118).

Despite their heavy reliance on social transfers and assistance benefits Dutch solo mothers, in sharp contrast to those in the USA and to some degree the UK, have usually enjoyed a socially acceptable standard of living. The poverty rate of solo mothers in the early 1980s was relatively modest – 6 percent – and contrary to the situation in most industrial countries, Dutch lone parents were not overrepresented among the poor (Mitchell 1991: 67–8). Due to the low level of employment among Dutch solo mothers, their pre-transfer poverty rate was extremely high at nearly 75 percent. However, Dutch transfers were highly effective in eliminating poverty among mother only families, and benefits lifted 94 percent out of poverty.

The economic well-being of Dutch solo mothers and their families has been characterized by market independence. Judged by this criterion, the Dutch social minimum has had pronounced decommodifying effects for solo mothers. Of the four countries, Dutch mothers were the least likely to be in the labor market and dependent upon paid work for their livelihood. According to aggregate measures, they possessed roughly the same economic standard irrespective of whether they chose welfare or work. Nor was there any difference in the poverty rates of working and non-working solo mothers (Hobson 1994).

The social entitlements of solo mothers have made them largely independent of the market but this is less true of family relationships.

Admittedly the eligibility conditions for the social minimum run counter to the preferential treatment of marriage in the breadwinner model, but by relieving solo mothers of the necessity of having to register for work eligibility rules have preserved the traditional gendered division of labor in the family. The principle of maintenance has also continued to affect the economic resources of solo mothers. Until the early 1980s, as long as the mother was not the insured person, the father was formally the recipient of child allowance even if the child was not in his household.

Reliance on assistance has also entailed assessment of needs based on the maintenance principle and support obligations of the ex-husband if his financial resources were sufficient. Efficient child support collection machinery has also made fathers' contributions more commonplace than in the other three countries. In the 1980s seven out of ten children involved in parental divorces were estimated to receive child support (Wiebrens 1988: 139). Since the mid-1980s divorced mothers have had to claim alimony as a condition of receiving assistance, and if they have not claimed alimony the local authorities administering the assistance scheme have done so on their behalf (Holtmaat 1992: 347). In these ways, the economic well-being of divorced mothers has not been fully independent of that of their former partners.

The UK: benefits and earnings versus assistance

On a continuum of providing benefits based on the principle of care the UK follows Sweden – although the distance between the policies of the two countries is substantial. The introduction of the child benefit, replacing family allowances, strengthened social entitlements based on the principle of care. Phased in during 1977–9, the reform extended entitlement to the first child and upgraded benefit levels. Besides child benefit, lone mothers could also claim the child benefit increase (renamed the one parent benefit in 1981). Because of these benefits, virtually all solo mothers have received social benefits other than assistance. However, these benefits have been pitted against assistance, and they only increased the incomes of mothers not receiving assistance. All cash benefits and any maintenance payments have counted as income in calculating the amount of assistance.

A much larger proportion of British solo mothers – slightly over double that of Dutch single mothers – were employed in the early 1980s. Nearly 50 percent of British mothers were in the labor market (table 4.1) and had earnings. Thus British solo mothers were more likely to have state benefits and employment than their Dutch counterparts, but because income – both benefits and earnings – reduced means tested allowances, many British single mothers were no better off.

As displayed in table 4.1, slightly less than half of all British solo mothers received assistance, or as it was then called supplementary benefit, around 1980, and this was the main source of income for many. Besides a weekly allowance and additions for each child, supplementary benefit generally covered housing costs and automatically qualified the recipient for benefits in kind, such as free prescriptions, glasses, and dental care, school lunches, and welfare milk. Mothers on benefit also received help in paying "rates" – local government taxes and utility fees. Finally, supplementary benefit also contained a discretionary component to meet exceptional needs, for example heating, special diets, or maternity expenses.

A detailed analysis of low income mother only families around 1980 (Millar 1989) revealed the importance of state benefits and multiple sources of income to these families. In the sample of low income families the proportion of lone mothers on supplementary benefit increased to 80 percent. Mothers who were worst off generally had only one source of income. For solo mothers with earnings, universal non-contributory benefits and national insurance benefits contributed more to their net disposable income than did means tested benefits. For example, the child benefit and child benefit increase were especially important, accounting for around 20 percent of their net disposable income (Millar 1989: 60, 63, 87, 90).

The effect of transfers on the poverty status of single mothers in the UK is shown in table 4.1. The reduction of poverty was not nearly so dramatic as in the Dutch case, but 65 percent of mother only families were removed from poverty. One possible explanation of the proportion who remained in poverty is the low take up rates of means tested benefits and the one parent benefit. In her analysis, Jane Millar estimated that lone parents lost substantial potential additions to their income through unclaimed benefits (1989: 91–7). According to official statistics, take up rates of family income supplement (FIS) were notoriously low, at only about 50 percent, the one parent benefit was around 60 percent, and supplementary benefits 75 percent (DHSS 1981: 253). In any event, as distinct from the Netherlands where the choice between work and welfare resulted in similar disposable income above the poverty line, a choice for welfare in the UK increased the odds of being poor. The poverty rate of solo mothers whose main source of livelihood was social transfers was higher than those whose main source of livelihood was earnings (Hobson 1994: 178).

Assistance benefits in the UK have been characterized by both an "unemployment" trap and a poverty trap which affect the income of solo mothers. A peculiarity of the national assistance scheme and its successors (supplementary benefit and income support) has been the ineligibility of individuals in full-time employment – but not part-time employment. This regulation is one of several factors which may discourage full-time employment. During the 1980s, the economic activity rate of lone mothers dropped, and especially of those in full-time employment. A poverty trap exists when recipients of means tested benefits find that an increase in earnings is offset by simultaneous reductions in benefits and increased outlays due to income tax and national insurance contributions. The poverty trap has also been heightened by the additional benefits in kind and cash that more or less follow from assistance. On the other hand, solo mothers and their children have benefited enormously from medical services provided on the basis of citizenship, and these benefits have not contributed to the poverty trap.

As in the Netherlands, the dual roles of solo mothers as family providers and caregivers have resulted in contradictory legislative measures. In 1980 a more generous and tapered earnings disregard was introduced to encourage solo mothers to work. As family providers, they have also been able to claim a tax allowance comparable to the married man's allowance. Eligibility conditions for the family income supplement also favored single mothers over two parent families; a solo mother was eligible upon working fewer hours than the earner in a two parent family (Millar 1987: 173). By contrast, also in 1980 lone parents became eligible for the higher long-term rate of supplementary benefit after one year instead of two years – a measure which would seem to encourage utilization of assistance and longer spells on benefit. Nor have mothers had to register for work. The trends of the past decade entailed a shift from solo mothers as earners to caregivers – and a convergence toward the Dutch pattern with a heavier reliance on assistance benefits. Greater utilization of assistance also signified less independence from family relationships, especially after the Child Support Act came into effect in 1993. The Act made it mandatory for solo mothers receiving means tested benefits to authorize collection of maintenance payments.

The US: poor despite welfare or work

The single most important program for mother only families is Aid to Families with Dependent Children (AFDC). As a federal–state program administered at the state level, eligibility criteria and benefit levels vary from state to state. Benefits have been meager by most yardsticks – as a percentage of the average wage or the minimum wage – and the average benefits paid to recipients fell short of the program's own standards of need at the end of the 1970s (Duvall et al. 1982: 8–9). Even worse, AFDC benefits have generally been below the official poverty line, and benefit levels eroded during the late 1970s and the 1980s because AFDC payments were one of the few cash benefits which was not indexed by the 1980s.

Around 1980 roughly half of all mother only families received AFDC benefits, and this corresponded fairly closely to the number of potentially eligible families. Approximately 80 percent of the recipient mothers had no source of income other than AFDC payments. A mere 15 percent of the AFDC mothers had paid employment (Duvall et al. 1982: 6, 8), whereas the rate of employment among all solo mothers was higher than married mothers (table 4.1).

Because cash benefits are meager, relatively few solo mothers and their children were pulled out of poverty around 1980 (prior to the Reagan era). Of the four countries, and also in a ten-country study on income transfers (Mitchell 1991), US policies had the least impact in altering the income poverty of mother only families. Transfers reduced their poverty rate by 8 percent, and 14 percent of mother-only families were removed from poverty by cash payments (table 4.1; cf. Smeeding et al. 1990: 67).

Given the fact that AFDC benefits often leave recipients in poverty, why do single mothers go on welfare? Many solo mothers lack the possibility to support their family through employment. Equally important, AFDC has served as a passport to other benefits in kind – food stamps, Medicaid, job training, day care, and housing. Moreover, the value of benefits in kind has grown in contrast to the erosion of means tested cash benefits over the years (Burtless 1986: 21–4). For example, most AFDC families received food stamps, and 70 percent of the recipients were mother only families (Kamerman and Kahn 1988: 357–63). Similarly large numbers of children in AFDC families had medical protection through Medicaid (CPR 1982: 93).

The poverty trap of solo mothers in the USA is more pronounced than in the UK; it is exacerbated in two ways. First, eligibility for benefits in kind through AFDC pertains to a large range of goods and, second, their importance is magnified due to the lack of statutory benefits and private provision through the third tier of occupation welfare. Because benefits in the third tier are part of the reward system and are stratified according to one's position in the job hierarchy, the persons most in need of the benefits are those least likely to receive them. This arrangement worsens the poverty trap compared to a situation where benefits are statutory and publicly provided. The gulf between welfare and independent well-being through employment and access to standard social benefits is wider. It is a longer leap to employment which also provides adequate fringe benefits than to a job.

In contrast to the Netherlands and the UK, there has been stronger emphasis in public policy on solo mothers' role as earners. Already in the late 1960s and early 1970s, work incentives and work requirements in the AFDC program were enacted. To encourage work, Congress legislated the

"$30 and one-third" earnings disregard in 1967. The disregard allowed recipients to earn a net sum of $30 without losing benefit, and on subsequent net earnings to forfeit 66 cents of benefit for every dollar earned. In 1972 for the first time in the history of benefits to mothers with dependent children a work requirement was adopted. Mothers without children under the age of 6 were required to register for work, and the focus of public employment measures shifted to disadvantaged groups which included AFDC mothers (Adams and Winston 1980). Nonetheless, the work requirement has not been strictly enforced, as witnessed by the huge proportion of AFDC mothers who were not employed at the end of the 1970s.

The "choice" between employment and welfare faced by many mothers with preschool children and poor education or few vocational skills is grim. To support a family of three on an income above the official poverty line, a mother needed to work full time in a job paying considerably more than the minimum wage.[1] She would also incur childcare costs and other work expenses, social security, and income taxes (which may be offset by a refundable tax credit – the Earned Income Tax Credit), and she would lose food stamps and medical benefits. In short, there was little difference in the material well-being of a solo mother who worked full time in a minimum wage job and an AFDC mother without employment – and the AFDC mother could care for her children (Ellwood 1988: 138–40, 148).

Either way – through welfare or work – mother only families in the USA have run a strong risk of being poor. It is true that solo mothers had a higher employment rate than their British and Dutch counterparts, and working solo mothers had a lower poverty rate than AFDC mothers, but solo mothers with earnings had a higher poverty rate than mothers on welfare in the UK and the Netherlands (Hobson 1994). In other words, US solo mothers, whether they worked or not, were more likely to be poor than single mothers in the other two countries. In fact, the situation of US solo mothers was the reverse of Dutch solo mothers, who were probably not in poverty regardless of their decision to work or utilize welfare benefits. By contrast, assistance allowances in the USA have been set at such a low level that their decommodifying capacity has been non-existent, explicitly in an effort to make mothers choose work.

Nor do US policies promote independence from family relationships. Instead AFDC administrators have been concerned to establish paternity and to enforce support obligations to recipient children. As the AFDC rolls swelled in the 1970s, interest grew in measures to strengthen the collection of private support due to children on welfare. In 1975 Congress created the child support program, but already in the 1960s states were required to enforce child support and establish paternity. The 1975 legislation provided federal funding for these purposes and authorized the use of internal revenue service data to collect child support for AFDC recipients. These measures were extended to cover all mother only families in 1980. As proponents of stronger enforcement of collection have been quick to point out, such measures may improve the situation of mother only families. On the other hand, they are insufficient to secure a satisfactory standard of economic well-being for AFDC families. Most absent fathers of AFDC children do not earn enough to pay child support which is equivalent to assistance benefits (Garfinkel and McLanahan 1986: 118–19, 175–7).

Sweden: earnings supplemented by benefits

Nearly all Swedish solo mothers have been economically active, and as in the USA their employment rate has been higher than married mothers. Compared to their counterparts in the other countries, a larger proportion of Swedish solo mothers had earnings as their main source of income. As a result of their earnings, far fewer mother only families – around one-third – experienced pre-transfer poverty (table 4.1). Nonetheless, social benefits have been quite important in lifting lone mothers from pre-transfer poverty and improving the economic well-being of those above the poverty line. This is because, as distinct from the other three countries, benefits supplemented rather than replaced earnings. Table 4.1 indicates that cash transfers reduced the poverty rate to 5 percent among solo mothers, lifting 84 percent out of poverty. If these transfers had been means tested, it is unlikely they would have had this effect since most of these mothers had earnings.

Although Swedish lone mothers were more likely than other parents to utilize social assistance, the proportion and duration of assistance payments have been much lower than the other countries. In 1980 18 percent of all Swedish lone mothers received social assistance for an average of 4.2 months (compared to an average of 4.1 months for two parent families) (SCB 1981: 203, Kindlund 1988: 79), and of those only 4 percent – or 0.7 percent of all lone mothers – received payments for a 12-month period. The average amount of assistance received by solo mothers was between 3,000 and 4,000 crowns – or between one-half to two-thirds of the average net monthly earnings of solo mothers. In short, assistance payments have served as a temporary economic buffer – not as a major source of income of Swedish solo mothers.

Instead, a combination of other social benefits has bolstered the incomes of mother only families, and public services and amenities have enhanced their well-being. The most common benefits are the universal child allowance and the parental allowance, followed by an income tested housing allowance, and the advanced maintenance allowance. In the early 1980s 80 percent of solo mothers received a housing allowance, a much higher utilization rate than that found in two parent families. The allowance also covered a larger portion of the housing costs of solo mothers than those of two parent families. The advanced maintenance allowance ensures child support payments to single mothers in the absence of the father or his failure to fulfill maintenance obligations, and 56 percent of lone parents received the allowance. Single mothers' utilization rate of public day care was also high: 70 percent of the preschool children of single parents had public day care compared to 44 percent of all preschool children in the early 1980s (SCB 1986: 133, 148, Gustafsson 1990: 166–7).

Unlike the policy mixes of the other countries which often compel women to choose between work and welfare, Swedish policies have sought to facilitate solo mothers' dual roles as earner and caregiver. Before the expansion of day care in the 1970s solo mothers were a high priority group, and the higher incidence of solo mothers' preschoolers in public childcare arrangements in the early 1980s reflected the continued existence of this priority. Day care fees have usually been geared to ability to pay, which has benefited solo mothers. The proportion of solo mothers working full time is substantially higher than that of mothers in two parent families. Nonetheless, more than half of the solo mothers only work part time. Their roles as earners, however, have affected their roles as mothers. Because of economic constraints, they have had fewer options with respect to mothering. Compared to married mothers, a much smaller proportion of solo mothers were not working because they wanted to spend time at home with their children. Conversely, a much larger portion had increased their working hours because of insufficient income (Gustafsson 1990: 164).

Swedish policies are not decommodifying in the sense of providing market independence. Instead they have promoted labor market participation, and earnings are a crucial component in the income package of solo mothers. Equally important, social benefits supplement rather than substitute for earnings since so few mothers have been on assistance. Admittedly marginal effects can exist with respect to the housing allowance and day care fees, but they have been limited compared to the poverty trap phenomenon in the USA and the UK.

As a result of earnings combined with benefits, the disposable income of single parent households adjusted for family size was only slightly less than that of comparable two parent households, especially in the case of single parents with one or two children. The disposable income of these single parent households was about 90 percent of that of two parent households in the early 1980s. For families with three or more children the ratio fell to around 80 percent (Gustafsson 1990: 164; cf. Hauser and Fischer 1990:

133).[2] In other words, mother only families in Sweden not only experienced less poverty, their disposable income was closer to that of the average family.

The breadwinner model challenged: defamilialization and decommodification

In all four countries solo mothers' entitlements – and especially those of never married or divorced mothers – represent a challenge to the celebration of marriage. The strength of the challenge, however, depends upon two factors: whether entitlements provide a decent livelihood for mother only families; and whether entitlements meet the criterion of defamilialization – of autonomy in family relationships.

Looking at entitlements as mothers to means tested benefits in the Netherlands, the UK, and the USA we find that assistance programs often afford solo mothers a livelihood independent of a former partner, and there is evidence that many mothers on welfare perceive that they are better off than in their previous marriage or cohabitation arrangements. Notably, Jonathan Bradshaw and Jane Millar found that the most valued aspect of solo motherhood was "independence," and nearly half of the British mothers preferred lone parenthood to entering a new family relationship in the immediate future (1991: 14, 17; for the Netherlands, see Knijn 1994: 92–3).

Nonetheless, means tested benefits are scarcely independent of family relationships. Quite the contrary. Benefits are conditional upon *family* income, and the unit of benefit is the family. Remarriage or cohabitation can affect eligibility because a partner's earnings or other economic assets may disqualify a mother from benefits. The defamilializing capacity of means tested benefits is weakened in two additional ways. These benefits are usually targeted to a specific clientele confining their effects to these categories. The more specific the targeting, the more limited the effects. Low take up rates associated with means tested benefits can also reduce their impact. Second, as we have seen, means tested benefits, especially when characterized by a poverty trap, compel mothers to "choose" between work and welfare. When they opt out of the market, they forfeit not only earnings but also benefits based on labor market status – both of which would strengthen their autonomy in family relationships.

In several respects Swedish policies have stronger defamilializing effects. The policies have neither reinforced the separate gender roles of the traditional family nor treated marriage as the preferential family form. Swedish policies have sought to enable solo mothers to fulfill both earner and caregiver roles, and solo mothers have often exemplified the dual roles of earner–caregiver in the individual model of social policy. Marital status has scarcely influenced the social entitlements of solo mothers. For example, the advanced maintenance allowance is a benefit to support the child, which has not been affected by the marital status of the mother, an arrangement that enhances the integrity of a woman's private life. Nearly as large a percentage of step families (remarried mothers) received the allowance as single parent families. Similarly services – benefits in kind – have been available to all children and families: free medical services and dental care, school meals, day care services, home help for families, family education, and counseling. As distinct from the USA and the UK, Swedish social policy has moved away from means tests as a device for distributing benefits in kind to families, and consequently these services tend to benefit all mothers – irrespective of their marital status. Finally, in contrast to the other countries, the principle of maintenance has successively eroded. Advanced maintenance allowances paid by the government were initially restricted to poor mothers, but means testing was removed in the mid-1940s. Eventually a guaranteed standardized minimum was established, and the proportion collected from fathers has decreased over time (Gustafsson 1990: 166–7).

The experiences of one category of solo mothers – widows – in the other countries also underline the importance of non-means-tested benefits in contributing to the economic well-being of solo mothers. The economic situation of widows is generally better than other solo mothers, and a major source of their incomes is insurance benefits. In the USA social security benefits – including survivor benefits – were substantially improved through major increases and indexation during the 1970s. Compared to other solo mothers, a larger percentage of widows received social benefits, their level of benefits was higher, and their poverty rate was lower in the early 1980s (Garfinkel and McLanahan 1986: 26). In the UK earnings are not deducted from widow benefits, although benefits became liable to taxation in the event of employment. With the exception of widows, the employment rate of British mothers – both solo and married – dropped during the 1980s, and widows with dependent children had the highest rate of economic activity among solo mothers (GHS 1989: 104). In the Netherlands a widow with dependent children is entitled to a pension irrespective of the size of her earnings, but very few widows are employed. Nonetheless the disposable income of widows was substantially larger than other solo mothers, and their disposable income adjusted for family size approximated that of two parent families (SCP 1988b: 57). The economic situation of widows in the three countries is generally closer to that of Swedish solo mothers. On the other hand, a fundamental difference is that marital status has generally been a key to widow benefits, limiting their defamilializing potential. In all four countries, remarriage resulted in the termination of widow benefits.

   The differing situations of solo mothers in the four countries raise questions about Esping-Andersen's conceptualization of decommodification and its adequacy in assessing the quality of social rights. An essential limitation of his notion and operationalization of decommodification is that they are embedded in a particular set of policies – income maintenance programs. In effect, when he introduces decommodification as a measure of the quality of social rights, his welfare state regimes become income maintenance policy regimes. Although income maintenance policies are central to welfare states, social rights are not confined to this set of policies. Welfare states have also conferred rights to health care, housing, education, and employment. While the concept of decommodification can be fruitfully applied to medical services, housing, and education, the relationship between decommodification and the right to work is problematic. As stressed in chapter 1, commitment to full employment and the individual's right to work constitute a major welfare state variation. Indeed, Esping-Andersen acknowledges this welfare state variation, and its importance underlies his discussion of labor market policy regimes. Yet his conception of decommodification assumes prior commodification of one's labor. There is an inherent contradiction in the acknowledgment of full employment as a welfare state variation and the assumption of prior commodification as a given.

   The contradictions are even more glaring in the case of solo mothers' social entitlements. Policies with decommodifying effects in the sense of providing a genuine work–welfare choice can directly impede employment. Of the four countries Dutch solo mothers were the least likely to be in the labor market but they, together with Swedish mothers, were most likely to enjoy a socially acceptable standard of living. Accordingly, the social rights of Dutch solo mothers would seem to epitomize decommodification, and for them the work–welfare trade off was on the average close to nil. At the same time the Dutch social minimum, like assistance schemes in the other countries, creates a situation where solo mothers are often forced to choose either work or state benefits but not both.

   The Dutch case also makes it clear that largesse in public support is not enough; it is the structure of policies that counts. This becomes clear when we examine the parity in the incomes of single and two parent families in the Netherlands and Sweden. The disposable income of Dutch mother only families, after taking family size into account, was lower than two parent families; they have had 34 percent less to spend (SCP 1988b: 191) – substantially less than Swedish mother only families. Generous assistance benefits may eliminate poverty, but they have more difficulty in achieving parity between single and two parent families.

   Because of the economic hardships faced by mother only families and their overrepresentation in poverty statistics, the social entitlements of solo mothers have eclipsed the discussion of women's entitlements as mothers in general. To fully understand the social rights of women the entitlements of solo mothers must be put in the larger context of all mothers' entitlements to maternity benefits and services.

Maternity benefits

Historically women's entitlements as mothers developed as labor protection schemes to eliminate hazards to the health and well-being of mothers and their infants – and eventually to compensate for loss of earnings. Currently maternity benefits are available primarily through social insurance schemes or as occupational benefits provided by employers. Benefits of these sorts were commonly claimed by mothers in the four countries in the early 1980s. This shared pattern of claims obscures a vital difference in women's entitlements as mothers – the degree to which cash benefits are solely based on motherhood and available to all mothers. Nor do women's entitlements to maternity benefits in the four countries cluster as neatly into a clear pattern as policies to aid solo mothers. Instead, four distinctive policy constellations emerge.

The USA: bifurcation in a different guise

Maternity benefits and women's entitlements as mothers are characterized by a bifurcated structure in the USA. As distinct from income maintenance policies such as old age, disability, and survivor benefits, however, the components are not the two tiers of public provision. Instead, provision is bifurcated along lines of private and public provision, with public provision located primarily within the "welfare" tier and private provision through the third tier of occupational welfare. A bifurcation of this sort compounds all the disadvantages of the welfare tier with a new set of difficulties for women inherent in provision through occupational welfare.

Unlike the other countries, maternity benefits including hospital costs are a component of private or occupational welfare. Nor have employers been obligated by law to provide benefits and rights to all female employees under uniform qualifying conditions. Thus the incomplete nature of the US welfare state – the lack of national health insurance and family policy measures – has profound consequences for women *qua* mothers.

Because there is no public health insurance, the hospital costs of having a baby are not automatically covered for all women. Coverage has either been through private insurance companies or through employment as a fringe benefit, which has become increasingly common. On the basis of a careful perusal of existing but spotty data, Sheila Kamerman and her research colleagues estimated that around 1980 "some 10 percent of all employed women . . . in prime childbearing years lack any health insurance coverage in their own right or as dependents, and that a still higher percentage may be uncovered among the nonworking" (Kamerman et al. 1983: 50).

The USA was one of the few industrialized nations which had not legislated statutory maternity leave by 1980. In the late 1970s around 75 percent of women employees working at least twenty hours per week reported that they had some form of leave with the right to reinstatement (Kamerman and Kahn 1983: 52–3, 57). The proportion of women entitled to maternity pay diminishes sharply compared to those with some form of leave. Since 1978 federal legislation has required employers who offer leave and compensation for short-term disability or sickness to include pregnancy and childbirth in these benefits. But if employers do not provide disability benefits or sick pay, then women have no entitlement. In addition, a few states provide public temporary disability insurance, and many federal and state employees have leave benefits. Overall, it was estimated that only around 40 percent of employed women were entitled to paid maternity leave in the early 1980s (Gelb and Palley 1987: 172).

There is a substantial discrepancy, however, between estimates of coverage and utilization. Survey data suggest a much smaller percentage have actually received paid leave – between 15 and 30 percent of employed mothers (NCCS 1991: 371, 375; CPR 1990: 14, 17).[3] As in other areas of private or occupational welfare, the provision of maternity benefits and rights suffers from partial coverage and benefits reflecting job stratification. For example, the proportion of women with paid leave after the birth of their youngest child varied according to income, ranging from around 15 percent of mothers in the lowest income brackets to 40 percent in the highest brackets (NCCS 1991: 373).

In the early 1980s the USA was clearly a laggard in the provision of maternity benefits because of its lack of statutory entitlements, and it is difficult to imagine that access to maternity benefits could be similar in a country with comprehensive social insurance schemes offering generous benefits – and ranking high in the quality of social rights according to the mainstream literature.

The Netherlands: generous benefits but low recipient rates

The compulsory sickness insurance (ZW), an employee insurance, has provided generous maternity benefits. In fact, the replacement rate of 100 percent of the mother's pay up to a ceiling (for twelve weeks in 1980) is the most generous in the Dutch employee insurance schemes – and the replace-

Table 4.2 *Utilization rates of maternity benefits, 1980[a]*

	Recipients as a percentage of mothers giving birth during the year	
	All mothers	Employed mothers
USA		
Maternity leave (paid and unpaid)	20	50
Netherlands		
Maternity benefits (1979) (ZW and other employer sponsored schemes)	27	88
Great Britain		
Maternity grant	92	na
Maternity allowance	48	91
Earnings related supplement	28	53
Maternity pay	17	45
Sweden		
Parental allowance	95	na

Notes:
[a] The percentages for the USA and the Netherlands are rough estimates because of employer sponsored benefits for which there are no statistics. For the Netherlands the percentage receiving ZW maternity benefits is around 16 percent of all mothers but this figure does not include public employees and employer sponsored benefits outside the ZW.
Sources: Kamerman et al. 1983: 98, NCCS 1991: 371–5, CPR 1990: 14, 17, *Statistical Abstract of the United States* 1992: 72, *Statistical Yearbook* 1982: 368, 21, 41, Koesoebjono 1983, Kool 1983, Brown and Small 1985: 54, 67, Daniel 1980: 62, *Allmän försäkring* 1980: 50, *Statistisk årsbok* 1981: 83.

ment rates are more generous than in other countries. On the other hand, Dutch women did not have a statutory right to maternity leave beyond this. Nor was there a maternity grant or benefits for non-working mothers or mothers who were self-employed or family workers. Entitlement to maternity benefits was based entirely on labor market status as an employee, but eligibility requirements were not demanding: six months of insured employment, including part-time work and a modest earnings requirement (Maier 1991: 6).[4]

These relatively favorable qualifying conditions contrast markedly with the actual receipt of benefits. An inspection of table 4.2 reveals that slightly under 30 percent of all mothers were recipients, which is the second lowest percentage after the USA. However, most working mothers – around 90 percent – receive benefits (Kool 1983: 113–14), and the small percentage is explained by the fact that Dutch women have had one of the lowest labor market participation rates among the industrial countries – 35.7 percent in 1980 – and married women an even lower rate. Although nearly 75 percent of all mothers of first children were employed at the start of their pregnancy in the early 1980s, 60 percent stopped working (*Statistical Yearbook* 1990: 99), and Dutch mothers were usually not employed at the time of birth of subsequent children. Furthermore, married women have generally worked part time, and in the early 1980s two-thirds of working wives earned less than the minimum wage (SCP 1985: 52). Despite a generous benefit construction, women with low earnings have received low benefits.

Although Dutch mothers were not likely to receive maternity pay, the Netherlands differed from the USA in that costs of child delivery have been covered by the public health insurance (ZFW). Dutch health insurance was not universal, as it is in the UK and Sweden, but was available to families with medium and lower incomes – roughly 70 percent of the population (OECD 1985b: 64). Better off families have had to rely on private insurance. This system covered families and mothers who were most at risk and in need of protection, resulting in low infant mortality rates. Gradually, however, health programs for pregnant women and infants have been added to the universal health insurance scheme (AWBZ), and families receive assistance when the mother is ill or has given birth to a baby.

The UK: a fourfold benefit structure

Maternity benefits were an integral part of the national insurance scheme (until 1987), which included a maternity grant and a maternity allowance. In addition a mother might qualify for an earnings related supplement to the allowance and maternity pay. Thus in 1980 British maternity benefits consisted of a fourfold structure with varying severity in eligibility conditions which affected recipient rates (table 4.2).

The maternity grant was a lump sum to cover the extra costs of a new baby, and the maternity allowance replaced a woman's loss of income in connection with childbirth. Payment of both types of benefit depended upon fulfillment of contribution requirements. However, requirements for the grant were among the least demanding of national insurance benefits, and the grant could be claimed on the basis of the mother's or husband's contributions. In 1980 over 90 percent of all mothers received the grant. Since the grant was not indexed and had not been uprated since 1969, its value had diminished to virtually a symbolic sum by 1980.

Eligibility requirements for the maternity allowance consisted of labor market status and stiffer contributions. Perhaps the most cruel effect of the married woman's option was that it disqualified a woman from receiving the maternity allowance. Despite this, the number of women receiving the allowance climbed from approximately 15 percent in 1950 to around 50 percent of all mothers in 1980 (Brown and Small 1985: 38). As a national insurance benefit, it was indexed in the mid-1970s and the earnings related supplement introduced in 1966 was eventually applied to the maternity allowance in the 1970s.

Insurance benefits were also complemented by employer sponsored maternity pay schemes which were widespread in the public sector. By the early 1970s there was almost complete coverage but no uniformity. By contrast, sick pay schemes in the private sector did not cover pregnancy, and private companies only offered unpaid leave. This changed when the 1975 Employment Protection Act established the right to maternity pay for a duration of six weeks, the right to reinstatement to the same or a comparable job, and protection against unfair dismissal because of pregnancy. Work tests and the exemption of small enterprises, introduced in 1980, excluded a majority of female employees, and not all employed mothers meeting the qualifications were actually paid (Brown and Small 1985; Daniel 1980).[5] Less than one-fifth of all pregnant women received maternity pay in the early 1980s.

In 1980 a pregnant woman was potentially eligible for several benefits. A very small proportion of mothers received no benefits, while others received all (table 4.2). The main exclusionary mechanisms were labor market status and contribution requirements, even in the case of the maternity grant – the most frequently claimed benefit. Mothers ineligible for the maternity grant were young single women who had never worked or had not worked enough and non-working wives of students or the unemployed. Eligibility regulations for the grant also embodied the preferential treatment of marriage. Divorced women, cohabiting women, and single women even when paternity was established could not claim the grant on the basis of the father's contributions. Nonetheless British women's access to maternity benefits sharply contrasted with their availability in the USA and the Netherlands. Furthermore, as in the Netherlands, nearly all the working mothers received the maternity allowance.

In retrospect, the late 1970s stands out as a period of strengthening benefits tied to the principle of care. The child benefit reform not only extended coverage to all mothers, it upgraded benefit levels. As a result of these two changes, the benefits for two children as a percentage of the average net industrial wage rose from around 3 percent before the reform to over 10 percent in 1980 (Wennemo 1994: 164). Maternity pay, leave for forty weeks, and job reinstatement became statutory rights. Finally the state earnings related pension scheme (SERPS), adopted in 1975, recognized care responsibilities by giving credits to those caring full time for children, the sick, or the elderly.

Sweden: maternity benefits as parental insurance

In Sweden the 1974 Parental Insurance Act extended the principle of care to fathers, and maternity benefits were converted into parental benefits. The Act originally provided benefits for a duration of six months, but by 1980 the period of payment had been lengthened to twelve months. The 1974 reform also increased benefit levels, which resulted in parents taking leave for a longer duration. The parental allowance is either in the form of earnings related benefits to replace the parent's loss of income (90 percent up to a ceiling in 1980) or flat rate benefits for a parent without earnings. To qualify for the earnings related allowance the parent must have worked six months during the year or twelve months during the past two years.

Despite the changeover to parental benefits, it is overwhelmingly mothers, and nearly all mothers, who have been the beneficiaries. In 1980 95 percent of all mothers claimed the parent's allowance (table 4.2), and 97 percent of them took leave for at least six months. Table 4.2 summarizes women's access to maternity benefits in the four countries in terms of the recipient rates of all mothers and employed mothers. The rates of all mothers were relatively low in the USA and the Netherlands but for different reasons. The rate in the Netherlands reflects Dutch women's employment patterns, and public opinion has frowned upon mothers of small children working outside the home. US married women have been employed in much larger numbers, and the major obstacle has been the lack of statutory benefits. British women were more likely to receive maternity benefits; however, nearly half of the mothers received only the maternity grant, which was the modest sum of £25. Slightly less than half of all mothers received more generous benefits to replace their loss of income. A much larger proportion of Swedish mothers – approximately 85 percent – received earnings related allowances, and the remainder of mothers drew a flat rate allowance. Although the flat rate benefit is a nominal daily sum, the maximum duration of payment was one year. As a result, this flat rate benefit in many cases exceeded the maternity benefits of employed women in the UK and the Netherlands. The amount received by Swedish mothers without an employment record was more than a British mother claiming the maternity grant, the maternity allowance at the standard rate, and the maximum earnings related supplement would have received in 1980 (calculated from DHSS 1981: 10, 51, 53).

In conclusion, the fact that so many Swedish mothers have been entitled to an earnings related allowance by virtue of their employment obscures a very significant feature of Swedish benefits. In the other three countries a prerequisite for maternity benefits is labor market status. Moreover, this is a necessary but not a sufficient condition. In the USA a mother must have the "right" employer or live in the "right" state; in the UK a mother had to fulfill contribution requirements, and in the Netherlands a mother had to be an employee (not self-employed or a family worker) and to meet work tests, albeit modest ones. Only mother workers received benefits, and this is especially contradictory in the Dutch case where the mother's duty as care-giver has often precluded employment. By contrast, labor market status is not a requirement in Sweden; instead the underlying basis of entitlement is motherhood, or more precisely parenthood; but since the early 1970s earn-ings have definitely improved a mother's benefits.

Women's rights to maternity benefits conform to a larger pattern of entitlements as mothers and benefits tied to the principle of care. In the USA the only instances of social provision reflecting the principle of care are AFDC and survivor benefits for mothers with dependent children. In the Netherlands women's social rights were circumscribed as long as they were family members, and despite paid maternity leave, benefits attached to motherhood at the beginning of the 1980s were primarily utilized by mother only families. British policies in principle have more fully acknowl-edged mothers and women as caregivers through family allowances and subsequently child benefit, maternity grants and allowances, care credits in the pension system, and the invalid care allowance. Swedish policies contain the most comprehensive recognition of the principle of care, and benefits have been directed to all mothers. The four countries array them-selves along this dimension so that in the 1980s the policies of the USA least reflected the principle of care followed by the Netherlands and the UK, with Sweden as the opposite end of the continuum. Although British and Swedish policies have been similar in providing cash benefits according to the principle of care, a major dividing line between the two countries has been their approaches to childcare outside the home.

Childcare: private versus public responsibility

The childcare policies of the USA, the UK, and the Netherlands resemble one another in emphasizing private responsibility, whereas strong public involvement has characterized childcare in Sweden. The variations in systems of childcare can be categorized as the maximum private responsibility model and the maximum public responsibility model (Ergas 1990). This classification combines aspects of models based on the residual–institutional distinction in chapter 1 and the familial models pre-sented in chapter 2. The private responsibility model prescribes state inter-vention as a last resort in situations of need and to promote social protection of children at risk. The sanctity of the family and its responsibil-ity for the care and upbringing of children are emphasized. It is the duty of the mother to provide care, and the limited availability of childcare services reinforces the norm that the mother's place is in the home. Public childcare policies tend to be minimalist, and the preferred providers of childcare outside the home are private individuals or organizations.

The public responsibility model views children as a common resource and concern, and the financial burden of having children as one to be shared by all members of society. Public institutions play an important role in the provision of childcare services, and the objective is to provide services to all parents who wish to utilize them. In the public responsibility model, the state is directly involved in the provision and funding of services.

Looking at childcare for preschool youngsters in the early 1980s we find minimal state involvement in the USA, the Netherlands, and the UK. Apart from pre-primary education, public provision of day care was extremely limited. Formally organized and licensed care was also in short supply, and the most acute shortage was registered care for infants and toddlers (Kamerman and Kahn 1991, OECD 1990a: 133). As a result, working mothers have been compelled to rely on *ad hoc* arrangements, and the informal sector was dominant in all three countries.

The USA: for-profit childcare and fiscal welfare

Two distinctive trends in the USA, emerging during the 1970s, are the growth of for-profit childcare centers and fiscal welfare – tax expenditures – to ease the childcare costs of families. In accordance with the private responsibility and residual models, federally funded childcare services have been confined to welfare recipients and poverty status families, and the targeted programs have reached only a small portion of eligible children – an estimated 10–20 percent depending on the program (Hayes et al. 1990: 214–18). In the early 1980s organized group care accounted for roughly 15 percent of the care arrangements utilized by working mothers. By 1990 this form of care had nearly doubled, and it was now the most common arrangement together with parental care (CPR 1983a, NCCS 1991: 99). Organized group care was also accompanied by a steady expansion of for-profit care, and over half of the children in center based care were enrolled in for-profit centers (Adams and Winston 1980: 66, Ginsburg 1992: 125). The growth of center based care has not displaced the informal sector – especially family day care (childminding) – but there has been a decline in arrangements involving relatives. Informal unpaid care was less common than in the UK. In the early 1980s around two-thirds of employed mothers with preschool children reported paying for care (CPR 1983a: 14).

The onus of childcare costs has been on the parent/s, except for children in subsidized day care. The costs averaged about 10 percent of family income, but the burden was much heavier for poor and low income families, ranging between 30 and 50 percent for those with annual earnings under $5,000 and between 15 and 20 percent for those with earnings between $5,000 and $10,000. As in the case of easing the financial burden of families with dependent children, the major form of support has been tax expenditures. In 1976 tax deductions for day care were converted into tax credits, and the 1980s witnessed a rapid growth in families claiming childcare tax credits. However, since the credit is non-refundable, it has been less advantageous for low income parents. Consistently better off families have utilized the childcare income tax credit, and working mothers were more likely to claim the tax credit as family income increased. In the mid-1980s half of the families claiming the credit had an income of $25,000 or more. Moreover there was an appreciable gap between the proportion of families paying for childcare and that claiming tax credits (Kamerman and Kahn 1989: 241; Hayes et al. 1990: 202, 237, NCCS, 1991: 186–7). In other words, a substantial number of families did not receive any help in bearing their costs of day care, and it appears to have been poor families whose costs were a larger portion of their income.

The UK: informal care as the solution

The state's role in childcare in the UK has been largely limited to supervision and licensing childminders and care facilities. The structure of registered services in terms of type of care was dominated by playgroups (65 percent), followed by child minders (25 percent) and public nurseries (10 percent) (OECD 1990: 133). Registered full-time day care has been at a premium, and public day nurseries have been primarily reserved for children at risk. During the 1980s private provision of childcare services increased, while public provision stagnated, and the Thatcher government expressed a preference for childminders rather than group arrangements (Pichault 1984: 104). While the state has been involved in supervision and a limited delivery of services, childcare has not been supported through tax expenditures. On the contrary, childcare services provided by employers were liable to taxation until 1990 (OECD 1990a: 139).

What stands out in the UK is the size of the informal sector and the amount of unpaid care. In 1980 only 30 percent of working mothers with preschool children paid for care. Instead they enlisted the help of their husband, other relatives or friends, and nearly 15 percent cared for the child while working (Martin and Roberts 1984: 40–1). Two factors seem important in determining this pattern – widespread part-time employment and the inadequate supply of formal care. In 1980 registered care services covered less than 20 percent of preschool children (Cohen and Clarke 1986: 77), and British mothers reported little utilization of center based services.

The Netherlands: playgroups for all mothers

The predominant arrangement of childcare in the Netherlands has been playgroups and pre-primary education for older preschool children. Both working and non-working mothers use these facilities, but they offer limited care since they only operate on a part-time basis. Registered care for children under 3 was virtually non-existent. An EC survey of childcare facilities in the early 1980s revealed that the level of provision for infants and toddlers in the Netherlands was the lowest of the member countries (Pichault 1984, SCP 1993a: 205).

The labor market participation of Dutch mothers with preschool children was extremely low in the early 1980s. Only 17 percent of mothers with preschool children were in paid employment and a mere 3 percent were full timers (SCP 1993a: 58). Although the number of preschool children enrolled in playgroups and childcare centers corresponded to the proportion of mothers in the workforce, this does not mean that employed mothers exclusively utilize these forms of care; quite the contrary, since both working and non-working mothers utilize playgroups. In fact there is little difference in the pattern of childcare of working mothers and non-working mothers (Maassen van den Brink 1994: 46). Large numbers of employed mothers appear to have solved their care problems through informal arrangements during the 1980s (SCP 1993a: 202–6).

The development of childcare policies is of recent origin. Initially the government opted for a "private" solution by introducing an extra tax allowance for childcare expenses for dual earner families in the mid-1980s. Toward the end of the decade tax concessions accounted for two-thirds of public financial support for childcare, and the remaining one-third consisted of grants to local governments or childcare institutions (OECD 1990: 131). With this policy, it is hardly surprising that there was little increase in the availability of center based childcare during the decade.

Sweden: increasing public responsibility

In several respects childcare policies in Sweden are the reverse of the private responsibility model yet, contrary to the image of collective childcare, parental insurance has enabled many parents, usually mothers, to care for infants until their first birthday. In fact, a surprisingly large proportion of preschool children were cared for by their parents. In 1980 half of the parents cared for their own children (this figure includes parents on paid

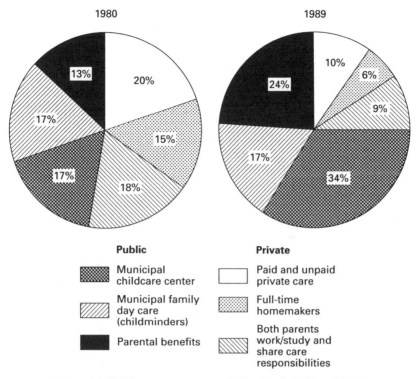

Figure 4.1 Childcare arrangements in Sweden in 1980 and 1989
Sources: SCB 1980, 1983a, and 1989a: 2, 7.

leave, families where both parents worked or were students and alternated in caring for their child, and full time homemakers) (figure 4.1). The most striking difference, compared to the other countries, was that public provision of day care was more commonplace than private and informal arrangements. Only 14 percent of the parents of preschool children made use of private care services, and an additional 6 percent relied on unpaid care provided by relatives or friends (SCB 1989a: 7). As we have seen, relatives and friends – either paid or unpaid – were one of the most common solutions to the childcare problems of employed mothers in the other three countries. A second major difference was the small proportion of Swedish preschool children who were cared for by mothers who were full-time homemakers – 15 percent.

The public sector has been heavily involved in the provision, funding, and regulation of childcare. Enrollment in public day care either in municipal childcare centers (*daghem*) or family day care (*familjedaghem*) – in the homes of childminders in municipal employment – amounted to one-third of preschool children in 1980. The costs of day care have been funded mainly through tax revenues, and parents' fees for public day care accounted for less than 10 percent of the costs. Local governments have determined the structure and amount of fees, which have often been graduated according to income and the number of children a family had in day care. On average, parents' fees were approximately 5 percent of family income for both lone parents and two parent families (calculated from Gustafsson 1990: 160, OECD 1984b). On the other hand, because of the sliding scale of fees, high income families might pay as much as 40 percent of the actual costs, while low income parents paid as little as 3 or 4 percent (Gustafsson and Stafford 1993: 21).

The 1980s witnessed increased public involvement. At the end of the 1980s the care of three-fourths of Swedish preschool children was supported by public measures – either through public day care or parental allowances – and informal arrangements and private childcare services continued to decline. The proportion of full-time homemakers also decreased.

Perhaps the greatest paradox is that the public responsibility model – often portrayed by its critics as detrimental to the traditional family – resulted in more Swedish mothers than US mothers caring for their children as infants in the home in the early 1990s. In 1991 roughly 95 percent of Swedish infants were exclusively cared for by their parents (SCB 1991: 3), whereas in 1990 this was true for only 55 percent of US infants. Furthermore, the primary care arrangement of nearly 20 percent of the US infants was either childcare centers or family day care, and the time spent in these care arrangements outside the home averaged more than 40 hours per week (calculated from NCCS 1991: 36, 106).

Childcare policies and maternity benefits in the USA, the UK, and the Netherlands reveal an enormous contradiction. On the one hand, childcare policies emphasizing private responsibility make it difficult to combine motherhood and employment. On the other hand, maternity benefits are solely available to mothers with labor market status. Public care arrangements have been limited to children at risk and needy mothers. Yet in the 1980s solo mothers on assistance were often not in employment.

Need and labor market status have been the key criteria shaping women's entitlements as mothers in the three countries, and benefits based solely on motherhood have been conspicuously absent in the USA – and in the past also in the Netherlands. At first glance, the UK by virtue of its introduction of universal family allowances in 1945 and subsequent reforms enhancing the principle of care seems markedly different. Yet family services and benefits in kind have been targeted to families in need. Universalism in the UK has not applied to services for families, reinforcing the norm of care in the private sphere for the vast majority of British families. Nor, apart from the maternity grant abolished in the late 1980s and the national health service, has universalism, in the sense of encompassing all mothers, shaped benefits related to childbirth and caring for infants.

The changing boundary between private and public responsibility

Charting the variations in women's entitlements as mothers in our four countries discloses crucial differences. In three important ways Swedish entitlements contrast with those in the other countries. *First*, the social rights of solo mothers have generally descended from poor laws, and in the countries where assistance schemes are the main form of social provision their rights have been modernized, but the basis of entitlement continues to be need. By contrast, Swedish policies have transcended the poor law framework, broadening and redefining the scope of public responsibility.

Vital to this process was the establishment of motherhood as the basis of entitlement to benefits and services, and the population policies of the 1930s represented a major turning point. Of special relevance, the notion of compensation attached to benefits changed. Maternity grants compensated for the costs of motherhood rather than the loss of earned income, and thus potentially encompassed all mothers. Until the introduction of universal maternity insurance in the mid-1950s, claims to maternity benefits were differentiated, however. Mothers claimed benefits either as members of a voluntary sickness fund or as "less well-off" mothers – a category including most mothers. For mothers outside the voluntary insurance system, cash benefits were income tested rather than means tested, and no distinction was made between married and unwed mothers. Under this system approximately 90 percent of all mothers received benefits.

The same entitlement to maternity grants by all "less well-off" mothers – irrespective of their marital status – weakened the principle of maintenance and the enforcement of support obligations of fathers. An argument against enforcing the maintenance obligations of absent fathers, such as repayment of assistance to the state, was that it was unreasonable to require all fathers to repay maternity grants (Abukhanfusa 1987: 158–78). The principle of maintenance was further eroded by the introduction of advanced maintenance allowances in the late 1930s. These reforms signaled a shift in the notions of the boundary of public responsibility. The state did not waive support obligations of fathers but gave precedence to guaranteeing the maintenance of solo mothers and their children regardless of the fathers' fulfillment of their obligations.

In summary, benefits based on motherhood transformed solo mothers' social rights so that they were not exclusively attached to need, and they shared entitlements with all mothers. Simultaneously within this universal framework, selective measures have been targeted at solo mothers but means testing has either been done away with or replaced by income testing – with the income ceiling set relatively high. As in the case of the social rights of married women, the diminished role of means tested benefits has strengthened solo mothers' entitlements but in this case because benefits are not jeopardized by earnings.

Second, women's entitlement to maternity benefits in the three other countries has been based on labor market status, and compensation for the loss of earnings has been the rationale behind benefits (with the exception of the British maternity grant). Swedish insurance benefits, while now based on the principle of income replacement, also provide allowances for non-working mothers. This unusual feature is largely the legacy of the maternity grants of the 1930s which were carried over to the compulsory maternity insurance and subsequently to parental insurance. Maternity insurance benefits consisted of a basic allowance equal for all mothers and an additional allowance. The additional allowance was paid to both home-makers and working mothers. Mothers in the home received a flat rate amount, and working mothers received an amount related to their earnings. Mothers who already had children were also entitled to child supplements.

This system of allowances together with sickness cash benefits were the first benefits explicitly recognizing work in the home as a basis of entitle-ment. The allowances put unpaid work in the home on a par with paid work outside the home, but benefit levels indicate that paid work was more highly valued. Since the mid-1950s benefit levels related to work outside the home have outstripped those of a mother without paid work. The growing gap should not obscure the important fact that the benefits of the non-working Swedish mother have been generally higher than those of working mothers receiving maternity benefits in the other three countries. The more advan-tageous position of the Swedish mother is due to the duration of benefits. As the period of leave has lengthened (from three months in the mid-1950s to eighteen months in the 1990s), parental benefits can be interpreted as compensation for care in the home or paid care work. Parents have increas-ingly cared for their children during the first months after birth, and the number of infants in day care has decreased since the early 1970s.

Third, mothers' entitlements to benefits in kind and services have often been reserved for the needy in the other three countries, although there is a trend toward universalization in the Netherlands. In Sweden these benefits and services eventually became available as universal social rights, recon-stituting the very character of the welfare state as a "social service state." As social rights, a number of services have been largely removed from the market – or decommodified. Decommodification in this sense has been especially important to mothers' options and well-being and, ironically, to women's commodification.

The origins of the "social service state" can also be traced to the population policies of the 1930s and benefits attached to motherhood. Among the instruments of population policy were collective goods in kind available to all mothers. These collective goods, such as free child delivery, pre- and postnatal medical check ups, and free vitamins and minerals for mother and child, formed part of the nucleus of what was to develop into the "social service state." During the 1940s collective goods aimed at families and children expanded to include free school lunches, school medical services, social services for families, and day nurseries. Through state grants the government also encouraged the local authorities to provide services to families, and to do so through training and employing staff to assist in the home. In these instances care in the home was paid work performed by public employees. Although family services were in limited supply, the goal was that they should be available to all families. Means tests disappeared in the early 1960s but service fees were often graduated according to income and certain categories of user had priority.

Benefits based on motherhood set in motion a new dynamic of interdependence between the private and public spheres. Population and later family policies caused a blurring of the boundary between the private and public spheres. The population crisis elevated the importance of motherhood and paved the way for benefits to all mothers. By the end of the 1930s the state had assumed a larger responsibility for the well-being of mothers and their infants, and in the 1940s state responsibility as reflected in policies was extended to the well-being of all families. Cash benefits and services eased the financial burden of having children for families, and the costs were shared by all members of society.

Both population and family policies consisted of benefits in cash and kind. Collective benefits in kind – in the form of services – converted care into paid work in the public sector, and cash benefits compensated for care work done in the home. The expansion of care work in the public sector created new employment opportunities for women, and as benefits became increasingly related to earnings, employment strengthened women's benefit levels and claims for compensation for care work in the home.

5 Women's employment and entitlements as workers

Women's massive influx into the labor market during the post-World War II period has often been described as a revolution (Smith 1979, Mott 1982, Fuchs 1988, Esping-Andersen 1990, Lewis 1992b), and dramatic changes in women's labor market status have occurred in all four countries. Women's employment, at least in theory, enhances their social entitlement because labor market status confers a variety of social rights. The centrality of entitlements based on work in the social insurance schemes of many countries and the legitimacy of these entitlements as earned rights have caused feminists to emphasize the necessity of improving women's status and claims as workers through their full integration in the labor force. Current typologies based on the breadwinner model also highlight women's entitlements as workers as the most important dimension of variation between welfare states (Lewis and Ostner 1991, 1995, Lewis 1992a). In effect, the substitution of the male breadwinner model for a universal breadwinner model has been high on the agenda of many feminists (Fraser 1994).

This chapter examines how and to what degree women's labor market participation has altered their entitlement to social benefits. More specifically, to what extent have women workers been included or excluded in social provision through work related schemes? How has women's incorporation varied across the four countries? What policy constructions or mechanisms result in women workers' inclusion or exclusion? Finally, what is the defamilializing impact of women's entitlements as workers? Have such entitlements lessened married women's dependency on benefits based on their husbands' social rights?

In work related insurance schemes and in the third tier of welfare provision – occupational welfare – labor market status is a prerequisite for individual entitlement. Although it is a necessary condition it is rarely sufficient for eligibility. Additional qualifying conditions usually determine which workers and what proportion of the labor force are actually eligible for benefits. Among the most important qualifying conditions are work tests (minimum hours or years of employment), earnings requirements, and contribution rules. The interplay between additional eligibility require-

Table 5.1 *Women's labor market participation rates, 1960–90 (ages 16–64)*[a]

	1960	1970	1980	1990[b]	
USA					
Women	43	49	60	68	+25
Married women	34	44	55	66	+32
UK					
Women	46	51	58	65	+19
Married women	35	49	62	69	+34
Netherlands					
Women	26	31	36	53	+27
Married women	7	17	33	47	+40
Sweden					
Women	50	59	74	81	+31
Married women	41	55	76	87	+46

Notes:
[a] Figures for UK are women aged 16–59 because the pension age was 60.
[b] For the USA the figures are for 1991 and for the UK 1989.
Sources: OECD, 1992b: 276, 1993: 192; EG 1990 (12): 626; SCP 1993a: 22; 1985: 41; AKU 1960, 1970, 1980, *Statistisk årsbok* 1992: 162, *Statistical Abstract of the United States* 1961: 34, 1971: 32, 1981: 38, 1992: 43, 387.

ments and the working patterns of women – especially the degree of their integration into the labor market – is decisive to women's ability to claim benefits and in some instances the benefit amounts they can claim.

Employment patterns and trends

Women's employment revolution is most evident in the magnitude of the changes in female labor market participation during the past three decades.[1] Since 1960 the proportion of women in the workforce has increased by at least 20 percentage points in all four countries. In other words, an additional one-fifth to one-third of the adult female population had joined the labor force in comparison to thirty years ago. The increase in married women entering the labor market during this period has been even more impressive, with gains between roughly 30 to 45 percentage points (table 5.1).

Labor market participation is an initial threshold to social entitlements and an important variation. Turning back the clock to the early 1980s, we find that the proportion who had crossed this threshold of potential eligibility ranged from slightly over one-third to nearly three-fourths of working age women in 1980 (table 5.1). How many of these women gained entitlements as workers? And what are the emancipatory effects of social rights as workers for married women? Because work tests and earnings requirements can disqualify workers, we must look more closely at the time women spend in market work and their pay.

Part-time employment and hours of work

The number of part-time jobs has grown dramatically during the past three decades, and the proportion of women workers who were part-timers in the four countries varied between one-quarter and one-half of the female labor force in 1980. The most spectacular increase in part-time employment has occurred in the Netherlands. Around 20 percent of Dutch women workers held part-time jobs in the early 1970s, and a decade later nearly 50 percent were part-timers (*Statistical Yearbook* 1982: 138, 1984: 136). This trend continued during the 1980s so that in the early 1990s 60 percent of Dutch female workers were part-timers (Plantenga and van Velzen 1994: 2–3), and of all the OECD countries part-time employment as a percentage of total employment was highest in the Netherlands (OECD 1994a: 198). Simultaneously there has been a stagnation in the number of women working thirty-five hours or more (*Statistical Yearbook* 1982: 140, Eurostat 1988: 143, 173; cf. Maier 1992: 90).

Parallel trends in the growth of women's part-time employment can be observed in the UK, where part-time jobs accounted for virtually the entire increase in women's employment. In Britain roughly 25 percent of women workers were part-timers in 1960 and by 1980 the percentage had grown to approximately 45 percent. The size of the British full-time female work-force has hovered around 5.6 million since 1960, and in the mid-1990s the number of women in full-time jobs was actually lower than in the 1950s (Hakim 1993, Land 1995).

The proportion of Swedish women in part-time employment also grew as women's labor market participation rate increased through the early 1980s. In 1960, when 50 percent of women were in the labor force, slightly over 30 percent worked part time. Two decades later when nearly 75 percent of Swedish women were in the labor force, slightly over 45 percent held part-time jobs. In contrast to the Netherlands and the UK, however, the expansion of part-time employment has been accompanied by a steady increase in the number of women in full-time work (AKU 1960, SCB 1989b: 158).

At first glance the employment patterns of US women appear to deviate markedly on three counts. A much smaller portion of the female labor force was in part-time employment. In 1980 only around 25 percent of women workers were part-timers, compared to between 45 and 50 percent in the other three countries. Second, the percentage of employed married women who were part-timers in the USA was only slightly higher than that of other women workers, while part-time employment was more typical of working wives in the three other countries where a majority of married women were part-timers (table 5.2). Upon closer scrutiny, however, we find that although a larger percentage of US women worked full-time schedules, many women were not year round workers. Only 45 percent of the female labor force was working full time during the entire year in 1980 (CPR 1982: 19), and this pattern was replicated for working wives (Hayghe 1993: 42). Third, the contribution of part-time employment to the overall growth of women's labor market participation is more modest in the USA. Nonetheless the number of part-time jobs has doubled since the late 1960s (Nardone 1986), and the expansion of part-time employment has been heavily concentrated to sales and services jobs with low pay (Mellor and Stamas 1982: 21). In effect, the expansion of part-time employment has largely meant an increase in poorly paid jobs (Smith 1984, Tilly 1991), and women in these jobs have been marginalized workers.

The category of part-time employment conceals more than it reveals because there is no standardized definition of part-time employment, and part-time employment encompasses a wide variety of jobs, ranging from those consisting of a few hours a week to those with nearly full-time work schedules. A useful alternative is to look at the actual number of working hours and changes over time. In most industrial countries the average number of hours women worked declined or stagnated during the the 1980s (OECD 1990a: 26–7). The drop was sharpest in the Netherlands, and the female labor force as a whole and part-time employees worked fewer hours than in nearly all other OECD countries. The same trends are evident in the UK, although they are less pronounced than in the Netherlands. By contrast, the average number of hours worked by US and Swedish women increased during the decade (table 5.3).

An inspection of table 5.3 discloses a major dividing line between the four countries based on hours actually worked by women in the labor force and the female/male differential of time in paid work per week.[2] US women in the labor force worked the longest hours, and the differential in women's and men's working hours was smallest – followed by Swedish women workers. Indeed, what is surprising is that the differences in the working hours of US and Swedish women are not greater, considering the much higher rate of female part-time employment in Sweden. Conversely, the UK and the Netherlands cluster together as countries where women's attachment to the labor market was substantially weaker, as measured in hours of paid work, and where there are wider differentials in the average working hours of women and men.

Table 5.2 Women's labor market status and entitlements as workers, ages 16–64, 1980[a]

	% of women in labor force	% of married women in the labor force	% of women in part-time employment[b]	% of married women in part-time employment[b]	% working women with entitlements as workers	% all women with social rights as workers
USA	60	55	27	29	70[c]	42
Great Britain	65	62	44	55	50	33
Netherlands	36	33	50	63	75	25
Sweden	74	76	46	57	90	67

Notes:

[a] For Britain the relevant age group is 16–59.

[b] Part-time employment is defined as working less than thirty-five hours per week except in Britain (where self-definition was used in the survey).

[c] % women workers who were fully insured in OASI.

Sources: OECD 1991b: 39, Martin and Roberts 1984: 17, AKU 1980: 1–2, Statistisk årsbok 1991: 176, CBS 1985: 29, SCP 1993a: 22, 1985: 41, Statistical Abstract of the United States 1981: 38, 386, USDL 1981, (1): 191.

Table 5.3 *Women's average hours of market work and the female/male difference in hours*

	1979 Actual hours worked per week	1983 Actual hours worked per week	1988 Actual hours worked per week
USA			
Full-time female employees	40.3	40.6	41.6
Part-time female employees	19.2	19.4	19.9
All women workers	34.5	34.5	35.7
All men workers	42.0	41.2	42.0
Female/male difference in hours	−7.5	−6.7	−6.3
Sweden			
Full-time female employees	39.4	39.3	39.5
Part-time female employees	21.1	21.9	24.7
All women workers	31.1	31.4	33.2
All men workers	40.5	40.5	41.0
Female/male difference in hours	−9.4	−9.1	−7.8
UK			
Full-time female employees	37.5	37.7	38.6
Part-time female employees	18.6	17.3	17.1
All women workers	30.1	29.0	29.2
All men workers	43.3	42.1	42.9
Female/male difference in hours	−13.2	−13.1	−13.7
Netherlands			
Full-time female employees	36.4	40.5	39.1
Part-time female employees	18.2	17.4	16.6
All women workers	30.8	28.9	26.3
All men workers	42.0	42.0	38.8
Female/male difference in hours	−11.2	−13.1	−12.5

Source: OECD 1990a 26–7.

Finally, in assessing women's integration into the labor force it is important to examine the share of women in jobs involving a small number of hours because these workers are likely to have poor earnings and least likely to meet eligibility requirements for social benefits and employment protection. In the Netherlands and the UK "short" part-time employment (defined as working fewer than twenty hours per week) expanded during the 1980s. At the end of the decade around 40 percent of Dutch women in the labor force worked fewer than twenty hours a week (Eurostat 1988: 103, 139, 177), and the figure was nearly 25 percent in Great Britain (EG 1990: 639). Both countries had a larger portion of part-timers who worked less than ten hours than was typical of other OECD countries (OECD 1990a:

25). The most extreme case was Dutch women employees, of whom 20 percent worked for ten hours or less. The average number of hours worked by US part-timers, presented in table 5.3, suggests that around 20 percent of the female labor force worked "short" part time. By contrast, around 5 percent of Swedish women worked fewer than twenty hours, and this represents a decrease since the mid-1970s (SCB 1989b: 158). Moreover, as can be observed in Table 5.3, Swedish female part-time employees worked the highest average number of hours in the late 1980s, diminishing the differences in hours worked by full-time and part-time women workers, while the gap increased in the other countries.

To sum up, labor market participation rates are a poor measure of women's integration into the workforce. Participation rates fail to take into account cross-national differences in actual working hours. While participation rates of all four countries show an increasing incorporation of women into the labor market and suggest a revolution in women's employment, other measures do not. Using hours actually worked or full-time equivalents instead of head counts points to a weakening in women's position on the labor market in the UK and the Netherlands during the 1980s and 1990s.

Earnings and pay differentials

Women's earnings are also an aspect of their employment that can scarcely be depicted as a revolution. In all four countries women's earnings lag behind men's, but there is considerable variation across countries, jobs, and time. In the long term perspective earnings differentials of women and men were largely frozen in the USA from 1960 to 1980, but wage differentials declined in the 1980s and 1990s. In the UK years of stagnation in wage differences were followed by a brief period of improvement after the introduction of equal pay legislation in the mid-1970s and subsequent slippage in the early 1980s. Wage differences successively narrowed in the Netherlands and Sweden until the first years of the 1980s. Stagnation set in, and only minor advances were made during the decade (Jansson and Sandqvist 1993: 25; Gustafsson and Bruyn-Hundt 1991: 45).

In the USA the female to male ratio of hourly earnings of full-time year-round workers was actually higher in the mid-1950s than in 1980, and from 1960 through 1980 it gravitated around 0.65 (O'Neill 1985: S94). The earnings of part-time workers were even lower. The average hourly wages of female part-timers were around 75 percent of those received by female full-time workers and 50 percent of those paid male full-timers (calculated from Mellor and Haugen 1986: 24). Due to differences in hours at work, women working part time earned on average only one-quarter of the earnings of

Table 5.4 *Women's earnings as a proportion of men's (full time)*

	1980	1990
USA		
Full-time women workers		
Average hourly earnings	0.65	0.77
Average weekly earnings	0.62	0.72
Median annual earnings	0.60	0.72
Part-time women workers		
Average hourly earnings	0.51 (1984)	–
Average weekly earnings	0.24	0.25
All women workers		
Median annual earnings[a]	0.47	0.57
Great Britain		
Full-time women workers		
Average hourly earnings	0.71	0.77
Average weekly earnings	0.63	0.68
Part-time women workers		
Average hourly earnings	0.58	0.57
All women workers		
Average weekly earnings[a]	0.48 (1983)	0.55
Netherlands		
Full-time women workers		
Average annual earnings	–	0.72
All women workers		
Average hourly earnings	0.78	0.77
Average annual earnings[a]	–	0.52
Sweden		
Full-time women workers		
Average annual earnings	0.81	0.79
Part-time women workers		
Average annual earnings	0.50	0.48
All women workers		
Average annual earnings[a]	0.68	0.69

Note:
[a] Earnings of all women workers as a percentage of all male workers' earnings.
Sources: Statistical Abstract of the United States 1982–3: 403, 1993: 414, USDL 1981 (1): 81–2, 1991 (1): 222–3, 1994: 33, FES 1984, 1991, Bruegel 1983: 137, EOC 1991: 2, SCP 1993a: 141, *Statistical Yearbook* 1993: 127, 1994: 111, SCB 1993a: 72–3.

men working full time (table 5.4). In 1980 the female-to-male ratio of annual median earnings of full-time year-round workers was 0.60, but it dropped to a mere 0.47 when all workers were included (calculated from *Statistical Abstract of the United States* 1982–3: 403).

For full-time British workers the 1970s saw an improvement in women's earnings *vis-à-vis* men's. In 1980 the average hourly wages of women were roughly 70 percent of men's (Rubery and Tarling 1988: 120). Otherwise there are a number of striking similarities between the female/male earnings differentials in the UK and the USA. In both countries the weekly earnings of women full-timers were around 60 percent of men's. The earnings of part-timers also reveal a parallel development. A major trend of the 1980s was a deterioration in the earnings of British women in part-time employment. Their hourly earnings were 74 percent of the earnings of female full-time workers and only 56 percent of the earnings of male full-time workers (Robinson 1988: 123; cf. Hutton 1994). Finally, the overall differentials in the earnings of women and men were nearly identical. In the UK it was 0.48 in the early 1980s (calculated from FES 1984: 63–4, 66).

In the Netherlands the ratio of women's average gross hourly wage had climbed from 0.60 in 1960 to nearly 0.80 in 1980, and it has been argued that the improvement in women's real wages was a major reason for their entry into the labor market (Hartog and Theeuwes 1985: S243). Although both the UK and the Netherlands experienced a surge in female part-time employment in the 1980s, part-timers' earnings followed different courses. During most of the decade the average hourly earnings of Dutch female part-timers were slightly higher than those of full-time women employees. Nor was there a major drop in female part-time earnings in relation to male full-time earnings. The ratio of women's hourly earnings – both full- and part-time workers – to male full-time hourly earnings was 0.74 in the mid-1980s. On the other hand, the number of flexible workers, or "standby" workers as they are called in Dutch statistics, grew during the decade, and their hourly earnings were substantially lower – 48 percent of male full-time hourly earnings (*Statistical Yearbook* 1983: 351, 1988: 348). The difference in average annual income of economically active women relative to men was 0.51 (SCP 1993a: 141, 153).

The earnings of Swedish women workers have generally been less unequal, but inequalities persist, and the 1980s were a decade of stagnation and reversals. The earnings of women workers employed on a full-time basis were roughly 80 percent of their male counterparts in the early 1980s (Gustafsson and Jacobsson 1985: S261). As in the Netherlands there is little difference in the hourly pay of women who work part-time schedules compared to those on a full-time basis. The pay of part-time workers is a *pro rata* amount, based on hours of work, of what they would have received as full-timers in the same job. Nevertheless, part-time employment impacts negatively on women's pay compared to men's, and the effects are most apparent in the female–male ratio for annual median income from work, which was only around 0.70 (calculated from SCB 1993a: 73).

As we can see in table 5.4, female/male differentials in average annual earnings have been widest – and they have been smallest with respect to hourly earnings – in all four countries. The greater disparity in annual earnings reflects differences in pay, number of working hours, and location of jobs in the occupational hierarchy and sectors of employment. Women workers' average annual earnings ranged from slightly below 50 to 70 percent of men's in the 1980s. While the female/male ratio of hourly earnings is smallest, part-time employees in the USA and the UK have particularly low hourly earnings in relation to full-time workers. The wage situation of standby workers in the Netherlands was quite similar, and at the end of the 1980s nearly 15 percent of the female labor force worked irregular hours (*Statistical Yearbook* 1992: 111). Low earnings in many instances bar or limit women's access to work related benefits and cause married women workers to fall back on their entitlements as wives.

Additional qualifying conditions and women's entitlements

Additional qualifying conditions often determine eligibility in work related schemes. These conditions vary in their exclusionary effects, partly because of differing degrees in stringency of requirements, partly because of dissimilarities in women's employment patterns. In the most extreme cases of exclusion in the four countries as many as half of the women workers failed to meet eligibility requirements for state benefits, and around two-thirds were excluded from private schemes. By contrast, the least exclusionary requirements disqualified approximately 10 percent of the female workforce.

The USA: covered employment, insured status and occupational welfare

Labor market status is potentially more decisive to social entitlements in the USA for three reasons. The lack of universal non-contributory benefits makes social insurance benefits the only public provision alternative to "welfare." Second, social insurance benefits have been exclusively tied to employment except for wife supplements. Third, occupational welfare is especially important because of the incomplete nature of the public provision of benefits.

The most fundamental qualifying condition for social security benefits has been having a job in "covered employment." Originally the Social Security Act of 1935 only covered workers in commerce and industry; but over the years covered employment has been extended to more and more categories of workers, including the self-employed. Coverage is compulsory, and *all* earnings below a ceiling have been liable to contributions in the form of social security taxes. In 1980 around 90 percent of all jobs in the USA were officially covered. The most important categories exempted and unlikely to be covered by other schemes were employees in non-profit organizations and self-employed persons, farm employees, and household workers not meeting minimum earnings requirements. Low earnings have not excluded workers from coverage, with the exception of farm and household workers.

The second major qualifying condition has been "insured status," and the underlying principle is that the worker must demonstrate an enduring attachment to the labor force. Insured status is acquired on the basis of years of employment in covered employment. Accordingly, benefits are dependent upon one's work history in jobs covered by social security, and workers, such as women, with interrupted employment records are disadvantaged. In 1980 only around 70 percent of all women workers were fully insured for old age benefits, and with increasing age, the figure dropped (SSB, *Annual Statistical Supplement* 1983: 93). Finally, eligibility requirements for disability benefits have consisted of insured status plus a stiff work test, and in 1980 only slightly over one half of the women paying social security taxes were insured in the event of disability (Irick 1986: 23; cf. SSB, 1986: 9).

The growth of US women's labor market participation since 1960 has not been matched by a similar increase in individual entitlement to old age benefits as workers. In 1960 slightly under 40 percent of all women claimed old age benefits solely on the basis of their own work record; in 1980 such entitlements had risen only by a few percentage points despite an increase in the female workforce of nearly 20 percentage points. Instead women's dual entitlement – as workers and wives – had climbed from 5 percent in 1960 to over 15 percent by 1980. Despite their longer working hours than women in the labor forces of the other countries, US women's benefits as workers were often less than their benefits as wives. The main impediments have been breaks in employment and lower earnings than their husbands'.

Several qualifying conditions combined with the nature of women's unemployment limit women's entitlement to unemployment benefits. Federal legislation makes unemployment insurance mandatory, but the individual states are responsible for specific rules and administration of the program. Three-fourths of the states have enacted a minimum earnings requirement which tends to discriminate against part-time workers, and in some states the minimum earnings requirement is as high as 50 percent of median earnings (*Statistical Abstract*, 1988: 350, 331–2; MacLennan and Weitzel 1984: 207–8, 212). Moreover, since 1960 the states have tightened rules concerning disqualification for refusal to accept suitable work and voluntarily leaving a job (Price 1985). Stiffer availability for work tests and disqualification for voluntary quits disadvantage women. Family tasks can set limits on the ability to take an available job, and domestic reasons often cause women to leave a job. Among job leavers, women outnumbered men, and domestic quits have not been recognized as involuntary. Third, characteristics of women's unemployment undermine their entitlement to benefits. Women were less frequently covered by unemployment insurance because both in relative and absolute terms they were overrepresented among entrants and reentrants to the labor market (*Statistical Abstract* 1982–3: 391, 1988: 339, 350, 382, 384).

Women workers' entitlements to occupational or private benefits – such as medical insurance, paid leave, and pension plans – have been even more tenuous than their claims to public benefits. Because private benefits have not been statutory, many employers – especially small firms – do not offer benefits or have been extremely selective in their coverage. In 1980 over 50 percent of all women workers participated in a health plan, and slightly under 40 percent were covered by an occupational pension plan. A mere 10 percent of female part-time employees were covered, and only half of all women full-time workers. The sectors of employment with the poorest coverage were sales and domestic services (calculated from CPR 1982: 19, 59, 75) – sectors dominated by women workers.

It also needs to be stressed that coverage in pension plans is not the same as entitlement and actual receipt of benefits. Vesting rules, which confer a non-forfeitable right to pension benefits, have been quite demanding in the USA compared to other countries (Daily and Turner 1992: 43). In 1980 vesting rules required ten years of service with the same employer, and only around 20 percent of women workers had job tenure of ten years or more (calculated from Woods 1989: 11). Available statistics, which only included full-time private sector employees, reveal sharp discrepancies between coverage and vesting. Around 40 percent of female full-time private sector employees were covered but only slightly over 15 percent were vested for benefits (Woods 1993: 15). The recipient rate for occupational pensions was much lower than social security retirement benefits among women workers in the 1980s. Their entitlement to occupational pensions, however, had slowly inched upwards since the 1960s, whereas their entitlement to social security pensions solely as workers had largely stagnated.

In summary, labor market status is crucial to women's individual entitlement to social benefits which are not means tested, and from 1960 to 1980 women's labor market participation rate increased from 43 to 60 percent. In contrast to this continuous increase, the proportion of women whose entitlements were entirely based on their status as workers in 1980 was slightly less than in 1970 (Lingg 1985: 29). In the early 1980s slightly over 40 percent of all women beneficiaries claimed old age social security benefits in their own right. Despite the compulsory nature of OASDI, around 30 percent of all working women did not have fully insured status in 1980, and additional work tests disqualified women workers from disability benefits so that only 55 percent of women workers met the requirements. Finally, looking at retired women as a whole, the change in recipient rates of occupational pensions is not all that impressive. In the early 1960s a minuscule 5 percent of women aged 65 or older received private pension benefits, and by the 1980s their recipient rate had risen to less than 15 percent (Woods 1989: 3), although among new beneficiaries nearly 25 percent received a private pension (Woods 1988: 7). As in the case of earnings, women's employment revolution since 1960 has not been translated into comparable social rights and entitlements (table 5.2).

On the other hand, there has been a marked reduction in the share of women claiming social security benefits solely as wives from over 55 percent of all women OASI beneficiaries in 1960 to approximately 40 percent in the early 1980s (SSB, *Annual Statistical Supplement* 1993: 199). For large numbers of married women, however, social security benefits have had a limited defamilializing impact in the sense of totally eliminating dependency upon their husbands' social rights. The combination of earnings related benefits and the spouse benefit poses a difficult hurdle to the working wife's entitlement as a worker. She must earn around 30 percent of her husband's earnings for her benefits as a worker to exceed her spouse benefit – her benefits as a wife.[3] Among new beneficiaries in the early 1980s, approximately half of the working wives crossed this threshold (SSB 1985: 20).

However, social security benefits compared to earnings enlarged women's financial contribution to family income (Sørensen and McLanahan 1987: 670). The social security check of women with individual entitlement amounted on average to nearly half (44 percent) of the couple's social security income, while the check of women with dual entitlement contributed around one-third (35 percent). In all instances, social security benefits contributed a larger share than wives' earnings to joint income. In 1980 working wives' contributions to family income averaged slightly over one-quarter, and this share had been relatively constant during the previous two decades (SIT 1968: 138, Hayghe 1993: 42).

The UK: contribution requirements, part-time employment, and continuous service

Despite the common image of the postwar British welfare state as embodying universalist principles, the UK does not have any "citizen" insurance programs. The national insurance scheme is basically work related, and contributions have been a centerpiece of British social insurance schemes. Payment of insurance benefits depends upon meeting contribution requirements in full (with the exception of the state retirement pension and widow's benefits), but prior to the mid-1980s partial contributions resulted in partial benefits.

Contribution requirements and the construction of contributions have disadvantaged women workers in several ways. As distinct from the other countries, national insurance contributions have a lower income limit. Workers whose earnings are below the limit are not liable to pay contributions, and they are without entitlement. The lower income limit was introduced during the mid-1970s in connection with the change to a system of fully earnings related contributions and the phasing out of the married woman's option. The lower limit has posed a major obstacle to women's eligibility to national insurance benefits and eventually to other statutory benefits. In 1980 40 percent of female part-time workers and 20 percent of all working women did not pay contributions because their earnings were below the lower limit (Martin and Roberts, 1984: 43). At the end of the decade the proportion of female part-time workers whose earnings were below the contributions threshold increased to nearly 50 percent (Land 1994a: 114, Lister 1992: 27).

Not only do contributions exclude women, they are also a source of injustice for many women workers who pay contributions. The abolition of flat rate contributions changed the minimum contributions from a number of payments to the value of the payments (Micklewright 1989: 539). Previously the minimum requirement was payment of contributions for a period of fifty weeks or nearly a year; the requirement was changed to payment of an amount equal to fifty times the minimum weekly contribution. Consequently, workers with earnings just above the lower limit must still pay contributions for nearly a year to be eligible for benefits, whereas those with high incomes have met the minimum requirement more quickly. Women have also paid contributions amounting to a larger portion of their earnings because their pay has seldom been above the upper limit (Lister 1992: 32, 28). Finally, employees whose employer contracted out of the state occupational pension scheme have paid lower national insurance contributions, and contributions to employer sponsored schemes often afforded tax advantages. A smaller portion of female employees have worked for employers who have contracted out. In 1981–2 only around one-third of women workers enjoyed this advantage (DSS 1992: 289).

As well as resulting in exclusion and injustice, aspects of the construction of contributions make part-time work attractive to both employee and employer. The lower income limit (about £25 per week in 1980 and nearly £60 in the mid-1990s) has been attributed with encouraging earnings below the limit because neither employer nor employee need pay national insurance contributions.[4] Moreover, in the early 1980s the threshold for payment of contributions and income tax was nearly identical; and the average earnings of female part-time workers were very close to the contributions and income tax thresholds.[5] Part-time employment has also often absolved employers from providing occupational benefits, thus lowering labor costs. In any event, a survey of European employers in the early 1990s indicated the importance of contributions. Nearly half of the British employers claimed that the cost effectiveness of part-time jobs arising from lower social security contributions was the main reason for employing part-timers (Maier 1992: 73).

Contribution requirements are a barrier to women's entitlement as workers, but in the case of unemployment benefits – a part of the national insurance scheme – two additional qualifying conditions have operated to exclude women. The first is that the worker must register as unemployed. Studies have found a general reluctance among women to register (Martin and Roberts 1984: 84), and married women are more unlikely to register. The second qualifying condition is an availability for work test, which has at times been interpreted to the disadvantage of women workers (Callender 1987: 143, 148–9). Of the women workers who were registered as unemployed only around 40 percent received insurance benefits in 1980 (DHSS 1981: 14).

Women's access to occupational welfare benefits – such as paid vacations, sick pay, and pensions – has been limited by part-time employment. In all instances part-timers were much less likely to receive these benefits. The smallest disparity concerned paid holidays, but there were wide differences in women's coverage in occupational pension schemes. Pension regulations have generally allowed employers to exclude part-time employees, and less than 10 percent of part-timers were covered.

Of all working women, only around one-third were members of a pension scheme, and among full-timers coverage was slightly over 50 percent in the early 1980s (Martin and Roberts 1984: 49). As these figures reveal, other mechanisms were at work than merely the broad exclusion of part-timers. Further exclusion from private schemes can result because provision need not be the same for all categories of employees within an organization. This has opened the possibility of excluding women from pension coverage on grounds of job classification. Non-membership stemmed from no available scheme (no scheme for a particular job category), age requirements (under 26), insufficient service (less than five years in the early 1980s but now two years), or part-time work. Women employees in the private sector were much less likely to be a member of an occupational pension scheme – 25 percent – compared to those in the public sector where 55 percent were members (Groves 1983: 55–6).

The lack of an occupational pension is especially grave in the UK because of the low benefit levels of the basic state retirement pension

(Palme 1990b). In the early 1980s the poverty rate among pensioners was higher in the UK than in the other countries (Hedström and Ringen 1990: 94), and roughly 40 percent of elderly women were living at or below the poverty line defined as the standard assistance benefit (Walker 1987: 180–1).

Length of service and continuous employment as a qualifying condition was not limited to occupational pensions. Other benefits and rights – such as paid holidays, maternity rights, severance pay, and employment protection – have required two years of continuous service for those working sixteen hours or more or five years of service for employees working eight hours per week. In 1980 around 35 percent of all working women did not meet the requirement of two years of employment with their present employer, and by 1989 the percentage had risen to over 40 percent (calculated from Martin and Roberts 1984: 45, EG 1990: 633). Few women have qualified on the basis of the five years' rule (see Daniel 1980).

In the early 1980s over 60 percent of British women were in the labor force, and thus potentially eligible for work-related benefits. However, the lower income limit and continued use of the married woman's option, disqualified roughly half of all working women from national insurance benefits. Thus slightly over 30 percent of all British women were entitled to national insurance benefits as workers (table 5.2). The unified structure of the national insurance scheme, often viewed as an admirable feature promoting comprehensive coverage, resulted in women's exclusion from nearly all insurance benefits. The picture for occupational pensions was even more bleak. Approximately two-thirds of working women were excluded, and only slightly over 20 percent of all British women were members of occupational pension schemes (calculated from Martin and Roberts 1984: 43, 49; cf. HMSO 1991: 4).

Of the employed women excluded from work related entitlements, the vast majority were married women. They either continued to use the married woman's option or they worked part time. Among working married women 55 percent held part-time jobs and 20 percent worked too few hours (under sixteen) to meet the requirement of two years of continuous service (Martin and Roberts 1984: 17). Slightly over 10 percent of elderly married women received occupational pension benefits as workers compared to nearly 50 percent of elderly single women in the mid-1980s (Ginn and Arber 1991: 383). For substantial numbers of working wives, entry into the labor market did not provide them with entitlements as workers to reduce their dependency on benefits via their husbands.

Women's entitlement to benefits as workers has thus not paralleled their influx into the labor market. Their entitlements, especially in the case of pensions, were initially stymied by the married woman's option and sub-sequently by contribution requirements. The abolition of the married woman's option was, however, accompanied by advances for women as claimants of several short-term insurance benefits. As we saw in chapter 4, women's entitlement to the maternity allowance, which could only be claimed on their own insurance, grew during the 1970s. Women's claims to sickness and unemployment benefits also increased compared to the early 1970s (cf. DHSS 1973: 37, 26–7). In short, although the entitlement of British women as workers was not especially impressive in 1980, it was an improvement in comparison to the days when the married woman's option was in full force.

The Netherlands: low thresholds of employee insurance schemes

In 1980 only one-third of Dutch women were economically active, and around half of them were in part-time employment. Nor did labor market status always enhance married women's social rights; however, women workers – irrespective of marital status – were potentially eligible for ben-efits in the employee insurance schemes covering sickness, disability, and short-term unemployment. The qualifying conditions for benefits in the employee insurance schemes appear to be modest, especially compared to those in the USA and the UK. The crucial question is whether modest qual-ifying conditions constitute sufficiently low thresholds, given the marginal position of many Dutch women on the labor market.

The official definition of employees is decisive in terms of who is included and who is not. On the one hand, the definition has been inclu-sive, encompassing work which is contracted out, done on a commission basis, or in sheltered employment, and mediated through an employment agency. In 1980 the minimum requirements for employees to qualify was that they had to have worked at least two days (sixteen hours) per week for a period longer than one month and as a rule also earned 40 percent of the minimum wage (SZW 1982: 30–1). This represents a low hurdle with regard to duration of employment, and because of the relatively good hourly earn-ings of many part-timers, they would probably have qualified. On the other hand, standby workers, although less numerous in the early 1980s, would have had difficulty in meeting the earnings requirement. The definition of an employee also explicitly excluded domestic workers employed by a private individual for fewer than three days per week and "home workers" earning less than 40 percent of the minimum wage.

It also needs to be pointed out that beneficiaries in most work related schemes have been restricted to employees. Economically active persons who are self-employed or family workers have not been covered by the employee insurance schemes. Such workers amounted to slightly over 10 percent of the female labor force in the early 1980s (van der Burg et al. 1992: 96), and they were ineligible for sickness, maternity, and unemployment benefits. Coverage of the self-employed has been more limited than several programs in the other countries.

The explicit exclusions and minimum requirements affected primarily women workers, and the exclusion of domestic workers can be interpreted as reaffirming the position of care work in the private sphere. In the early 1980s around 15 percent of women employees worked less than the minimum hours' requirement (CBS 1985: 39), and the vast majority of domestic workers worked part time (van der Burg et al. 1992: 20, 22). The combined effect of restricting the insurance schemes to employees and the official definition of employees seems to have excluded slightly less than 25 percent of all economically active women in the early 1980s. Employment trends during the decade signified an increase in women's labor market participation – rising to over 50 percent – but simultaneously short working hours became more common (SCP 1993a: 25, 53). At the same time, qualifying conditions were made more lenient so that shorter working hours have not accelerated the exclusion of employed women because they worked too few hours.[6]

In 1980 earnings related benefits provided 80 percent of the worker's daily wage up to a ceiling in return for earnings related contributions. Women's low earnings affect the benefits they receive. Of workers receiving the minimum wage two-thirds were women. Moreover, many women may not have had the right to a minimum wage. Until 1993 the right to a minimum wage required that the employee work at least one-third of the "normal hours" of work for the particular job (Plantenga and van Velzen 1993).

Turning to occupational welfare, we find that larger proportions of both employees in general and women workers were part of an occupational pension scheme in the Netherlands, compared to the UK and the USA (Daily and Turner 1992). Slightly over 60 percent of female employees above the age of 24 were covered by such a pension scheme in the mid-1980s, while the rate of coverage of married working women was only around 50 percent (SCP 1993a: 159). It appears that women's higher coverage in the Netherlands was favored by the greater availability of pension plans compared to the UK and the USA. On the other hand, job tenure is crucial to receiving an occupational pension, and Dutch women workers have a very low rate of job tenure, in part because of their recent entry into the labor market (OECD 1994a: 120–1). Although one-third of retired women aged 66–70 received private pension benefits in the 1980s, these benefits mirrored the gendered outcomes of public pensions benefits. The recipient rates were highest among widows (71 percent), followed by single women (55 percent), and sharply declined for married women (7 percent) (SCP 1993a: 159).

Only 25 percent of all Dutch women had social entitlements as workers in the early 1980s – the smallest proportion of the four countries (table 5.2). Nonetheless, the effects of qualifying conditions were less exclusionary than in the UK and the USA in the early 1980s. Working hour requirements appear to have excluded around 15 percent of economically active women compared to the lower income limit of national insurance, which barred 20 percent of British women workers. Although Dutch female employees were more likely to be covered by occupational pensions than British women workers, coverage of all women in the two countries was similar – around 20 percent in the early 1980s. The defamilializing effects of Dutch women's entitlements as workers appear to be limited by the small percentage of married women who were employees and their marginal earnings.

Sweden: "double-decker" schemes and earnings related benefits

Since the mid-1950s reforms have introduced earnings related benefits as a complement to universal flat rate programs, resulting in double-decker schemes of public provision for old age and disability pensions, sickness benefits, and parental benefits. Earnings related benefits did not replace flat rate benefits, but by 1980 the former dominance of flat rate benefits in terms of the amount of money paid out as transfers had tipped toward earnings related benefits. The growing prominence of earnings related benefits has increased the importance of social rights deriving from labor market status.

The Swedish occupational pension scheme, known as ATP (the state supplementary pension), was enacted in the late 1950s. Unlike the British state pension scheme – SERPS – it covered all workers, and employers were not allowed to contract out. Although there were no contribution requirements for insured persons, two features of ATP have served as thresholds for eligibility. The first feature was an employment record of thirty years with adequate annual earnings. Upon failing to meet the required thirty years, a percentage was subtracted for missing years, and this clearly worked against older women who stayed home with their children and then entered the labor market. The second feature has been the requirement that annual earnings must be over a lower limit – the so-called base amount. In 1980 the amount was nearly 14,000 crowns (around US$2,500 or £1,400), and around 10 percent of working women failed to meet the earnings requirement that year (SCB 1986: 130, 134).

The earnings requirement and years of employment were barriers to eligibility in 1980 but their exclusionary effects have successively diminished as women have entered the labor market. In 1970 only about 10 percent of all women pensioners had ATP benefits but ten years later around 35 percent had a supplementary pension, and among new female pensioners in 1980 nearly 60 percent had ATP benefits. Looking at the new pensioners without ATP benefits, we find over 25 percent had no claim to an occupational pension – and an additional 15 percent of the women failed to qualify because of inadequate earnings (Marklund and Svallfors 1987: 23, 24).

Besides old age benefits ATP provides disability pensions. Persons with labor market status are eligible for ATP disability benefits upon fulfillment of an earnings test (earnings corresponding to the base amount at the time of disablement) and a work test.[7] These qualifying conditions have not posed an insurmountable barrier to women's entitlement, as can be seen by comparing ATP beneficiaries with those receiving basic disability benefits who did not have to meet either an earnings requirement or a work test. In 1980 around 60 percent of the female recipients of basic disability benefits also received ATP benefits (calculated from *Allmän försäkring* 1980: 270, 291).

Unemployment compensation has consisted of insurance benefits and labor market allowances (*kontant arbetsmarknadsstöd,* or KAS), and these two programs have had dissimilar ramifications for women's entitlements. As in the other countries, several features of unemployment insurance have entailed disadvantages for women, whereas labor market allowances have tended to benefit women since neither contributions nor past employment were a requirement for eligibility.

Unemployment insurance, unlike other social policy programs in Sweden, has been voluntary and organized by the trade unions. Although membership in a particular insurance fund was not limited to union members, relatively few non-members enrolled in the funds. The requirement of membership in a union administered fund has meant that a large segment of the labor force has not been covered by unemployment insurance. In 1980 slightly under 50 percent of registered unemployed persons were not covered by unemployment insurance either because they were not members or not previously part of the workforce (cf. AMS 1980: 4, SCB 1989b: 70), and less than half of unemployed women received insurance benefits in 1980.

Besides membership in a fund for one year, eligibility was dependent upon previous employment and availability for work. Work tests, which consisted both of months of employment and amount of work time,[8] disqualified at most around 10 percent of economically active women in 1980. The requirement of availability for work was that the claimant had to be prepared to work at least seventeen hours a week. At the same time this requirement has generally assured that the worker was covered for other benefits, such as paid vacations, private pensions, etc.

To protect persons not covered by unemployment insurance the labor market allowance was introduced in 1974. Similar qualifications of previous employment and availability for work have determined eligibility, but education and training programs could replace the stipulation of previous employment. Thus, besides providing benefits for persons not covered by insurance, the allowance has provided support for people trying to enter or re-enter the labor market. This represented a radical departure in the area of unemployment benefits because it expanded the definition of the labor force (often equivalent to employees already working) by incorporating entrants. For women the allowance has been especially valuable, and 63 percent of the recipients of labor market allowances were women in 1980 (AMS 1981: 12).

Despite the comprehensive public provision, occupational welfare benefits have also grown. Employer sponsored sickness benefits and pensions covered large numbers of employees primarily as collectively bargained plans on a nationwide basis. As a result, around 95 percent of all employees were insured in an employer sponsored pension scheme in 1980 (calculated from Kangas and Palme 1989: 72). Part-time workers must work at least 40 percent of the normal working hours (sixteen hours a week) to qualify for coverage – a requirement which excluded less than 10 percent of women employees. In the early 1980s 30 percent of women pensioners received benefits from these schemes as workers not wives (SCB 1986: 134), and the proportion had increased to nearly 45 percent in 1990 (calculated from Ståhlberg 1994: 22).

In conclusion, the high female labor market participation rate has meant that a larger proportion of Swedish women has been potentially eligible for social benefits as workers. At the same time relatively few working women – usually around 10 percent – were excluded from work related schemes due to additional qualifying conditions in 1980 (table 5.2). One important factor mitigating against exclusion has been the comprehensiveness of both public and private schemes. Swedish employees have not faced a situation where benefits were not available because their job was not covered. Nor did they confront contribution requirements, and minimum employment or earnings requirements have usually not barred women workers from benefits. In some instances, the requirements have posed low thresholds. More decisive, however, is the much smaller proportion of women workers who have experienced extreme marginalization on the labor market in terms of short working hours and meager pay. Availability for work tests and subsidized day care have required women to take jobs which are not "short" part-time employment. In contrast to the UK and the Netherlands, the proportion of women working short hours has declined during the past two decades. Moreover, jobs which provide poor earnings in other countries have tended to be better paid in Sweden (Persson 1993: 43).

Entitlement as workers: altered social rights?

Close to one-quarter of the adult female population in all four countries entered the labor market over a period of three decades (from 1960 to the 1990s). In the 1980s the participation rate of Swedish women in the labor market approached that of men, and a larger proportion of Swedish women were potentially eligible for benefits as employees and economically active persons than in the other countries. In one respect, this is quite paradoxical. As we have seen, Swedish women have stronger entitlements based on citizenship and the principle of care, whereas labor market status and the principle of maintenance have played a much larger role in determining eligibility for benefits in the other countries. That is, in the countries where labor market status has been central to the entitlement of social insurance benefits, women were less likely to be in the labor market. In several instances, additional qualifying conditions have been more difficult for larger numbers of women to meet than in the Swedish case. The differences are not solely the result of a larger proportion of potentially eligible Swedish women due to a higher labor market participation rate; they arise from the fuller integration of Swedish women workers into the labor force and in some cases less exclusionary policy constructions than in the UK and the USA.

In 1980 insured status requirements adversely affected a larger proportion of US women workers – 30 percent – than the earnings threshold in the national insurance scheme, which disqualified around 20 percent of British women workers. The combined effects of the lower income limit and the married woman's option, however, took a heavier toll, severely curtailing the social entitlements of half of the British female workforce. In fact, the UK is distinguished by more severe work tests than the Netherlands and Sweden. For low income workers contribution requirements in effect entailed a work test of nearly a year. The continuous service requirement amounted to an even stiffer work test of two to five years. Similarly, the work test for disability insurance benefits in the USA barred nearly half of all women workers.

The pattern of coverage in the third tier of occupational welfare is remarkably similar in the USA and the UK. Only around 50 percent of women full-time workers and 10 percent of women part-time workers were covered in the early 1980s. Yet this similar pattern has different repercussions because part-time employment is more widespread in the UK.

Equally ironically, Swedish women's entitlements as workers in the third tier of welfare are also greater in that they were more likely to have both a second and a third pension of their own. Since ATP was compulsory women did not face the problem of no coverage because the employer lacked a scheme. In the early 1980s nearly 30 percent of retired women received additional benefits from employer sponsored pensions.

A further contrast between Sweden and the other countries is the failure of women's entry into the labor market to be matched by parallel increases in their entitlements as workers. US and British women workers' entitlements have inched forward and in a few instances stagnated. In benefit area after benefit area, we find a pattern of steady advances in Swedish women's entitlements as workers as they have entered the labor market.

Finally, in assessing how labor market participation has altered women's social entitlements and its emancipatory effect, it is necessary to consider women's social rights as workers in relation to their existing rights. In the Netherlands entitlement as workers was in theory especially important because married women lacked social rights. The earnings related construction of the employee insurance schemes, however, offers meager benefits for working wives with low pay. In the USA and UK married women have major entitlements as wives, and there is a tension between their rights as workers and as wives because they pertain to the same benefits. Despite US women workers on average putting in the longest hours on the labor market, married women's benefits based on their rights as workers have often been less than their benefits as wives. In the UK qualifying conditions have excluded a large number of married women who have then fallen back upon their rights as wives. For many working wives in the USA and the UK their entitlements as workers have not displaced their entitlements as wives. Swedish women's social rights have stemmed from citizenship and the principle of care, and their entitlements as workers have pertained to a new set of benefits, augmenting their prior entitlements as citizens.

Part III

Stratification and redistributive outcomes

6   Access to benefits and the stratifying effects of bases of entitlement

Social entitlements stratify categories of persons by either granting or denying access to benefits. Keenly aware of differences in women's and men's social entitlements, feminists have argued that a gendered pattern of stratification pervades social provision. Women and men are channeled into separate programs, resulting in a system of dual welfare. Men's maintenance by the state is through social insurance schemes based on claims as earners, while women make their claims on the basis of domestic work and rely more heavily on public assistance programs (Nelson 1984, 1990, Pearce 1985: 457–9, Pateman 1988: 241–2, Fraser 1989: 152, Bryson 1992). Social insurance and assistance programs are further differentiated in terms of benefit levels, political legitimacy, and administrative intervention in private lives. The benefits of social insurance schemes are usually more generous, while assistance benefits, perhaps reflecting their lineage from poor laws, are often meager. Social insurance programs enjoy widespread popular support and legitimacy as "earned rights." By contrast, assistance programs frequently are viewed negatively and their recipients with suspicion. Standard routines with little or no intervention in one's private life characterize the administration of social insurance, but assistance is means-tested involving a detailed investigation of an individual's resources and the resources of relatives. In effect, feminists have theorized that dual welfare and its far-reaching implications for women and men as beneficiaries are intrinsic to social provision and the welfare state.

In mainstream analysis the work of Esping-Andersen has emphasized the welfare state as a system of stratification, but his regime typology underlines stratification as a welfare state variation (1990: chapter 3). Each regime type is associated with a dominant pattern of stratification. In the liberal welfare state regime stratification is characterized by a series of dualisms reinforcing the division between the poor and non-poor. The conservative corporatist welfare state regime reproduces class and status differentials through separate schemes for specific occupational groups and benefits corresponding to existing pay differences. The social democratic welfare state regime combines universal entitlements with high earnings-graduated benefits to promote solidarity and minimize stratification. As is obvious from this description, Esping-Andersen deals exclusively with class and social status without considering stratification with respect to women and men and the gendered division of labor in the family and society.

The purpose of this chapter is to explore how women's and men's social entitlements are differentiated and to cast light on the dynamics of different bases of entitlement in patterning stratification. I argue that the bases of entitlement are central to understanding welfare states as systems of stratification, and that a fuller understanding of the stratification of women and men requires the analysis to encompass a broader range of bases of entitlement by combining feminist and mainstream perspectives.

The empirical focus is on women's access to and utilization of income maintenance benefits compared with men's in the early 1980s. This comparison provides a foundation to assess feminist claims concerning the existence of a gendered system of dual welfare and Esping-Andersen's theorizing on stratification in his three regime types. On the basis of such a comparison we can delineate the patterns of gender stratification in access to benefits in the four countries, and we can establish the nature of variations and commonalities in gender stratification across the countries.

Dual welfare and access to social benefits

Is a gendered system of dual welfare segregating women and men as beneficiaries of different types of social provision an intrinsic feature of the welfare state or a welfare state variation? To answer this question the analysis initially deals with women's and men's access and recipient rates in major social insurance schemes, and subsequently turns to a comparison of the sex of recipients of means tested benefits in the four countries.

Access to social benefits and beneficiary status are determined by rules of eligibility. In the three preceding chapters we have focused on women's entitlements as wives, mothers, and workers – and the importance and interplay of three criteria of eligibility: need, labor market status, and citizenship. Here we examine the differences in how women's various types of entitlement are translated into benefits as compared to men's entitlements. What benefits do women receive and what benefits do men receive?

Insurance benefits: access and utilization

We begin by looking at the degree to which women and men are incorporated into major social insurance schemes – old age pensions, sickness and disability insurance, and unemployment benefits. For the most part, we shall deal with individual entitlement in the major social insurance programs because the dual welfare thesis is primarily concerned with the direct rights of women and men. In fact, this is one limitation of the thesis, since it ignores women's entitlements as wives derived from their husband's rights.

Retirement pensions

Women's access to retirement pensions, the basis of their entitlement, and the gender gap in pension rights varied widely between the four countries around 1980 (table 6.1). Most elderly American women and men receive social security benefits but, as can be seen in table 6.1, approximately 10 percent of the pension age population did not in the early 1980s. A large share of the elderly without social security benefits were women. Historically women have been less likely to be "fully insured" for benefits. In 1980 slightly over 90 percent of men workers were fully insured compared to 70 percent of women workers (SSB, *Annual Statistical Supplement* 1983: 93). The basis of entitlement for a majority of women was as wives. Only a little over 40 percent received social security benefits exclusively on the basis of individual entitlement (Lingg 1990: 4). Roughly the same proportion were eligible for benefits solely as spouses. The remaining women had dual entitlement, i.e. rights based on their own and their husbands' work records.

In 1980 slightly less than one-third of all British women receiving retirement benefits had a pension in their own right; instead 70 percent based their claims on their husband's insurance (DHSS 1981: 80–1). This pattern of claims and the low incidence of individual entitlement were largely due to the married woman's option and women's difficulties in meeting contribution requirements. Although abolished in 1975, the married woman's option influenced the pension entitlements of nearly two generations, so its effects have only slowly diminished. The earnings threshold of national insurance contributions has excluded many more women than men. As we saw in chapter 5, roughly 20 percent of all working women had earnings below the national insurance income threshold in the 1980s, compared to a mere 2 percent of working men (Hakim 1989: 479).

Dutch national old age insurance (AOW) in 1980 was an example of extremely harsh discrimination, inasmuch as married women had no individual entitlement to a national old age pension.[1] Because of married women's lack of entitlement, the gender gap in access to pensions was widest in the Netherlands. All men of retirement age received a pension but only slightly over half of all women did. This is one of the most striking cross-national differences evident in table 6.1. In the other three countries women constituted a majority of the pension beneficiaries, whereas in the

Table 6.1 *Recipients of old age insurance benefits around 1980[a]*

	Pension aged persons[b]			Pension beneficiaries			% Women with individual entitlement
	N	% of population	% women	Total N	Women N	%	
US							
OASI (includes aged survivors)	25,545	11.3	59.7	23,818	14,274	59.9	41[c]
Great Britain[d]	9,459	17.4	66.6				
Retirement pensions				9,098	5,885	64.6	31
Netherlands	1,614	11.5	58.8				
National old age insurance (AOW) (including "invisible" recipients, i.e. married women)				1,333	616	46.2	100
				(1,858)	(1,141)	(61.4)	(52)
Sweden	1,362	16.4	56.6				
Basic old age pension (*Folkpension*)				1,351	763	56.4	100
Supplementary old age pension (ATP)				748	255	34.1	100
ATP including widows' pensions				884	391	44.2	65

Notes:

[a] N in thousands.

[b] Pension-aged population is defined as 65 years or older for the USA, the Netherlands and Sweden, despite the fact that younger persons receive reduced old-age pensions. In the case of Great Britain pension aged population is comprised of men who are 65 years or older and women who are 60 years or older.

[c] This figure includes only women entitled to a pension based solely on their work records.

[d] Figures are for 1981 to take advantage of the 1981 census data.

Sources: Statistical Abstract of the United States 1982–3: 27, SSB Annual Statistical Supplement 1982: 132, Annual Abstract of Statistics 1984: 10; DHSS 1982: 80–3, Statistical Yearbook 1984: 20, 25, 358, Statistisk årsbok 1981: 41, Allmän försäkring 1980: 280, 291, 298, 300.

Netherlands male old age beneficiaries outnumbered female beneficiaries. Of elderly Dutch women, it was only those without a husband who received a pension of their own. Nonetheless, and quite paradoxically, the proportion of Dutch women with individual entitlement to an old age pension – 52 percent – was higher compared to US and British women due to the "citizen" pension scheme in the Netherlands. Thus in the early 1980s Dutch national old age insurance was a peculiar combination of harsher discriminatory measures and a more inclusive construction *vis-à-vis* women.

The individual access of Swedish women is better than that in the other countries but it has differed according to the type of pension, illuminating the importance of the basis of entitlement. In the case of the basic pension, when entitlement was based on citizenship (since 1993 on residence) there was little difference between the sexes. On the other hand, entitlement to the national supplementary pension, ATP, entails labor market status as well as a minimum earnings requirement, and women's access lags behind men's. In 1980 slightly less than 35 percent of female old age pensioners had ATP compared to nearly 85 percent of their male counterparts (*Allmän försäkring* 1980: 280, 291) – a female/male ratio similar to those in the USA and the UK.

Table 6.1 presents women's utilization of retirement benefits as a percentage of pension beneficiaries and the proportion of women whose claims are based on individual entitlement. At first glance, US and British women seem to be advantaged because of their higher numbers compared to men, but these figures merely reflect sex ratios among the aged in these countries. In the British case the higher proportion of women is also the result of different retirement ages for women (60 years) and men (65 years). Looking at recipient rates, this favorable picture is reversed. As can be seen from the table, nearly 2 million Americans aged 65 or over did not receive OASI benefits in 1980, and around two-thirds of them were women. Similarly, and contrary to the image of universalism of the British national insurance scheme, a comparison of the resident elderly population with pension benefits reveals a discrepancy between the number of elderly women and the number of female beneficiaries, but no such disparity for men.

In summary, the old age insurance schemes of the USA and the UK have been shaped by a philosophy of earned rights based on labor market status, income, and contributions. Individuals without paid work are not covered by the schemes (unless they are married women whose husbands are eligible for benefits), and those with insufficient contributions receive reduced pension benefits. Their main recourse is old age assistance programs for the needy. By contrast, the basic pension schemes in Sweden and the Netherlands are "people's pensions," covering in principle the entire population irrespective of income or labor market status. An essential difference, easily obscured by the unjust treatment of Dutch married women, is that women's claims to old age pensions in the Netherlands and Sweden were based solely on individual entitlement (table 6.1), whereas the majority of British and American women claimed pensions on the basis of their entitlements as wives. The twist in the Dutch case was that only women who were not wives had pension rights, while in Sweden marital status did not affect women's entitlements.

Sickness and disability benefits

The lack of a national sickness insurance program in the USA has resulted in a proliferation of mainly private schemes to protect workers from loss of income during short-term illness.[2] In the early 1980s around 60 percent of all workers were covered by some sort of formal plan, and benefits from such plans are estimated to have replaced nearly 40 percent of income losses in 1980 (Price 1984, 23–8). Unfortunately little information is available about women's involvement in these plans. However, existing evidence suggests that only around 40 percent of female workers have been covered by such schemes (Perman and Stevens 1989, Newton 1988, Gelb and Palley 1987: 172). In other words, women's overall access to sickness benefits is substantially worse than their access to old age benefits, although the difference is negligible if we confine the comparison to women's access based on individual entitlement.

By contrast, in the UK sickness benefits for the entire working population were provided by the national insurance scheme until 1983. Given the existence of a national insurance scheme one would expect women's access to be much better than in the USA. However, the negative features of the contribution requirements also affect the availability of sickness benefits. This anomaly shows up in a gender skew in the proportion of the claimants of sickness benefits in 1980: although women constituted about 40 percent of the workforce, only one-third of the beneficiaries were women (calculated from DHSS 1981: 26). Because of contribution requirements it is open to question whether British women's access to sickness benefits in the early 1980s was much better than in the USA, despite the existence of a statutory program.

In the Netherlands statutory sickness insurance (Sickness Benefits Act, ZW), which covers employees against loss of income due to sickness or accidents, provides more generous benefits for a longer duration than the schemes in the UK. Unfortunately most available statistics that provide a breakdown of sickness insurance claimants by sex include maternity benefits, making valid comparisons difficult.

Although entitlement to benefits under the Swedish sickness insurance

Table 6.2 *Recipients of disability insurance benefits, 1980*

	Total *N*	*N* women	% women
USA			
OASDI	2,869,253	931,635	32.6
Great Britain			
Invalidity benefit	615,000	109,000	17.7
Non-contributory invalidity pension	131,000	68,000	51.9
Housewives non-contributory invalidity pension	45,000	45,000	100.0
Total disability benefits	791,000	222,000	28.1
Netherlands			
AAW + WAO	660,300	172,338	26.1
Sweden			
Basic disability pension	293,334	143,808	49.0
ATP disability pension	208,563	87,605	42.0

Sources: SSB *Annual Statistical Supplement* 1980: 161, DHSS 1981: 43, 49, *Statistical Yearbook* 1984: 360, *Allmän försäkring* 1980: 281–3, 291.

scheme was not restricted to employees, as in the Netherlands, or the working population, as in the UK, most women were insured as economically active persons by 1980.[3] Nor did women have to meet contribution requirements. Until the 1980s women's utilization rate of sickness benefits was slightly lower than that of men, despite the fact that women outnumbered men as insured persons. However, differences in women and men claiming sickness benefits were much smaller than in the UK, largely because women were more fully incorporated in the Swedish insurance scheme. Major yardsticks – such as the numbers of cases of benefits, the average number of days of incapacity per insured person, and the percentage of insured persons not claiming benefits during the year – reveal a change during the past decade. Since 1980 the number of cases of benefits for women has been higher than that for men, and since the mid-1980s the average number of days of incapacity for women in all benefit categories has been higher.

Women's access to disability insurance benefits is severely curtailed, and it is in this area that we find the most glaring differences in women's and men's entitlements to insurance benefits (table 6.2). In the USA to be eligible for benefits a person must be fully insured and also meet a test of substantial recent work before disablement. Women have fared worse than men in their right to claim OASDI disability benefits. In 1980 only around 55 percent of the women workers were insured in the event of disability compared to 85 percent of the men (calculated from Irick 1986: 23; cf. SSB 1986: 9), and this unfavorable ratio in coverage is reflected in the sex composition of beneficiaries. Of those receiving disability benefits that year, around one-third were women (SSB 1986: 13). This discrepancy is particularly alarming because the proportion of women between the ages of 16 and 64 who were disabled was larger than the proportion of men (*Statistical Abstract of the United States* 1982–3: 336; cf. Berkowitz et al. 1976: 11).

This disparity cannot be entirely explained by the gap in insured status of women and men. The number of female and male workers insured for disability has steadily risen, and the rate of growth in insured status has been much higher for women. Although the number of female disability beneficiaries grew dramatically between 1960 and 1980, increasing nearly tenfold (Lonsdale and Seddon 1994: 153), the recipient rate as a percentage of insured women actually declined. This was not the case for men, whose rate was slightly higher in 1980 compared to 1960 (calculated from Lingg 1990: 7, SSB, *Annual Statistical Supplement* 1968: 44).

In the UK incapacitated persons can apply for an invalidity benefit, which is also a national insurance benefit, or for a non-contributory invalidity pension providing a smaller benefit. As in the USA, British women have had higher rates of disability (Martin et al. 1988: 22) but they are much less likely to be recipients of disability benefits than men. The situation in the UK was slightly more unfavorable than in the USA. In 1980 less than 30 percent of the recipients were women, despite the existence of non-contributory programs, and a mere 18 percent of the recipients of insurance benefits were women.

The Netherlands has a double-decker system of disability benefits. In the mid-1970s a general disability program (General Disablement Benefits Act, AAW) covering all citizens was introduced to supplement the employee scheme (Disablement Insurance Act, WAO). The AAW provides flat rate benefits, which the employee scheme tops up with earnings related benefits. In looking at the recipients of benefits from both schemes, we find as previously that a very low proportion are women: slightly over one-fourth of the claimants were women in 1980 (Emanuel et al. 1984: 420–5).[4]

In view of the General Disablement Benefits Act covering all citizens and legislation introducing equal rights to disability benefits for women and men in 1980,[5] it initially comes as a surprise to discover so few women as claimants of benefits. However, the general scheme includes a modest income requirement earned in the year preceding incapacity, and even the most modest of income requirements may exclude Dutch women. In a survey from the early 1980s, over half of the women reported that they had no individual income (SCP 1985: 51). Training and previous occupation also seem important in establishing incapacity for work. A disabled person who is unable to earn the same income from suitable employment as a healthy person is regarded as incapacitated, but suitable employment has been determined by a person's training and previous occupation (SZW 1982: 64–5). Beneficiary statistics prior to the enactment of AAW reveal that this "universal" program did little to improve women's access to disability benefits (*Statistical Yearbook* 1982: 368).

In Sweden disability benefits have been linked to the pension system. Like the Netherlands, Sweden has a double-decker system of general and work-related disability benefits through ATP. But in contrast to the Netherlands, the general program of disability benefits has no income or work requirement. As can be observed in table 6.2, this construction of disability pensions boosts the proportion of beneficiaries who are women and the gender gap nearly disappears. In contrast to the other three countries, Swedish women are much more likely to receive disability benefits. In the case of the basic pension benefits 49 percent of the recipients were women in 1980, and as many as 42 percent of the recipients of ATP benefits were women, that is, a substantially higher percentage than in the case of old age ATP benefits (table 6.1). By the 1990s a majority of the recipients of disability pensions were women (Lonsdale and Seddon 1994: 153).

Unemployment benefits

In all four countries the chief instrument for protecting workers against loss of income when jobless has been unemployment insurance. However, in the USA unemployment insurance provides the sole statutory benefits available to the jobless, while the other countries have additional income support programs to aid unemployed persons who cannot claim insurance benefits. In the UK and the Netherlands, these programs are integrated in means tested assistance schemes. In Sweden the labor market cash allowance exists as a separate program without any connection to social assistance. In the USA unemployed persons *qua* unemployed persons have no recourse to federal assistance programs. The overall importance of these differences shows up in the coverage or availability of benefits to the unemployed. It also has an impact on the sex composition of recipients of public assistance programs.

In the USA women's official rate of unemployment has usually been higher than men's, as it was in 1980 (table 6.3), but women have been less likely to receive unemployment benefits for several reasons. First, unemployment insurance covers only those who hold jobs. In 1980 the average rate of unemployment was 7.1 percent but the rate of unemployment among insured persons was only 3.9 percent. Put differently, and

Table 6.3 Recipients of unemployment insurance benefits by sex, 1980

	Labor market participation rate			Unemployment rate			% of the unemployed receiving benefits		
	Total	Women	Men	Total[a]	Women	Men	Total	Women	Men
USA	72.3	59.7	85.3	7.0 7.1	7.4	6.9	43.9	–	–
Great Britain	74.4	58.3	90.5	7.0 7.3	5.3	7.5	45.4	41.7	47.0
Netherlands	57.7	35.5	79.4	4.7 4.6	5.3	4.4	62.6	49.1	70.1
Sweden	81.0	74.1	87.8	2.0 2.0	2.3	1.7	51.2	48.0	53.9

Notes:
[a] The first column is the OECD standardized unemployment rate and the second column is the rate reported in national statistics.
Sources: OECD 1992b: 90, 330, 394, 454, 1983: 18, 23, 86, Statistical Abstract of the United States 1982–3: 391, Annual Abstract of Statistics 1982: 163–4, DHSS 1981: 14, Statistical Yearbook 1984: 141, 359, Arbetsmarknaden i siffror 1970–1988: 70–1, 73, AMS, 1980.

more crucially, among the unemployed only slightly over 40 percent were covered by unemployment insurance (*Statistical Abstract of the United States* 1982–3: 323, 392). In 1982–3 nearly 50 percent of the female unemployed in 1980 were either re-entrants or entrants compared to around 25 percent of the male unemployed (*Statistical Abstract of the United States* 1982–3: 391). The likelihood of receiving unemployment benefits was tipped in favor of men who were 60 percent of the beneficiaries but roughly half of the unemployed (MacLennan and Weitzel 1984: 214, Nelson 1984: 222).

In the UK the claimants of unemployment benefits have been overwhelmingly men, and unlike most industrial countries their official unemployment rates have been higher than women's (OECD 1988: 143).[6] However, these rates are based on the number of persons registered as looking for work at the local offices of the employment service. The inclusion of "discouraged workers" in unemployment statistics would increase female unemployment relative to men (OECD 1987: 129; cf. Callender 1987). Around 70 percent of the registered unemployed and 75 percent of the persons receiving insurance benefits in the UK were men in 1980. However, calculating the recipiency rate as a percentage of the registered unemployed for each sex in November that year, we find that women were only at a minor disadvantage (41.7 for women as opposed to 47.0 for men) (calculated from *Annual Abstract of Statistics* 1982: 164; DHSS 1981: 14). In other words, women confronted a high initial threshold in becoming registered as employed; but once they had crossed it, they were only slightly disadvantaged in receiving insurance benefits.

The Dutch system of unemployment compensation is complex. In the early 1980s, the system was comprised of three major components: unemployment insurance proper (WW) which provided short-term benefits (a period of twenty-six weeks); unemployment provision (WWV) consisting of extended benefits for a maximum period of two years; and unemployment assistance (RWW) (Roebroek and Berben 1987: 685–6). In 1980 the rate of unemployment for women was slightly higher than for men (table 6.3). Despite this, men were the main recipients of insurance benefits; 70 percent of the male registered unemployed received either WW or WWV benefits, compared to just under 50 percent of the women who were registered as unemployed. In short, gender inequalities were more pronounced than in the other countries. Part of the explanation might lie in the fact that until 1987 married women were excluded from extended benefits (WWV) unless they had breadwinner status, i.e. earned more than their husbands. But even in the case of short-term benefits women's utilization rate was lower (22 percent as opposed to 30 percent). Nonetheless Dutch women's utilization rate of unemployment insurance benefits as a percentage of the female registered unemployed was higher than in the UK and also higher than in Sweden during the early 1980s.

Table 6.3 compares the unemployment rates and access to insurance benefits of the registered unemployed by sex in 1980. On the surface, differences in access between women and men appear less in the UK, but this needs to be taken with a pinch of salt because a major problem for women is the prior step of registering as unemployed. The picture would also be altered if we included other income support programs for the unemployed. In the UK the inclusion of the public assistance benefits to the jobless results in a widening of differences between the sexes as recipients – 69.9 percent for women as against 80.7 percent for men (calculated from DHSS 1981: 14). By contrast, the inclusion of the Swedish cash labor market allowance narrows the gender gap. The allowance improves women's access to unemployment benefits since, as we saw in chapter 5, a substantially larger share of its recipients have been women.

Furthermore, in Sweden the percentage of unemployed persons who could claim insurance benefits had risen to roughly 65 percent and those not entitled to any unemployment compensation had fallen to around 25 percent in the mid-1980s. This stands in marked contrast to the other countries where the proportion of unemployed claiming insurance benefits eroded dramatically because of very high rates of unemployment (much higher than those presented in table 6.3). The gender gap in Sweden sharply declined among the unemployed without any benefits or only able to claim compensation through the labor market allowance. In 1975 60 percent of the female unemployed were in this position, whereas the figure was 36 percent among the male unemployed. In the mid-1980s the percentages for women and men were nearly the same – 37 and 34 percent respectively (Marklund and Svallfors 1987: 32–3).

In conclusion, looking at insurance benefits on the whole, we can observe a pattern where women have been consistently disadvantaged in terms of *individual* access to benefits in three of the countries – the UK, the USA, and the Netherlands. The utilization rates of women have been lower than those of men for insurance benefits that women could not claim via their husbands in the three countries. In the Swedish case the pattern is mixed: access to benefits has been similar between the sexes in the case of basic pensions covering old age and disability, women's access to ATP benefits trailed behind men's, equality in access to unemployment insurance benefits replaced a former male dominance in the mid-1980s, and women's utilization rate of sickness benefits was slightly higher than men's in the 1980s.

Means tested assistance programs: access and utilization

Turning to the other component of the dual welfare system, table 6.4 sets out the utilization rates of social assistance. Contrary to what we have seen in the case of social insurance benefits, it is primarily women who were the recipients of public assistance in three countries, and as shown in table 6.4, this is overwhelmingly the case in the USA and the Netherlands (for ABW). Sweden, however, deviates from this pattern, and women recipients were slightly fewer than men.

Women's and men's access to social benefits reveals a stratification pattern which resembled a system of dual welfare where men are claimants of insurance benefits and women are recipients of assistance in three of the countries – the Netherlands, the USA, and the UK. The Swedish pattern of access, however, fails to conform to the thesis. Swedish women's access to benefits and their utilization rates of insurance benefits based on individual entitlement approximated men's with the exception of ATP old age pensions. Nor were women disproportionately claimants of assistance. Contrary to the claims of the dual welfare thesis, the Swedish case underscores the fact that a gendered two track system of welfare channeling men into social insurance schemes and women into assistance programs is a welfare state variation and not an inherent feature of social provision. Indeed, a closer examination of the fit of the other three countries to the thesis discloses other interesting variations and limitations.

The dual welfare thesis re-examined

The differentiation in women's and men's social rights – and the resulting dualism – was strongest in the Netherlands (see Bussemaker and van Kersbergen 1994). Social rights were the prerogative of men as family providers and workers, and men's entitlements were virtually universal. Women lacked entitlement because married women's rights were largely familialized, and the strongly gendered division of labor between the sexes resulted in women's extremely low labor market participation excluding them from work related schemes. At the same time, the right of every Dutch citizen to a social minimum has strengthened women's entitlements based on need.

This particular pattern of entitlement produced a disparity in women's and men's ability to successfully claim benefits and a differentiation in the main type of benefit claimed by each sex. In the working age population social benefits were the major source of income for 12 percent of men compared to 5 percent of women (SCP 1985: 51). Looking at long-term utilization of benefits in 1980, we find a strong tendency toward sex segregation

Table 6.4 *Recipients of public assistance benefits, 1980*

	Individuals		Households	Sex of claimants	Sex of adults provided for
	N	% of pop.	N	% women	% women
USA					
SSI	4,142,000			–	65.5
AFDC	10,923,000		3,712,000	81.1	81.1
Total	15,065,000	6.5			76.6
Great Britain					
Supplementary					
benefit	4,863,000	8.9	3,118,000	60.0	66.2
Netherlands					
Social assistance					
ABW	348,600	2.5		80.9[a]	83.8[a]
RWW			101,200	43.0	51.4
Total				64.3	68.5
Sweden					
Social assistance					
(*Socialhjälp*)	343,600	4.1	178,366	–	48.2

Notes:
[a] Regular assistance payments. Does not include institutionalized persons nor those receiving single payments, whereas the number of individuals includes these categories.
Sources: For Sweden, *Statistisk årsbok* 1989: 313; for the USA, *Statistical Abstract of the United States* 1988: 354, SSB *Annual Statistical Supplement* 1980: 227, for Britain calculated from DHSS 1981: 201, 202, 180, for the Netherlands, calculated from *Statistical Yearbook* 1984: 361–2, *Statistisch zakboek* 1984: 327.

according to type of benefit which corresponds to the results presented in tables 6.2–6.4. Men comprised 75 percent of the long-term beneficiaries in disability and unemployment schemes, and women accounted for nearly 90 percent of the long-term recipients of the general assistance scheme (ABW) (SCP 1993b: 146 and 1993a: 158).

A major paradox emerges, however, in the Dutch case. In several areas of provision there was a greater disparity between women's and men's entitlements, but Dutch women's coverage and recipient rates were higher than the other countries, especially the USA and the UK. Although Dutch policies created the largest gender gap in pension rights, the proportion of Dutch women with individual entitlement to pensions exceeded that of women in the UK and the USA. Similarly, gender inequalities in receipt of unemployment benefits were sharpest in the Netherlands but a larger share of unemployed Dutch women received insurance benefits than their counterparts in the UK and Sweden. Finally, Dutch working women were more likely to be members of an occupational pension scheme than US and British women, but the gender gap in coverage was similar to that in the UK and larger than in the USA.

Several aspects of social provision in the USA confirm the dual welfare thesis – and it has most relevance in the case of women's and men's individual entitlements (see Orloff 1993: 315). On the one hand, insurance benefits are based on earnings and substantial work tests, which pose a major obstacle to women's individual entitlement despite the smaller female/male differential in hours of market work. On the other hand, assistance programs in the USA are by category – not universal as in the Netherlands and the UK. US programs are targeted to specific categories deemed worthy of aid, which includes families with dependent children. Unlike the other countries, the unemployed do not have the right to assistance – an arrangement which tends to exclude men. A further limitation of the dual welfare thesis is that it neglects the importance of women's entitlements via their husbands and the fact that women beneficiaries predominate in both tiers of public provision.

British social provision in 1980 fits the thesis in that men were primarily the claimants of short-term benefits in the national insurance scheme, and women were a majority of the persons provided for through assistance. This pattern of access evolved through women's exclusion due to contribution requirements and the married women's option, while assistance benefits have been universally available. However, with unprecedented rates of unemployment in the early 1980s men also joined the ranks of recipients of assistance benefits, so that women were no longer overrepresented.

In many ways the Swedish case is the most interesting because it runs counter to the dual welfare thesis. Women in their own right were often as likely to receive insurance benefits, and men were slightly more likely to be recipients of assistance. The Swedish case underlines the importance of the bases of entitlement in reducing a sharp differentiation in women's and men's access to benefits. First, and most important, income maintenance programs where eligibility is based on citizenship or residence promote equal access to benefits. Citizenship as the basis of entitlement, as brought out in chapter 3, has also undermined the influence of marital or family status in shaping social rights, which has differentiated women's and men's entitlements. Moreover the receipt of these benefits had made it less necessary to claim assistance.

No doubt the most important program of this sort in eliminating women's necessity to rely on public assistance has been the basic pension. In addition, for persons with no or low supplementary pension (ATP) benefits, the basic pension allowance has been topped up by a pension supplement. Nor was the supplement a means tested benefit; it has been automatically awarded to pensioners without ATP or low ATP benefits on an individual basis irrespective of marital status (Ståhlberg 1993: 24). Basic pension benefits have been more adequate compared to minimum pension benefits in the USA and the UK (Palme 1990b, 48–9), and the recipient rate of the basic pension has been higher than for old age insurance benefits in the USA and the UK. In the 1980s and 1990s British and American women with inadequate pensions have been a major contributing factor to the skew between the sexes in utilization of the social assistance benefits.

A similar pattern emerges with respect to disability benefits where women's coverage in social insurance schemes has been particularly inadequate. Poor access to insurance benefits was most pronounced in the Netherlands and the UK, followed by the USA, and it shows up in the type of benefit awarded to disabled individuals. Men are covered by disability insurance which provides more generous benefits than old age insurance, while women are less likely to be covered by social insurance programs. They mainly receive meager means tested benefits in the USA under Supplemental Security Income (SSI) or lower non-contributory benefits in the UK. This tendency is most pronounced in the USA, where women constituted one-third of the recipients of OASDI disability benefits but nearly two-thirds of the needy disabled receiving SSI in 1980. In Sweden women's access to disability benefits has long been almost on a par with men's because, like the old age basic pension, citizenship has been the basis of entitlement.

Several Swedish programs – the advanced maintenance allowance, the housing allowance, and the provision of public day care – reduce the likelihood of single parents having to turn to public assistance, whereas solo mothers constitute a large and expanding group of the women receiving means tested benefits in the other three countries. Although the housing allowance is income tested, most social transfers making up the income package of Swedish solo mothers as well as public provision of childcare are citizenship/residence entitlements. Similarly, the rationale behind the advanced maintenance allowance has been that the child has a right to a social minimum.

As made clear in chapter 5, more Swedish women in their own right are eligible for benefits whose basis of entitlement is labor market status. Women's high rate of employment, approximating men's, and their fuller integration in the labor market, undercut the emergence of a new gender gap in access to insurance benefits, as more programs offered benefits based on labor market status. Women's high rate of labor market participation not only helps to incorporate them in major income maintenance schemes but also provides them with an income, making them less likely to need to fall back on public assistance (cf. Casper et al. 1994: 599–600). Sweden's employment policy has facilitated women's entry into the labor market. Training and job creation schemes have benefited both women and men in roughly equal proportions, whereas such schemes have been more heavily aimed at men in Britain (Ruggie, 1984, chapters 3 and 4). This configuration of policies has combated the gendered differentiation in entitlements as set forth by the dual welfare thesis.

The stratifying effects of the bases of entitlement

In analyzing welfare state stratification, the dual welfare thesis and Esping-Andersen's regime typology are too limited in their conceptualization of the bases of entitlement. The logic of the dual welfare thesis presumes that social provision essentially consists of two components whose key features are diametrically opposed, and accordingly centers on only two bases of entitlement: need and labor market status. The thesis also assumes that these bases of entitlement correspond to a claim structure based on a gendered division of labor. This focus is too narrow; not only does it ignore the principle of maintenance, it also overlooks the basis of entitlement that is so crucial to women's social rights – citizenship. In Esping-Andersen's regime typology a single predominant basis of entitlement underpins and shapes the stratification distinctive to each regime type: need in the liberal regime, labor market status or work performance in the conservative corporatist regime, and citizenship in the social democratic regime. The typology excludes a consideration of the interplay between eligibility principles; and it totally neglects women's entitlements via their husbands and the principle of care. Instead an understanding of variations in the differences in women's and men's social rights requires that we examine the stratifying effects of a wider array of bases of entitlement – labor market status, the principle of maintenance, need, the principle of care, and citizenship – and how they intersect.

In all four countries labor market status is a pivotal basis of entitlement and extremely important in patterning stratification and producing differences in women's and men's access to benefits. Since entitlements as workers have coincided with male tasks in the traditional division of labor between the sexes, this condition of eligibility has buttressed men's social rights. As women have entered the labor market, they have gained entitlements as workers. Nonetheless, in the 1990s the differentials in women's and men's labor market participation ranged between 5 percent in Sweden and 30 percent in the Netherlands. In 1980 the differentials were wider, ranging between roughly 15 and 45 percentage points. Equally important, additional qualifying conditions in work related schemes have consistently excluded more women workers than men workers in all four countries. For women and men in the labor force, the gender gap in entitlements as workers caused by failure to meet eligibility requirements has ranged from a differential of a few percentage points to percentage differences as high as 30 in the 1980s and 1990s. These differences in the disqualification of women and men workers caution against equating labor market participation rates with the acquisition of social rights as workers. The current gender stratification in entitlement as workers stems from both differences in labor market participation and in the exclusionary impact of additional qualifying conditions in work related schemes – differences which reflect the gendered division of labor in the family and society.

The principle of maintenance as embodied in the breadwinner model has sharp stratifying effects. Clearly, social policies reflecting the breadwinner model have been especially detrimental to women because of unequal entitlement of women and men in marriage, with principal social rights vested in the husband. The breadwinner model not only results in differentiated social rights between men and women – bestowing full rights on men who are breadwinners and usually half rights but in some instances no rights for women who are dependants. The model also produces a stratification of benefits among women, differentiating between married mothers and unmarried mothers. In the absence of the male breadwinner, married mothers are awarded social insurance benefits, which are often more generous and not means tested, whereas unmarried mothers receive public assistance. In systems of social provision where married mothers lack benefits as long as the family remains intact, such as the USA and the Netherlands, the results are paradoxical since only unmarried mothers (never married, divorced, separated, or widows) are recipients of social benefits. The discrepancy is especially accentuated in the USA since so many public services – health care, employment programs, and daycare – are means tested benefits not available to married mothers.

Entitlements based on need established through means testing, as noted by Esping-Andersen, can create divisions between the poor and the non-poor. The dual welfare thesis maintains that this division is gendered. The existence of a gendered differentiation in entitlements based on need depends upon the construction of means tested programs – whether they are universal or selective. The Dutch constitution guarantees every citizen the right to a social minimum, and in 1966 British assistance benefits were made a matter of right (Gordon 1988: 313). Accordingly women and men as householders have equal recourse to entitlements based on need in the event of inadequate resources. US means tested programs have combined the principle of care with entitlements based on need, which results in a gendered differentiation.

The principle of care, because of the traditional gendered division of labor, has enhanced the social rights of women. The interplay with other bases of entitlement has been decisive in determining how comprehensive or narrow the extension of social rights has been. The principle of care combined with citizen entitlements encompasses all caregivers, whereas in combination with entitlements based on need, rights pertain to fewer women and are conditional upon family relationships.

Social rights based on citizenship or residence have fewer stratifying effects.[7] Discussions on the capacity of universal entitlements to minimize stratification and to generate solidarity have almost entirely pertained to classes and occupational groups. Entitlements based on citizenship can be equally important in eliminating a gendered differentiation in access to benefits. This is because social rights based on citizenship or residence have provided equal access to benefits irrespective of the traditional gendered division of labor in the family and society. This condition of eligibility equalizes social rights in marriage by granting uniform entitlements to husband and wife. Second, by neutralizing marital status as a criterion of eligibility, citizen benefits also preclude a differentiation in the rights of married and unmarried persons. Third, this basis of entitlement does not privilege paid work above unpaid work; it accords equal rights to those doing paid and unpaid labor. Besides reducing differences in women's and men's social rights, entitlements based on citizenship eliminate divisions among women and promote solidarity. Social provision where marital status affects entitlements produces schisms between married and unmarried women, and similarly between married and unmarried mothers. In short, the consequences of entitlements based on citizenship and residence for gender stratification are virtually the opposite of the principle of maintenance in the breadwinner model.

7   Benefit inequalities and redistributive outcomes

Benefit inequalities constitute a major source of welfare stratification, and different levels of benefits received by women and men are a key aspect of gender stratification. In one of the clearest formulations on the importance of types of benefit in producing differences in distributional outcomes for women and men, Sandra Hutton and Peter Whiteford present a number of working hypotheses. First, they hypothesize that earnings related benefits will lead to unequal outcomes by favoring men, because this type of benefit reproduces the differentials in women's and men's paid work. The degree of inequality generated by earnings related benefits, however, will depend on specific features of these benefits, such as the range between minimum and maximum benefits and benefit formulas. Second, Hutton and Whiteford hold that flat rate benefits will tend to produce gender equality in distributional outcomes. Third, they postulate that means tested programs have a stronger equalizing effect on women's and men's benefit incomes than either flat rate or earnings related schemes (Hutton and Whiteford 1994: 206–7).

Two central issues are addressed in this chapter. How far-reaching are benefit inequalities between women and men in the four countries and how do benefit inequalities affect redistributive outcomes for women and men? To answer these questions, the first part of the chapter examines differences in women's and men's benefit levels in the early 1980s and trends over time. The second part concentrates on redistributive outcomes by examining how welfare state policies reduce income inequalities and poverty rates.

The answers to these two questions reveal a redistributive paradox. Of the four countries the gender benefit gap is quite pronounced in Sweden, yet Swedish policies have a stronger redistributive impact than the other countries, and the distributional outcomes for women and men are less unequal. This paradox requires us to look more closely at the particular *combination* of policies – the structure of benefit income and taxation – which produces these redistributive outcomes.

Differences in benefit levels

Differences in benefit levels are affected by the construction of social benefits – whether they are means tested, flat rate, or earnings related. However, inequalities in the benefit levels of women and men are also the product of gendered differentiation in entitlements – women's entitlements are based on their status as dependants in the family and men's entitlements stem from their capacity as family providers and primary earners. In mapping out the benefit inequalities between women and men it is necessary to examine the interplay between gendered differentiation in entitlements and the benefit construction in the social provision of each country.

The UK: flat rate programs and equal benefits?

Is the gender benefit gap smaller in the UK because of the centrality of flat rate benefits? In principle flat rate benefits are equalizing because each beneficiary – male or female – receives the same benefits. The flat rate benefits of the British national insurance scheme and the principle of uniform benefits would seem to epitomize equal benefits.

Gendered differentiation in entitlements, however, counteracts benefit equality between women and men in several ways. As we saw in the preceding chapter, women have poorer access to insurance benefits because of weaker entitlements as workers compared to men. This has resulted in concentrations of women and men in separate programs. In the past, and currently, disability benefits furnish one of the clearest examples of gender stratification by benefit level in the UK. Disability benefits have privileged workers and paid work, and the highest benefits have been awarded to persons whose disablement occurred through work. An inspection of table 7.1 reveals a monotonic pattern in the benefit levels for claimants of each sex in the early 1980s. As benefits increase, the proportion of women diminishes, while the opposite is true for men. Only around 10 percent of the recipients in the highest benefit category were women, while roughly 60 percent of the beneficiaries in the lowest category were women.[1]

These differences in disability allowances represent one of the largest benefit inequalities in the British social security system, and the differential is much wider than that reported by Esping-Andersen (1990: 70). The benefit amount of the non-contributory invalidity pension – since 1984 the severe disablement benefit – has been around one-third of the industrial disablement benefit. Benefit inequalities are further magnified by vestiges of the male breadwinner model – additional allowances for adult dependants, whose generosity corresponds to the benefit level of each program. A married male beneficiary in the industrial disablement program would

Table 7.1 *Recipients of disability benefits and benefit levels by sex in Great Britain, 1980*[a]

	% Women	% Men	Number of women	Total number
Industrial disablement benefit (£44.30)	10.3	89.7	20,000	195,000
Invalidity benefit (£26.00)	17.7	82.3	109,000	615,000
Non-contributory invalidity pension (£16.30)	51.9	49.1	68,000	131,000
Housewives non-contributory invalidity pension (£16.30)	100.0	0.0	45,000	45,000
Total	24.3	75.7	242,000	986,000

Note:
[a] The benefit amounts are in the event of full disability.
Sources: DHSS 1981: 43, 49, 94–5; 1982: 133.

in many cases have received both the benefit and a dependant's allowance totaling £70 per week. A married female beneficiary in a non-contributory program would usually have been paid a benefit without the addition – that is £16. Under these circumstances, which are not unlikely, the range of benefit inequality increases so that the woman receives an amount which is less than 25 percent of that paid to the man. In short, women encounter a double hurdle with respect to disability benefits. Women have not only been less likely to receive disability benefits, but as brought out in chapter 6, their benefits in general were also substantially lower than those of men.

Second, flat rate benefits are the rule but higher and lower rates have proliferated for a variety of reasons. Failure to meet contribution requirements, for example, resulted in two lower rates of benefits, and the lowest rate cut benefits in half. In this way the lower earnings of women have been incorporated in a flat rate program. In 1980 only 82 percent of women pensioners whose claims were based on their own insurance received the full rate as compared to nearly all male pensioners. Equally important, gendered differentiation in entitlements is reflected in the lower rate for adult dependants, traditionally 60 percent of the full rate.

The combined effect of different rates in the national insurance scheme on state retirement pension benefits in 1980 was that only 55 percent of women were in payment of the standard flat rate amount compared to 97 percent of the men (calculated from DHSS 1981: 83). Despite an increase in the proportion of women claiming a pension on their own insurance since 1980, the percentage of women receiving the standard amount had fallen to 44 percent in the early 1990s (calculated from DSS 1994: 120). Moreover, many women claiming pensions on their own insurance without full benefits have experienced a deterioration in benefits. In the early 1990s, one in four of these women without full benefits was receiving less than one-third of the basic pension (Webb 1994: 24).

Although women often fail to meet requirements for full insurance benefits, the availability of means tested pensions lessens inequalities in the benefit incomes of women and men. The flat rate allowances provided by public assistance, and the fact that their amount has been close to that of benefits in the national insurance scheme and at times actually higher than insurance benefits, strengthens equalization. While women are less likely to receive full insurance benefits, there is evidence that elderly men and women receive quite similar amounts of social transfers. For example, in the mid-1980s median weekly state benefits, including national insurance and means tested benefits, amounted to £40 for men and £37 for women (Ginn and Arber 1991: 379). The transfer package of women differs, however, because they receive more means tested benefits than men (Hutton and Whiteford 1994: 211–12). In other words, inequalities in receipt of the national insurance benefits are frequently offset by means tested benefits.

An additional factor which undercuts the equalizing effects of flat rate benefits is that they are often supplemented by earnings related benefits. These benefits are more likely to be received by men, and their benefits are on average higher than those of women. In 1980 the impact of this type of benefit was confined to the earnings related supplement (ERS) in the national insurance scheme (later abolished), state superannuation schemes, and the third tier of welfare, such as occupational pensions and sick pay.

In the early 1980s benefits paid to pensioners through state superannuation schemes, primarily through the graduated pension, were the infinitesimal sums of £0.40 for women and £1.03 for men per week (DHSS 1981: 85). Yet, as evident from these figures, they reflected a glaring inequality in benefit levels. The gap stems partly from women's lower earnings relative to men's, partly from the contribution rules of the graduated pension. According to the rules, women paid more in contributions to get the same benefits as men. Benefits have been calculated on the basis of every £7.50 paid in contributions between 1961 and 1975 for men and every £9 for women. In the 1990s this formula continued to produce benefit inequality where the average amount received by women is only 40 percent of that of men (calculated from DSS 1993: 120), and a larger proportion of pensioners received graduated retirement benefits compared to an additional pension provided by the state earnings related pension scheme (SERPS).[2]

Table 7.2 *State retirement benefits by sex in Great Britain (average weekly rates)[a]*

	1980	1993
Amount		
Standard rate	£27.15	£56.10
All men	£28.21	£70.24
All women	£23.64	£50.88
Women on own insurance	£26.28	£55.99
Wives on husband's insurance	£16.51	£35.28
Widows on husband's insurance	£27.57	£61.35
Female/male benefit ratio		
All women	0.84	0.72−12
Women on own insurance	0.93	0.80−13
Wives on husband's insurance	0.59	0.50 −9
Widows on husband's insurance	0.98	0.87 −11

Note:
[a] Includes graduated pension, additional pension (SERPS), increments, age addition, invalidity allowance, attendance allowance but excluding increases for dependants.
Sources: DHSS 1981: 87, DSS 1994: 117.

Table 7.2 shows the average weekly rates of state retirement benefits – including earnings related benefits – payable to female and male pensioners in the early 1980s and 1990s. Overall, equality in benefits has decreased during the past decade. For all women beneficiaries, their benefits as a ratio of men's have declined, but the decline has been severest for women on their own insurance. The changes in benefit inequality presented in table 7.2 are mainly attributable to earnings related benefits in the state pension system. Increasingly, male pensioners have received benefits which exceed the standard rate of the basic pension. By contrast, women's benefits in relation to the standard rate have scarcely changed since the early 1980s.

Finally, occupational pension benefits further undermined benefit equality. Many occupation pensions are interlocked with the state system. The SERPS reform of the mid-1970s was a compromise between advocates of an additional tier of pensions through state provision and proponents of expanding occupational pensions. As a concession, employers were allowed to contract out of the state system under the condition that they provide as good a pension as SERPS. The flaw in this arrangement is that there is no requirement that the contracted out schemes cover all employees. In the late 1980s most occupational pensions were contracted out schemes, but coverage had not expanded. In fact, both the total number of members and the proportion of the labor force covered by occupational pensions have largely stagnated since the mid-1960s (HMSO 1991: 4–5), and coverage is currently greatest among high paid job categories (Ginn and Arber 1993: 57). Furthermore marital status affected women's and men's likelihood of receiving a non-state pension. While there was hardly any difference in the recipient rates of never married women and men (47 and 46 percent respectively), married men were most likely to have an occupational pension (67 percent) and married women least likely (12 percent) (Ginn and Arber 1991: 383).

In conclusion, flat rate benefits in the national insurance scheme have not led to benefit equality between the sexes, and a major obstacle is the continued influence of the male breadwinner model on benefit construction. In the case of state retirement pensions large numbers of women do not receive full benefits, while most men do. A disconcerting development since 1980 has been a deterioration in the pension benefits of women on their own insurance. Uniformity of benefits is a myth for a majority of British women – and for most married women.

The degree of benefit equality between women and men in British social provision is instead the product of means tested programs whose benefit levels have been roughly equivalent to those of the national insurance scheme. Assistance allowances either provide a single source of state income or they top up inadequate insurance benefits. On the other hand, flat rate benefits have been more equalizing than earnings related benefits. During the past decade the range of inequality in pension benefits has widened as earnings related benefits provided by both state and private occupational pension schemes have become a larger source of retirement income. In these respects the British case fits quite neatly Hutton and Whiteford's hypotheses. On the other hand, the equalization of benefit income is accompanied by greater differentiation in the bases of entitlement: women's claims are based on need and men's as earners.

The Netherlands: both more and less equal

During the postwar period flat rate benefits have become an increasingly important ingredient in Dutch social provision. Inspired by the Beveridge model of social provision, the Dutch introduced a new set of policies to complement their Bismarckian style employee insurance schemes. As in the UK, state pensions provide flat rate benefits, flat rate assistance allowances have been roughly the same amount as pension allowances, and standardized assistance benefits have been universally available. The Netherlands differs in several significant ways, and these differences result in both more and less equality in the benefits received by women and men than in the British social security system.

The single most important difference is the lack of gendered differentiation in entitlement to state pension benefits after the 1985 pension reform. The pension allowance for married couples was divided equally between husband and wife. A second crucial difference is the more generous benefit levels of Dutch pensions. Adequate pensions have two major repercussions for gender equality; they preclude a differentiation in the bases of entitlement. Very few old age pensioners need to utilize assistance, and the elderly comprise a minute fraction of the persons on welfare (CBS 1993: 52). Neither female or male pensioners received means tested benefits, while in the UK women's lower benefits required them to seek assistance (see Hutton and Whiteford 1994). Adequate benefits also eliminate differences in elderly Dutch women's and men's poverty rates.

A third difference, which operates in the direction of less benefit equality, is the greater role of earning related benefits. Looking at pensioners first, we find that despite the stronger equalizing effects of taxes and transfers in the Dutch case than the UK, gender inequality in disposable income among single male and female pensioners was larger in the Netherlands (Hutton and Whiteford 1994: 213). A key source of unequal retirement income is third tier pensions. In the mid-1980s only one-third of elderly women had an occupational pension, as compared to four-fifths of elderly men, and women's benefits from such pensions were 70 percent of men's (SCP 1993a: 159).

Turning to the population at large, benefit inequality among women and men caused by earnings related benefits is also pronounced. According to Esping-Andersen the average range of benefit inequality in Dutch social provision is somewhat wider than in the UK (1990: 70). All the employee insurance schemes provide earnings related benefits. Officially the range of benefit inequality extends from the minimum wage – roughly the social minimum – to currently 70 percent of earnings up to a fairly generous ceiling. This is a range of roughly 0.50 (the amount of the minimum benefit was about 50 percent of the maximum). In reality the range is greater because many working wives would not qualify for benefits equivalent to the minimum wage.

Among women and men whose primary source of income was social transfers in the early 1990s, statistics reveal substantial inequalities in benefit levels. The largest disparity was in disability benefits, where women's benefit income was slightly over 60 percent of men's. The differential in unemployment compensation was less; women's benefits relative to men's were around 80 percent.[3] Only in the case of assistance benefits did women fare better than men – possibly because of the higher rates paid to solo mothers (calculated from *Statistical Yearbook* 1994: 308).

The USA: inequalities of earnings related benefits modified by the breadwinner model

Of the four countries, the USA is unique in that social insurance provides only earnings related benefits. Moreover, according to Esping-Andersen's index of benefit equality, the USA ranked lowest of the eighteen OECD countries he analyzed. What is the degree of benefit inequality between women and men in the OASDI program?

Social security benefits do not exactly mirror paid work. Three factors prevent earnings inequalities from being directly reproduced in benefits. The first is that the benefit calculation is weighted in favor of low wage workers. Weighting results in different replacement rates depending upon an individual worker's earnings: roughly 53 percent for a low wage worker, 40 percent for an average wage worker, and 26 percent for a high wage worker (Steuerle and Bakija 1994: 96). Second, maximum benefits furnish a ceiling which compresses the range of dispersion in income compared to the market. The third factor is, ironically, the male breadwinner model and women's entitlements as wives. The benefits of working wives with low earnings are often higher than they would have been if their benefits had been based exclusively on their work records.

As a result of these three factors, the average monthly benefit of retired women workers relative to men's was 0.78 in 1980. The gender gap in the benefits of disabled workers was slightly wider – 0.73 (calculated from SSB, *Annual Statistical Supplement* 1982: 114–15, 130). In other words, benefit inequalities were substantially less pronounced compared to female/male earnings differentials for that year which were 0.47 for all workers and 0.60 for full-time year-round workers.

The ratio of the average monthly benefit of *all* women, including women without previous income, compared to men was approximately 0.70 – still appreciably more favorable than earnings ratios. This benefit ratio is the product of two contradictory aspects of wives' entitlements. On the one hand, the spouse benefit pulls average benefits down. The average monthly benefit of wives compared to men's was 0.46. On the other hand, survivor benefits for the aged push the average benefit level up. In 1980 the average monthly benefit of women who were aged widows was higher than the average benefit of women workers, and it was 0.82 of the average benefit of retired male workers. This pattern of gender ratios in social security benefits has been fairly constant over the past decade, and these differentials characterized social security benefits in the mid-1990s.

In short, the interplay between the breadwinner model and earnings related benefits creates a huge catch 22 situation for women in the social security system. Their entitlements as wives mitigate the gender inequalities in earnings related benefits. At the same time, earnings related benefits pose a major barrier to transforming women's entitlements as wives into entitlements as workers. Their entitlements as wives also bias the redistributive effects of the social security system in favor of the middle class (Steuerle and Bakija 1994: 108–11).

The third tier of welfare in the USA superimposes an additional layer of earnings related benefits on top of social security benefits, and the gender benefit ratio of employer sponsored pensions is far more unfavorable to women than social security. In the early 1980s the average employee pension benefits of unmarried women were only around 60 percent of unmarried men's, whereas their social security benefits were 95 percent of unmarried men's. Although it is difficult to disaggregate available data for married couples, in the few instances when married women had an employee pension their benefits averaged around 40 percent of those of married men (Maxfield and Reno 1985: 10–11). In other words, the factors which militate against benefit inequality in the social security system are absent from private pensions, and women's benefits as a percentage of men's fall sharply. Unlike social security, the gender gap in private pension benefits approximates the earnings differentials of women and men.

Sweden: an access–benefit levels trade off?

Universal policies in Sweden have promoted equal access, while earnings related benefits entail different benefit levels. The earnings related component of Swedish income maintenance policies has steadily grown since the mid-1950s. Swedish benefits also reflect more perfectly the earnings of workers than the US social security system, and the earnings related construction affects a wider array of state benefits compared to the Netherlands. How has the growing prominence of earnings related benefits been translated into inequalities in benefit levels of women and men and has an access–benefit level trade off emerged? That is, has increased equality in access to earnings related benefits led to a greater gender benefit gap?

The emergence of an access–benefit levels trade off has depended upon whether women and men previously had uniform entitlements or a gendered differentiation in entitlements existed. Sickness insurance and old age benefits – schemes combining earnings related and flat rate benefits – provide two interesting examples of contrasts in the impact over time. The gap in women's and men's sickness benefits has shrunk during the past three decades, whereas the Swedish double-decker pension system has successively increased inequalities in women's and men's pension incomes.

Inequalities in the level of sickness benefits of *all* women relative to *all* men have decreased since the mid-1960s. There has been a general rise in the level of benefits received by women and a trend toward equalization of the average insurance benefits to which women and men are entitled. In 1965 the average benefits to which women were entitled were only 0.50 of those of men, whereas in 1990 the ratio was approximately 0.80 (calculated from *Allmän försäkring* 1965: 17 and SOS 1993: 23). The wide discrepancy in the 1960s was a result of the gendered differentiation in entitlements. As housewives, approximately half of the insured women were only entitled to minimum flat rate benefits (*grundsjukpenning*), whereas nearly all men as workers were additionally entitled to earnings related benefits (*tilläggssjukpenning*). By 1990 the differences between women's and men's access to earnings related sickness benefits had almost vanished, and the benefit gap now reflected earnings differentials.

The difference in women's and men's recipient rates of ATP old age benefits, as we saw earlier, constituted the most clear-cut instance of gender stratification in access to social benefits in the 1970s and early 1980s. The percentage of women with individual entitlement to ATP benefits has risen, but the difference in access has persisted, so that by the early 1990s approximately 60 percent of women pensioners received ATP benefits in their own right compared to 95 percent of men (SCB 1993b: 103). At the same time as more women gained access, benefit inequality has increased.

Figure 7.1 allows us to compare the payout of benefits from the basic pension and ATP for both sexes over time. It clearly reveals that women are the winners with respect to basic pension benefits (see Ståhlberg 1988: 21), but losers in terms of total pension payments which include ATP. Figure 7.1 displays a steady rise in the inequality of benefits between women and men as the supplementary pension has come to maturity. In the early 1970s the differences between women's and men's total pension benefits were negligible, but by the 1990s the gender benefit gap had widened so that women's total pension benefits were only 60 percent of men's.

The range of benefit inequality in the ATP scheme has grown as the scheme has come into full operation, and since 1980 it has been possible to receive maximum benefits. For example, among the oldest pensioners with ATP pensions the female/male differential in average benefits is quite small, whereas it has widened among the new beneficiaries. The overall effect is that the female/male benefit ratio for pensioners with ATP dropped from 0.75 to 0.65 between the early 1980s and 1990 (calculated from SCB 1985: 202, SCB 1993b: 166).

The expansion of employer sponsored pensions has also contributed to the trend toward greater inequality in women's and men's pension income. Third tier pensions create greater stratification in access and benefit levels. Employer sponsored pensions for white collar workers have a much higher ceiling on pensionable income, resulting in a wider range of benefit inequal-

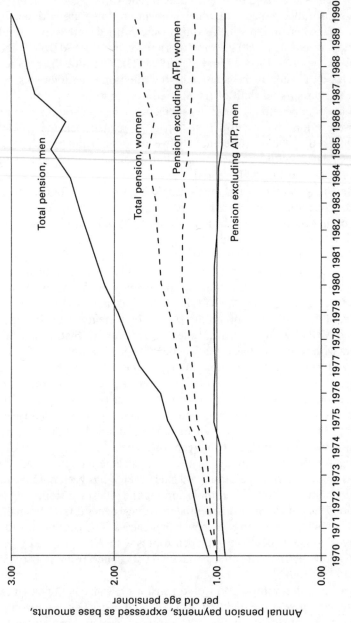

Figure 7.1 Annual pension payments by sex in Sweden, 1970–90
Sources: Allmän förskäring 1970–88, SOS 1989, 1990, RFV 1987.

ity than the ATP scheme. In theory, although seldom in reality, the benefits provided by the basic pension together with the supplement are a mere 5 percent of the maximum amount of employer sponsored pensions. Accordingly, the female/male differential in earnings related pension income (ATP and employer sponsored pensions) is much wider than for total pension income. In the early 1990s women's earnings related pension income was only 35 percent of men's (Ståhlberg 1994: 26). Clearly the flat rate benefits of the basic pension diminish gender inequalities in retirement incomes. Without them, Swedish female pensioners' situation would be on a par with that of German women (see Scheiwe 1994).[4]

Three conclusions can be drawn from this analysis of women's and men's benefit levels in the four countries. First, when gender is included, the range of benefit inequality is often wider than that reported by Esping-Andersen. His index of benefit equality is based on the minimum and maximum benefits received by the standard worker. But women frequently received reduced benefits which are lower than the official minimum, and this was often related to their family status as dependants.

Second, in line with Hutton and Whiteford's working hypothesis on the unfavorable consequences of earnings related benefits, we find that these benefits are associated with wider inequalities in all four countries. At best, the gender benefit gap was 20 percent: women's benefits were 80 percent of men's. In the most extreme instances, the differentials in average benefits were in the neighborhood of 60–65 percent, that is, women received benefits which were only 35 to 40 percent of those enjoyed by men.

Third, the growing importance of earnings related benefits has also undermined previous patterns of equal benefits. At the beginning of the 1980s the difference in the average amount of state benefits for elderly women and men was smallest in the UK. At that time retirement income consisted mainly of flat rate national insurance benefits and means tested benefits pegged at similar levels. Differences in women's and men's state pension benefits widened during the decade in the UK, and by the early 1990s the British gender ratio of average pension benefits was quite similar to the US ratio. Inequality in benefits increased in Sweden as reflected in pension incomes, and the difference in average pension benefits of women and men in the 1990s was wider than in either the UK or the USA. To what extent have benefit inequalities between the sexes resulted in negative redistributive outcomes for women *vis-à-vis* men?

Redistributive outcomes

An examination of the redistributive impact of welfare state policies and distributional outcomes in the four countries results in a puzzle. Despite the

Table 7.3 *Redistributive effects of transfers and taxes and rank order of the countries, around 1980[a]*

	Redistributive effects				
	Original income Gini coefficient	Disposable income Gini coefficient	Redistributive effect	Effect of transfers	Effect of taxes
Netherlands (1983)	0.467	0.293	0.37	0.29	0.10
Sweden (1981)	0.417	0.197	0.53	0.42	0.18
UK (1979)	0.393	0.264	0.33	0.25	0.08
USA (1979)	0.425	0.317	0.25	0.13	0.13

Rank order of the countries					
Rank	Least unequal original income distribution	Least unequal disposable income distribution	Overall redistribution	Redistribution via transfers	Redistribution via taxes
1	UK	Sweden	Sweden	Sweden	Sweden
2	Sweden	UK	Netherlands	Netherlands	USA
3	USA	Netherlands	UK	UK	Netherlands
4	Netherlands	USA	USA	USA	UK

Notes:
The effects of transfers and taxation do not always add up to the total redistributive effect because of different denominators. The total redistributive effect is computed by subtracting the Gini coefficient of disposable income distribution from the Gini coefficient of the original income distribution and dividing the difference by the original Gini coefficient.
Source: Mitchell 1991: 123, 127.

sharp gender benefit gap, Swedish policies have been more effective in reducing income inequality and poverty, and the distribution of disposable incomes of women and men is less unequal than in the other countries. Initially we examine the redistributive profiles of the four countries as reflected in the reduction of income inequality through transfers and taxes and the poverty rates of women and men. Subsequently we turn to the redistributive puzzle posed by the Swedish case and look at disposable income rather than benefit income.

The redistributive effects of transfers and taxation

Social benefits in cash and taxation modify the market distribution of income. To get an idea of the redistributive impact of these welfare state policies we can compare the degree of inequality in the distribution of original income (pre-transfer and pre-tax income) with the distribution of income after policy interventions (disposable income). A common measure of income inequality is the Gini coefficient whose value ranges from 0 to 1. The higher the Gini coefficient the greater the inequality in income distribution. The upper part of table 7.3 presents the Gini coefficients for original and disposable incomes along with the redistributive impact measured in terms of change.

The redistributive impact varied from a reduction in income inequality of over 50 percent to 25 percent in the four countries around 1980. Swedish policies produced the largest reduction of income inequality – over half – followed by the Netherlands – nearly two-fifths, the UK – around one-third, and the USA – a one-fourth reduction. Overall, the redistributive impact of welfare state policies is substantial, but so are the variations between the countries.

Table 7.3 also disaggregates the effects of transfers and taxes (columns 4 and 5). Sweden ranked highest both with respect to equalization through transfers and taxes. The rank ordering of redistributive effects of social security is the same as that of the reduction of income inequality, and generally transfers are more important in the process of redistribution. Although taxation overall did not play the same role for most countries, taxes were as redistributive as social transfers in the USA. Furthermore, the amount of redistribution achieved through taxation in the USA was greater than that of either the Netherlands or the UK.

Moving from the equalizing effects of transfers and taxation to the distributional outcome – the degree of equality in disposable income adjusted for family size – we find that the inequality in distribution of final income was considerably less in Sweden. Moreover, Swedes in the bottom quintile of income distribution were closer to median disposable income (Smeeding et al. 1990: 59). Income inequality of vulnerable groups such as the elderly (Hedström and Ringen 1990: 92), single parents, and families with several children has also been less in Sweden (Hauser and Fischer 1990: 150–1; Förster 1994: 200–1). Admittedly, the data in table 7.3 tell us nothing about the disposable incomes of women and men but among the vulnerable, such as the elderly and single parents, women outnumber men, and social transfers make up a larger portion of the income packages of female headed households in all four countries (Orloff 1994).

Poverty rates and gender poverty ratios

The incidence of poverty, using the relative measure of 50 percent of the median disposable income adjusted for family size, varied across the countries around 1980, as did the magnitude of women's likelihood of being poor compared to men. The countries arrayed themselves along a continuum where Sweden and the Netherlands had relatively low poverty rates (5.6 and 7.0 respectively), the UK a slightly higher rate (8.2), and the USA set itself apart with a much higher rate (17.0). The rank order of the countries in reducing poverty was the same. Sweden, the Netherlands, and the UK were relatively successful in lifting people out of poverty, while the USA lagged behind considerably (Mitchell 1991: 47).

The differences in women's and men's poverty rates for the working age population follow a similar pattern. The USA not only has the highest poverty rates, it also has the largest gender poverty gap. Women have been much more likely to be poor than men. The ratio of women's to men's poverty rates – the gender poverty gap – was 1.4 in the mid-1980s (figure 7.2). In other words, women were 40 percent more likely to be poor than men. In the UK the ratio was 1.19 or women's likelihood of experiencing poverty was nearly 20 percent higher than men's. The gender poverty gap in the Netherlands was virtually nil, while in Sweden the ratio was reversed, and women were less likely to be poor than men (Casper et al. 1994). While figure 7.2 shows that the Swedish poverty rate for the non-elderly population was slightly higher than the Netherlands in the mid-1980s,[5] the same data reveal substantially lower poverty rates of solo mothers (Hobson 1994: 178) and families with several children in Sweden compared to the Netherlands (Förster 1994: 199–201).

Turning to the elderly, they experienced only a small risk of poverty in Sweden and the Netherlands in the early 1980s. Data from the Luxembourg Income Study show virtually no poor among the elderly in Sweden, while other data indicate low poverty rates, but that the elderly were less likely to be poor compared to the rest of the population (SCB 1985: 185). Adequate

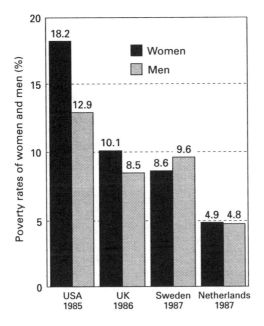

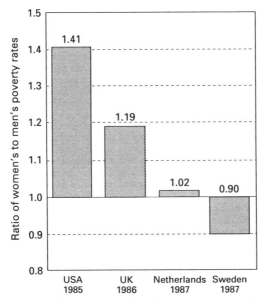

Figure 7.2 Women's and men's poverty rates and gender poverty ratio, working age population in the mid-1980s
Source: Casper et al. 1994: 597.

benefits have kept Dutch and Swedish pensioners of both sexes out of poverty.

By contrast, the poverty rates of the elderly were among the highest in the USA and the UK of the ten countries studied by Deborah Mitchell, and the situation of older pensioners (aged 75+) in both countries was worse (Hedström and Ringen 1990: 94). Nearly one-third of single aged persons in the USA had disposable income which was under half of the median (Mitchell 1991: 68), and US poverty statistics indicate an even larger gender gap – a ratio of 1.8 – among the aged than the non-elderly population (calculated from CPR 1983b: 13). In 1980 elderly women were 80 percent more likely to be poor than elderly men in the USA.

Although the poverty rates of the elderly were similar in the USA and the UK, it seems that in the USA the high rate stemmed from unequal income among the elderly, and in the UK from the low income level of the aged relative to the rest of the population (Hedström and Ringen 1990: 95). Nor did British poverty rates of elderly couples and single persons differ as sharply as in the USA at the beginning of the 1980s. Unfortunately we have no data to estimate the poverty gender ratio for the elderly in the UK for this period. However, elderly women's recipiency rate of assistance benefits was higher than men's (calculated from DHSS 1981: 80, 201–2), and between 60 and 70 percent of all persons receiving assistance (supplementary benefit) were in the bottom quintile of income distribution (DSS 1992a: 101).

In short, of the four countries the capacity of Swedish policies to reduce income inequalities and poverty stands out no matter what indicator we use. The distribution of disposable income is also significantly less unequal compared to the other countries, and Swedish policies seem to be more successful in eliminating women's poverty compared to men's. How do these findings square with the sizable gender benefit gap documented earlier?

The redistributive paradox: unequal benefits but "equal" outcomes

Equality in benefits is only one factor affecting redistributive outcomes. To assess the degree of equality in outcomes for women and men, we need to look at disposable income rather than benefit income and the equalizing effects of *both* transfers and taxes. Benefit income may be nearly identical to disposable income in some countries, but taxation substantially alters inequalities in benefit income in others. The crucial question is to what extent benefit income corresponds to disposable income. The best available data to answer this question are for pensioners. Equally important, pensioners constitute a suitable group to analyze because benefits form their major source of income and inequality in women's and men's pension benefits have increased since the introduction of ATP.

Figure 7.3 presents both the pension incomes and disposable incomes of elderly women and men. In the early 1980s the pension income of all women was 0.64 of men's, whereas their average disposable income was 0.94 of men's. Disposable income is equivalent net household income by sex, which is a contestable construction since it assumes married couples share equally their joint resources. However, the gender ratio in the average disposable incomes of single elderly women and men was the same (calculated from SCB 1985: 146). During the decade differences increased but there was still a sharp reduction in income inequality. In 1990 women's pension income averaged only 0.60 of men's, but their average disposable income was 0.90 of men's, and these trends applied to both married and single pensioners (calculated from SCB 1993b: 166 and SCB 1989c: 32).

Taxation and other social transfers account for the reduction of income inequalities. Higher gross pension benefits are clawed back by taxes, whereas the basic pension and the supplement for those without ATP or low ATP have not been subject to taxation for those without additional income. Non-taxable housing allowances also supplement the income of pensioners without ATP. The average amount of the housing allowance rises with age, contributing more to the resources of older pensioners who generally have the lowest incomes (SCB 1985: 134, SCB 1993b: 111). Breaking down the equalizing effects of taxes and non-taxable transfers, the redistributive impact of taxes was consistently greater during the period 1980–90. And in the early 1980s the impact of taxes was twice as large as non-taxable transfers (excluding pensions) (Jansson and Sandqvist 1993: 72).

The impressive reduction of inequalities in women's and men's disposable income compared to pension income in the Swedish case demonstrates the importance of including taxation of benefits as a dimension of variation in welfare state policies. In the early 1980s income taxation in all four countries was highly progressive, but the extent to which beneficiaries were taxed varied enormously. At the beginning of the 1980s the USA did not tax social security benefits and the UK taxed relatively few state benefits, whereas the policy of both Sweden and the Netherlands has been to tax most benefits.

As noted earlier, the effects of taxation in the Netherlands were less redistributive than in Sweden. A major difference between the two countries' tax systems concerns deductions and tax relief. Dutch taxpayers have enjoyed a wider range of allowances and deductions which have reduced the amount of taxable income in relation to gross earnings. Besides a generous personal tax allowance, nearly all social insurance contributions were tax

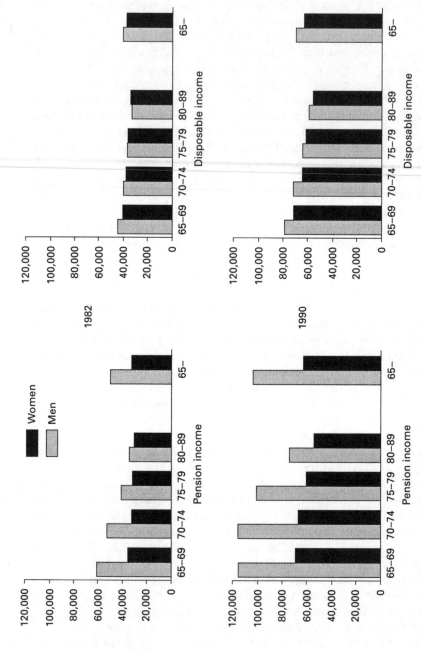

Figure 7.3 Pension incomes and disposable incomes of elderly Swedish women and men, 1982 and 1990
Sources: SCB 1985: 202–3, SCB 1993b: 166–7.

deductible in the Netherlands, and social security contributions amounted to roughly 25 percent of gross earnings up to a fairly high ceiling in the early 1980s (OECD 1984b: 82–3, 173–6). In effect higher income groups received a larger deduction because they paid more money in contributions. The steep progressivity of the tax system made these deductions especially important to the high income brackets.

Although US taxes were quite redistributive, as shown in table 7.3, taxation affected neither gender nor class inequalities in the social security system; but taxes may have reduced differences in retirement income due to private pensions. Prior to the mid-1980s social security benefits in the USA were non-taxable income, whereas private pensions and earnings were taxed (Pattison and Harrington 1993: 3–4). Both private pensions and earnings have been more important sources of retirement income in the USA than in the other countries, and upper income groups gained most from non-taxation. They received higher social security benefits and exemptions were worth more to high income groups because of progressivity in the tax system.

In 1980 most social benefits in the UK were not taxed. Unlike the USA, however, state pensions were liable to taxation, but the elderly (persons and couples 65 or older) received higher tax allowances. Age tax allowances boosted the ceiling of non-taxable income so that in many cases pension benefits were not subject to taxation. Thus taxes often did little to rectify the gender inequalities in benefits in Britain – but the gender gap in pension benefits was relatively small (table 7.2). On the other hand, the breadwinner model was also inscribed in taxation of pensions and the age tax allowances. The married man's allowance of an aged couple was increased to an amount nearly double that of an elderly single taxpayer, and the age tax allowance did not apply to single women between the ages of 60 and 64 (Atkinson 1989: 236).

In summary, both taxation of benefits and the structure of benefit income affect distributional outcomes. Several features of the double-decker structure of flat rate and earnings related programs – or what Walter Korpi and Joakim Palme (1994) term the encompassing model of social insurance – reduce inequalities in outcomes. Flat rate benefits provide the basic floor of income, but a comparison with the UK indicates that flat rate benefits in themselves are not sufficient. Flat rate programs must be truly universal in the sense that everyone is entitled to equal benefits, including wives and husbands. In addition, the amount of benefits must be clearly above the poverty line. These two preconditions are demonstrated by the contrast in outcomes between Swedish and Dutch basic pensions *vis-à-vis* the British state retirement pension, whose standard rate has been closer to the poverty line. An Achilles' heel of the British state pension is lower rates that reduce the benefit levels of many women putting them at risk of poverty. Earnings related benefits are important because they diminish the gap in income which arises between the working population and beneficiaries who only receive flat rate benefits (Korpi and Palme 1993: 149, 1994). Taxation of earnings related benefits counteracts income inequality among beneficiaries and groups with low earnings among the economically active.

Redistributive strategies and distributional dilemmas: equality and adequate benefits

The redistributive performance of Swedish policies raises a number of questions concerning commonplace assumptions about benefit constructions and their effects on distributional outcomes. According to conventional wisdom the construction of benefits in income maintenance policies – whether benefits are means tested, flat rate, or earnings related – is decisive in shaping redistribution. Means tested benefits targeted to the needy redress income inequalities and in the process achieve progressive or vertical redistribution – redistribution from higher to lower income groups. Flat rate benefits promote equal outcomes, but this assumption is subject to a major caveat. Obviously flat rate benefits only bring equality when there is no other source of income, such as earnings or earnings related benefits. Finally, earnings related benefits conserve income differences and are therefore regressive, or at best contribute to horizontal redistribution – that is, redistribution within the same income categories or redistribution over the lifetime of the individual. These assumptions form the standard "logic" of redistribution, and they have had a profound influence on theorizing about the redistributive impact of welfare states.

This logic of redistribution also informs the working hypotheses cited in the introduction of this chapter. Earnings related benefits are identified as the least favorable to women, followed by flat rate benefits. Hutton and Whiteford further argue the importance of means tested benefits in equalizing outcomes because they offset the higher benefits received by men. Their empirical analysis of the pension benefits in four countries – the UK, Australia, France, and the Netherlands – also suggests a distributional dilemma between gender equality and adequate benefits. British and Australian programs where means tested benefits are central had more equalizing effects but also the largest number of beneficiaries with low incomes. By contrast, French and Dutch schemes provided adequate benefits but resulted in greater inequality in distributional outcomes for women and men.

The Swedish case furnishes an additional test for the hypotheses. At first glance Swedish policies appear to offer some support. Means tested housing allowances supplement the benefits of the elderly with low pension incomes – primarily to the advantage of women. Without the allowance the incomes of pensioners would be decidedly more unequal and poverty would be more widespread among the elderly. Second, flat rate benefits are a major component of the Swedish social security system, and benefit equality exists among pensioners who receive only the basic pension. At the same time these pensioners are most at risk of being poor.

What is more interesting, however, are the ways in which the Swedish redistributive strategy does not substantiate the standard logic of redistribution or the working hypotheses. The distribution of women's and men's disposable income was less unequal, and women were less likely to be below the poverty line than men. Despite these outcomes, earnings related benefits are as much an integral part of the Swedish social security system as flat rate benefits.

That earnings related schemes can reduce income inequality and bring about vertical redistribution is an idea seldom contemplated, and it defies the logic of redistribution. Nonetheless earnings related schemes which protect income security reduce income inequality in the population as a whole. If benefits are flat rate and mediocre, inequalities develop because beneficiaries have a much lower income than the working population. This seems to have been the situation in the UK around 1980 when flat rate benefits were the major source of retirement income, and the income of many elderly persons was low relative to the national average. Similarly, the income of Swedish pensioners without ATP lags seriously behind that of the rest of the population, and must be topped up with flat rate and means tested supplements. Nor is vertical redistribution through earnings related schemes an impossibility. It can occur through higher utilization rates by low income groups. A case in point is the Swedish sickness insurance scheme. Despite the income replacement principle and the gender inequality in gross benefits, sickness compensation has equalizing effects because utilization rates are higher among low paid workers and women (Jansson and Sandqvist 1993: 33; cf. Söderström 1988: 107).

This sort of redistributive strategy points to an alternative solution to what appears as a distributional dilemma: the choice between adequate benefits and equal benefits for women and men. The strategy consists of combining flat rate benefits and earnings related benefits and taxing benefits instead of relying on flat rate benefits and means tested programs. It provides a way to minimize the possible trade off between unequal outcomes and adequate benefits. Admittedly the distributional outcome may be adequate benefits and modest inequality; but this seems to be a better choice than equal benefits and relatively high poverty rates.

Part IV

Welfare state restructuring

8   Gender equality reforms and their impact

Most discussions of welfare state restructuring during the past decade have reflected the view that the welfare state is in crisis, and that retrenchment measures are necessary. With this emphasis, little attention has been given to a possible restructuring of welfare states through gender equality reforms. Since the 1970s reforms to promote equality between the sexes have been on the policy agenda, and several countries have enacted reform legislation. Although evaluations and feminist critiques of the reforms exist for individual countries, along with surveys of international trends in social legislation (e.g. Brocas et al. 1990), gender equality reforms and their impact have seldom been analyzed from a cross-national perspective.

The object of this chapter is a comparative appraisal of gender equality reforms, focusing on their impact in terms of outcomes for women and men. At issue are two interlocking questions. The first is the extent to which the reforms of the past two decades have altered the patterns of inequality in women's and men's social rights described in the earlier chapters. The second is the nature and degree of change in the gendered differentiation of entitlements. The answers to these questions shed light on variations in welfare state restructuring affecting gender relations since the late 1960s. They also help us to understand which reforms have worked and which reforms have not – and the extent to which policies have evolved toward the individual model of social policy.

Reforms and outcomes

A useful point of departure in thinking about reforms to achieve parity in the social rights of women and men is a typology of strategies to influence gender relations, suggested by Prue Chamberlayne (1993). Here I apply the logic of her typology to social legislation, specifying and expanding the types of reform. The first type – gender neutrality – consists of reformulating laws in gender neutral terms. This involves changes in entitlements previously conferred upon only one of the sexes so that they are available to both women and men. This strategy is informed by a definition of equality between the sexes as formal equal access to benefits. In contrast to formal

173

equality, the second approach – gender recognition – assumes that equality can be achieved only by taking into account the differences between women and men. Measures aid or compensate the disadvantaged sex, and accordingly they have been aimed at women. The third strategy emphasizes overcoming inequalities between women and men that arise through unpaid work in the home and paid work in the market. It proposes to upgrade wifely and motherly labor, and it prescribes the conversion of women's unpaid domestic work into cash benefits and making this work the basis of entitlement to standard social security benefits – pensions, unemployment, and sickness benefits. This strategy – labeled gender reinforcement – is based on a separate roles gender ideology, and remedial action can assume two forms: the expansion of entitlements based on the principle of care, or the improvement of women's entitlements as wives. Such measures may buttress traditional gender relations, but as I have argued earlier this is not inevitably the case for entitlements based on the principle of care. The fourth and least prevalent type of reform – gender reconstruction – strives for equality through transforming the strict division of labor between the sexes so that the tasks of earning and caring are commonly shared by women and men. Or as expressed somewhat differently by Nancy Fraser (1994: 26), who calls for deconstructing gender, gender equity is promoted *"by dismantling the gendered opposition between breadwinning and caregiving"* (italics original). A fifth course of action advocates individualization, changes in legislation which make the individual the unit of entitlement and obligations (contributions and taxes) rather than the family or the household. This approach has special importance when the unit of policy is the family, but it is also crucial whether individualization results in an equalization of social rights or their elimination.

This typology is useful because it sets a number of strategies in sharp relief and clarifies their differences; but the dissimilar mixes of reform legislation in the four countries do not conform to these neat categories. Nevertheless, the typology offers a framework for categorizing the broad thrust of reform in each country. Below I analyze the strategies and reforms in an effort to assess to what extent the measures have altered inequalities between women and men in two respects. The first concerns improvements in women's access to benefits and benefit levels *vis-à-vis* men's. The second involves changes in the gendered differentiation of entitlements, that is, the extent to which social entitlements reflect and reinforce the traditional division of labor between the sexes.

The United States: gender neutral reforms and continued differentiation in social security benefits

In the USA the most acclaimed path of reform to achieve equality in women's and men's entitlements has been to reformulate social security legislation in gender neutral terms. This strategy has also been complemented by gender recognition reforms which take into consideration women's patterns of employment. Notably, however, this second approach has been confined to a single area of the third tier of welfare provision – private pensions. More significantly, and less trumpeted, reforms have simultaneously strengthened gender differentiation in the social security system and private pensions by improving women's entitlements as wives and inadvertently assigning more weight to husbands' earnings.

The initial rules equalizing access to benefits were introduced quite early (1950), and by the end of the 1970s gender neutral reforms had equalized access to OASDI benefits. Equal eligibility rules, however, have only produced negligible changes in the utilization patterns of women and men. Women remain overwhelmingly the recipients of spouse and survivor benefits. The arithmetic of benefits and earnings explains this huge disparity in women's and men's utilization rates presented in table 8.1. The aged surviving spouse has received 100 percent of the deceased worker's benefit, but since women's benefits were lower, men have done better by retaining their own benefit based on higher earnings. The average monthly benefit of the few men who received survivor benefits based on their wives' benefits was lower than the average monthly benefit of their female counterparts. In the case of widows and widowers with children, an earnings test accounts for the one-sided utilization rates. The amount of allowable earnings has been pegged at a level lower than average male earnings, and earnings above the

Table 8.1 *OASI beneficiaries and benefits by sex, 1993*

	Women (in thousands)	Average monthly benefit (US$)	Men (in thousands)	Average monthly benefit (US$)
Old age insurance				
Retired worker	12,460	581	13,500	759
Spouse benefit	3,065	349	30	212
Survivor insurance				
Aged survivors	5,040	632	37	461
Survivors with				
dependent children	274	456	16	315

Source: SSB *Annual Statistical Supplement*, 1994: 202.

Table 8.2 *US women's entitlements to social security benefits, 1960–90 (%)*

	1960	1970	1980	1990
Type of entitlement				
Entitled as worker only	38.8	42.1	41.0	36.9
Dual entitlement	4.6	8.5	15.9	23.4
Entitled as wife only	56.7	49.4	43.1	39.7

Sources: SSB, *Annual Statistical Supplement* 1993: 174, 199.

exempted amount reduce benefits ($1 for every $2 in earnings). Compared to widows, a widower would generally receive a smaller benefit based on his deceased wife's earnings, and most likely his higher earnings would reduce it to nil. In short, changes making legislation gender neutral have scarcely altered women's and men's recipient rates of social security benefits, and the changes have not aided women – the disadvantaged sex. Equalizing access has primarily extended entitlements to men.

Instead, reforms have reinforced the male breadwinner model and promoted a gendered differentiation in entitlements. Better survivor benefits and provisions for divorced spouses have strengthened women's entitlements as wives. To improve the adequacy of social provision, survivor benefits were upgraded from 80 percent to 100 percent of the benefit of the deceased insured worker in 1972. As brought out in chapter 3, widows experienced high rates of poverty in the 1960s, and during the decade the gender poverty gap among the elderly widened. Reforms of employer sponsored pensions have introduced similar improvements by recognizing the claims of divorced spouses and safeguarding survivor benefits. Simultaneously men's role as earners has been shored up through indexing social security benefits. The indexation of benefits in the 1970s has meant that the ceiling of taxable earnings has risen automatically, boosting the weight of the husband's benefits in calculating a couple's retirement income. The added importance of the husband's earnings has increased married women's dependency and the inequities between housewives and employed wives.

The existing inadequacy of women's social security benefits based on individual entitlement remains a major problem, and this difficulty is rooted in women's lower earnings relative to men's – and especially wives' lower earnings relative to husbands'. During the 1980s and 1990s the slippage in the proportion of women beneficiaries whose benefits were based solely on individual entitlement continued (SSB, *Annual Statistical Supplement* 1994: 203). In a long-term perspective, women's individual entitlement to social security benefits has virtually stood still during the past three decades, while dual entitlement increased (table 8.2).

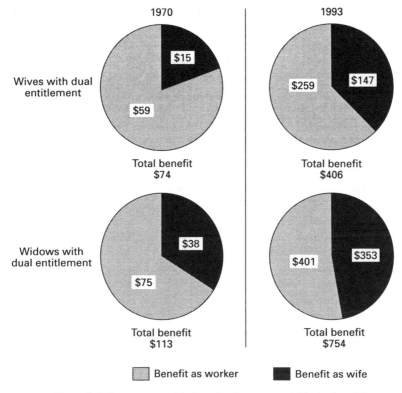

Figure 8.1 Average monthly benefits for women with dual entitlement: proportion of benefit claimed as worker and wife, 1970 and 1993
Sources: SSB *Annual Statistical Supplement* 1971: 99, 1994: 232.

The increase in dual entitlement reflects twin trends. First, the benefits of a growing number of married women based on their work record were not as much as their spouse benefits because their earnings were substantially lower than their husbands'. Greater numbers of married women entered the labor market, but working wives' contribution to family income stagnated from the mid-1960s to the mid-1980s (Hayghe 1993). Second, married women workers have increasingly claimed survivor benefits as wives because their benefits as workers were less than those of their husbands. Not only has the proportion of women with dual entitlement grown, the portion of the secondary benefit received as a wife has increased over the years (figure 8.1). In the late 1980s the secondary benefit of women with dual entitlement constituted on average 40 percent of their monthly benefit, but for a few women with the highest benefit levels the secondary benefit accounted for 60 percent of their monthly allowance (Lingg 1990: 11).

Today women have a stronger attachment to the labor market and higher earnings than earlier generations. Nonetheless, women's heavy reliance on their claims as wives seems likely to persist into the twenty-first century for two reasons. The required number of years of employment for full benefits has successively increased, and since 1991 (or for all persons born after 1928) the requirement is forty years of employment. Benefits are calculated on the best thirty-five years of earnings, with years of zero earnings averaged into the benefit calculation. The earnings records (up to 1990) of wives born in the 1930s who will reach retirement age in the 1990s, and even of those born in the 1940s, reveal that large numbers lack the necessary years in covered employment. Second, as long as wives have earnings which are 30 percent or less of their husbands', their benefits as wives exceed their benefits as workers. Cohort data indicate that the earnings of *two-thirds* of the oldest generation – women born in the 1930s – and *two-fifths* of the youngest generation – women born in the 1950s – were 30 percent or less of their husbands'. In other words, the current earnings records of married women suggest a continued increase in their claiming retirement benefits as wives. Only when women born in the 1950s retire in the 2010s and 2020s can a reversal of the trend be expected. Similarly few wives have earned as much as or more than their husbands – 10 percent of those born in the 1930s and under 20 percent of those born in the 1950s (Iams 1993: 24) – reinforcing the trend of women claiming survivor benefits as wives.

Because of these trends, attempts to reform the social security system by "individualizing" benefits and eliminating women's entitlements as wives would adversely affect a majority of female beneficiaries. Such reforms would worsen the social provision of many women who would not qualify for adequate social security benefits, and they would become dependent upon the assistance programs in the welfare tier. At the same time the inequities between women workers and wives as homemakers are as pronounced as three decades ago. For married women whose earnings are in the range of 30–50 percent of their husbands, their benefits as workers are only moderately higher than the benefits they would have received as wives, yet as workers they pay social security taxes. In the 1980s the average social security income of a newly retired dual earner couple was higher than a single earner couple, but the survivor benefits of women workers were often lower than those of women with dual entitlement and women entitled as wives (SSB 1985: 20). The conflict between the goals of women's independence from their husbands' social rights, adequate social provision in old age, and removal of inequities in women's rights as workers and as wives seems no nearer resolution than in the 1960s.

In the area of taxation, favoritism toward the one earner family has survived, while the strength of the marriage penalty has vacillated. More radical reform suggestions to abolish the community property principle and tax all earners as individuals, as favored by a task force on women in the Carter administration, never got off the ground (Leader 1983). Instead, legislation taxing social security benefits, introduced by the Reagan administration, reinforced joint taxation of married couples. Married persons who file separate returns are allowed zero earnings compared to $32,000 when a joint return is filed.

The main changes benefiting two earner couples with children were liberalizations of childcare deductions so that more taxpayers were eligible. In the early 1970s the earnings ceiling for tax deductions for childcare was raised, and in the mid-1970s deductions were converted into non-refundable tax credits. Although a principal argument for the conversion was that it would favor low and middle income families, it also eliminated the income ceiling so that the credit could be claimed by all earning parents. On balance, changes in legislation have at times aided dual income couples but without encroaching upon the tax advantages of the one earner family.

To sum up, US reforms have been limited in their scope, and change in outcomes has been minimal. Reforms have not tackled the major problems creating women's dependency and inequality in the "social security" tier. In attempting to reduce benefit inequalities between women and men, reforms strengthened the existing gendered structure of claims by promoting women's claims as wives and men's claims as earners. Reagan's victory and the subsequent attack on welfare spending scuttled proposals for structural changes in the social security system, such as the double-decker system proposed by the Carter administration. The proposal called for a flat rate benefit combined with earnings related benefits – a system similar to those of the UK and Sweden in the late 1970s (HEW 1979).

The 1980s saw a slippage in women's individual entitlement to old age social security benefits and a stagnation in their receipt of social security disability benefits and many employer sponsored fringe benefits. Joint taxation continues to be the rule, and the favorable tax position of the single earner family has not been altered. The major improvements in the situation of the two earner family and working single mothers have been the replacement of tax deductions with tax credits for day care. In the 1990s the USA stands out in the degree to which the male breadwinner model continues to structure social security and tax legislation.

The United Kingdom: reforms to end formal discrimination and extension of the principle of care

The British strategy, like the US approach, has consisted of gender neutral reforms and efforts to end formal discrimination. The single most important reform to establish equal treatment of the sexes in social provision was the abolition of the married woman's option. Equalizing access to British benefits, as distinct from US reforms, has more frequently enhanced women's formal eligibility.[1] Besides gender neutral reforms, the gender reinforcement approach has left an imprint on social legislation; but in contrast to the USA, British reforms have improved both women's entitlements based on the principle of care and as wives. Finally, individualization has largely been confined to the 1990 tax reform that introduced separate taxation, and to the elimination of several supplements for family members in the national insurance scheme.

The Social Security Pensions Act of 1975 abolished the married woman's option, ending formal discrimination of married women in the national insurance scheme. The Act immediately eliminated lower benefits for full contributions, but married women already utilizing the option could continue to do so. As we saw in chapter 5, 30 percent of the female labor force – or roughly 50 percent of working wives – used the married women's option in 1980 and did not pay full contributions. By the early 1990s only a small percentage of employed married women utilized the option. With the gradual phasing out of the married women's option, there has been an enormous increase in the number of married women paying standard contributions and a major shift in the female/male ratio of contributors to the national insurance scheme (table 8.3).

Have the near disappearance of the married women's option and the greater incidence in paying standard contributions meant a fundamental improvement in women receiving national insurance benefits? To assess changes since the early 1970s when the use of the option was widespread, table 8.3 presents data on women as a percentage of all employed earners paying standard contributions and the percentage of recipients of national insurance benefits who were women.

The table reveals a vast discrepancy in women's payment of contributions and their receipt of benefits, and the differences were exacerbated in the 1990s. For all types of insurance benefit women's proportion as beneficiaries was lower than their proportion as contributors in 1990. The greatest disparity concerns the industrial disablement benefit, with women accounting for approximately 10 percent of the beneficiaries over the three decades. The proportion of women as recipients of invalidity and unemployment benefits has edged upwards but still lags behind their percentage as contributors. Prior to the introduction of statutory sick pay, sickness benefits matched the ratio of beneficiaries to contributors almost perfectly. Similarly, during the 1980s there was only a moderate rise in the proportion of women making their claims to retirement pensions on the basis of their own insurance rather than their husband's (Sainsbury 1993a).

Table 8.3 *Women and the national insurance scheme, Great Britain,
1970–90*

	1970/1	1980	1990
Contributors			
% Working wives paying reduced contributions	76	52	14
% Women workers paying standard contributions	50	63	91
Women as a % of employed workers paying standard contributions[a]	22	31	42
Beneficiaries			
Women as a % of recipients of national insurance benefits			
Industrial disablement benefit	9	10	11
Invalidity benefit	20	18	24
Sickness benefit	22	30	32[b]
Unemployment benefit	14	28	28
Retirement pensions % claimed on own insurance[c]	41	30	37
Number of female beneficiaries (thousands)			
Industrial disablement benefit	19	20	21
Invalidity benefit	85	109	292
Sickness benefit	116	142	76[b]
Unemployment benefit	66	266	97
Retirement pensions % claimed on own insurance[c]	1999	1732	2386

Notes:
[a] Calculations are based on data showing persons who paid any contributions at any time
during the tax year.
[b] Sickness benefit only applies to the self-employed and employees not receiving statutory
sick pay since 1983.
[c] Figures not comparable because of a 1978 reclassification from own insurance to
husband's in cases where wives' pensions were topped up under new rules of the 1975 Social
Security Pensions Act.
Sources: DHSS 1972: 60, 78, 118, 182; 1973: 27, 1981: 14, 26, 43, 78, 229; 1982: 133, DSS
1990: 197–8, 1991: 176, 1992: 103, 137, 152, *Annual Abstract of Statistics* 1984: 51, 1993: 51.

Looking at women's benefits in the early 1990s, the single most important
action to end unequal treatment of women in the social security system –
the elimination of the married women's option – had yielded unexpectedly
few results.

Further changes in legislation to improve equal treatment of the sexes
included reforms to eliminate sole entitlement to benefits by the head of the
household. Since 1983 dependant allowances of insurance benefits and
public assistance benefits could be claimed by either spouse. For a variety
of reasons, the impact of these changes has been quite minimal. Most
fundamental is that the married women's entitlement has been grafted on

to a system of dependant additions, which was shaped by the notion of the "family wage" with the husband as the main breadwinner. Payment of the adult dependant allowance is conditional upon the spouse earning less than the allowance. As women have entered the labor market, fewer families conform to the male breadwinner model. Still, among married couples very few women are the primary earner, and few working husbands have earnings which are less than the dependant allowance. Because of these differences in women's and men's employment patterns, and their earnings, the dependant allowance is much less likely to be paid to wives than husbands. In the case of public assistance the number of women claiming means tested benefits on behalf of the couple has steadily increased since 1983 but they accounted for only 5 percent of the couples on assistance in 1990. A major difficulty is that the family is the unit whose income is assessed, and legislation in the 1980s extended the full-time work exclusion to a claimant's partner (Lister 1992: 42).

Other reforms did away with discrimination against married women's access to benefits for the disabled. In 1984 the housewives' non-contributory invalidity pension was replaced by the severe disablement allowance. This reform was expected to improve women's access to disability benefits, but scarcely changed their overall recipient rates (Sainsbury 1993a). One explanation is an increase in the severity of disability necessary to qualify for the allowance, and only a fraction of recipients of the housewives benefit were eligible for the allowance. Over 70 percent of the beneficiaries of the non-contributory invalidity pension were passported but only 6.5 percent of married women (Lonsdale 1990: 134).

A major gain for women occurred through the ending of discrimination against married women in applying for the invalid care allowance. After the change in legislation, the number of recipients increased more than tenfold. These gains have, however, been partially offset by overlapping benefits regulations which meant that the adult dependant allowance was no longer payable if a man's wife was in receipt of the invalid care allowance. Nonetheless, the reform represented an advance with respect to women's individual entitlement to social benefits. Other changes in overlapping benefit regulations may further discourage claims to the invalid care allowance. For example, public assistance supplements for severe disability require the absence of a carer receiving the invalid care allowance (Lister 1992: 40).

The past two decades marked the gradual extension of the care principle as a basis of entitlement to benefits. In the late 1970s the child benefit reform, which replaced the family allowance and child tax deductions usually claimed by the father, strengthened the benefits of mothers at the expense of fathers' tax advantages as family providers. A similar change occurred in assistance programs for families with children where a parent is in full-time employment. Earlier under the Family Income Supplement program, the benefit was paid to the breadwinner; under Family Credit it is paid to the carer (Lister 1992: 54). The rationale behind creating the invalid care allowance was to compensate a carer for loss of employment. Premiums in the income support program also acknowledge the importance of care of children and the disabled. Solo mothers and carers are eligible for premiums providing higher assistance benefits. Finally, persons with home responsibilities – caring for children or the infirm – have received credits counting toward their pension.

The first step toward separate taxation was taken in 1972 by providing an option for filing individual returns for earned income. However, the couple had to make the request *jointly*, implying the necessity of permission by the husband. Moreover, a wife's unearned income was deemed her husband's for tax purposes. The fact that the husband would lose the married man's allowance if the couple were taxed separately also encouraged joint taxation. It was not until the 1990 tax reform that the individual's income became the unit of taxation, thus eliminating joint taxation of spouses. The reform granted equal tax relief to each taxpayer but married couples were awarded an additional allowance. In other words the reform combined separate taxation with a privileged position for married couples (Dilnot 1989). Positively the reform provided a substantial measure of economic independence for working wives and wives with unearned income. Negatively, the husband received the married couple's allowance, thus reinforcing traditional notions of the man as family provider and affirming economic inequality among spouses in marriage.

In summary, the reformulation of laws extending married women's entitlement to benefits formerly claimed by the husband has not made much difference in terms of women as recipients. Nor did British women's utilization rates of national insurance benefits increase markedly in the 1980s and the 1990s. Inequalities in national insurance benefits, where men are predominantly the beneficiaries, persist despite the greater incorporation of women paying standard contributions. On the other hand, the increase in benefits attached to the principle of care has enhanced women's entitlement to non-contributory benefits – especially through the child benefit reform and the removal of restrictions on married women's eligibility for invalid care allowances. However, since non-contributory benefits are less generous than insurance benefits, this development could signal a new gender stratification of benefits (cf. Lister 1992, 1994a). Separate taxation was introduced, but the married man's allowance survived in the guise of the married couple's allowance, although its value is slowly diminishing. In the UK gender reinforcement reforms have dwarfed efforts at gender reconstruction. State policies have done little to encourage women to become earners and men to become carers. An exception is the home responsibility credit for carers in the state earnings related pension scheme, which has applied to both women and men.

Although the changes in legislation have been summed up as the formal demise of the male breadwinner model (Land 1994a), there is little sign of policies ushering in the individual model of social policy. Instead policy developments – with a few exceptions – signal a strengthening of benefits attached to the principle of care and the possible emergence of a separate gender roles model based on a familial ideology prescribing a traditional division of labor between husband and wife. This ideology is reflected in employment and training programs, along with wage formation, all of which prioritize men's earning capacity. The Child Support Act, which came into effect in 1993, reasserts the principle of maintenance and the obligations of the father as earner to provide for his offspring. Other policies emphasize women's role as caregivers and curb their possibilities of combining care and paid work. Women's underrepresentation in public training schemes and the lack of daycare facilities restrict their job opportunities. The restructuring of the economy through flexibilization and the deterioration of wages in part-time employment have reduced women's opportunities to become financially independent. During the 1980s and 1990s differences in women's and men's working hours and earnings have widened. Altering the role of men to encourage shared tasks in the family has received fairly little attention, and currently the UK is the only country of the four without some form of parental leave legislation.

The Netherlands: the quest for individualization

Dutch policies, as revealed in chapter 3, represented an extreme variant of the breadwinner model in the 1960s. Many reforms of the 1980s eroded the dominance of the male family provider as an ideal in structuring legislation. Because of this policy legacy, the Dutch strategy has centered on individualization of entitlements and obligations, and in the late 1980s there was talk of purely individualized policies for the generation coming of age from 1990 onwards (SCP 1988a: 382). Total individualization has also been accompanied by demands for gender reconstruction.

Since individualization has been introduced in several areas, the Netherlands offers an excellent opportunity of assessing its impact in relation to different policy constructions. Separate taxation was introduced in the early 1970s, and the Dual Wage Earners Act of 1984 granted both spouses the same basic tax allowance. The reforms of the 1980s ended the formal discrimination of married women in three major schemes – disability (1980), national retirement pensions (1985), and extended unemployment benefits (1987). Other reforms have changed the unit of contribution from the household to individuals. Contributions to the national insurance schemes were fully individualized in 1985 (de Kam et al. 1988: 200), but contributions and medical benefits under the Health Insurance Act (ZFW) remain familialized. Individualization has also affected means tested programs, but so far only obligations – and not rights. Increasingly the obligation to be available for work applies to both partners, while the unit of benefit is still the family.

The Dutch tax reforms, even more than the British reforms, underline the fallacy of automatically equating all separate or individual taxation reforms with major advances for women. In 1973 the Dutch introduced separate taxation but – in contrast to the Swedish reform – not on an equal basis for both spouses. The Dutch reform granted the working wife a small tax allowance which was one-fifth the size of her husband's, and separate taxation did not encroach upon the tax advantages of the family breadwinner. The 1984 tax reform equalized tax allowances for wife and husband when both were earners. But it left intact a generous spouse deduction for non-working married women, which was equivalent to the basic tax allowance. Although the husband loses this deduction if his wife works, a working wife can transfer any unused portion of her tax allowance to her husband (SCP 1985: 54–5; OECD 1984b: 173–4). In other words, as in the case of the 1990 British tax reform, the husband's privileged position was not abolished. The transferability of the Dutch couple's tax allowances also acts as a disincentive to the wife's entry into the labor market because it pits her earnings against a deterioration in her husband's tax position. The 1990 tax reform reduced the basic tax allowance making an additional income more attractive (Gustafsson and Bruyn-Hundt 1991: 53).

Individualization of the insurance schemes has differed in its equalizing effects on women's and men's access to benefits. The most successful reform in this respect was the 1985 old age pension reform which dramatically changed the sex composition of beneficiaries. From being totally excluded, the proportion of married women increased to over 40 percent. The 1987 unemployment benefits reform eliminated breadwinner status as a condition of entitlement to extended benefits and introduced credits for childcare. Earlier differences in women's and men's recipient rates of unemployment benefits narrowed after the reform. Finally, the 1980 reform of disability benefits initially produced only a marginal improvement in women as beneficiaries. The proportion of women as beneficiaries crept upwards from roughly 25 percent in 1980 to around 30 percent in 1990 (Sainsbury 1993a).

Another gauge – long-term utilization of benefits – points to similar

Table 8.4 *Long-term utilization of social benefits in the Netherlands, 1970–90*

	1970	1980	1990
Disability benefits			
% long term beneficiaries of all persons receiving disability benefits	53	58	75
Women as a % of all receiving long-term benefits	27	27	31
Unemployment benefits			
% long-term beneficiaries of all persons receiving unemployment benefits	3	9	27
Women as a % of all receiving long-term benefits	26	25	34
Assistance, ABW			
% of long-term beneficiaries of all assistance recipients	41	44	55
Women as a % of all receiving long-term benefits	80	89	93
% women of all long-term beneficiaries	39	34	38

Sources: SCP 1993a: 158, 1993b: 146.

results. The reforms seem to have only marginally altered male/female differentials in utilization rates of disability benefits. In 1970 and 1980 women beneficiaries receiving disability benefits for more than three years totaled 27 percent of all recipients, and in 1990 their percentage was 31 percent. The record was slightly better in the case of long-term utilization of unemployment benefits (SCP 1993b: 146, 1993a: 158).

What accounts for the dissimilarities in outcomes and how have they been influenced by different pre-existing policy constructions? Let us begin with what was initially the least successful of the reforms – disablement benefits. A major difficulty – especially during the first half of the 1980s – was the criteria and assessment procedures for entitlement. Married women were not awarded benefits as frequently as single women or married men. Only a small portion of male married breadwinners (nearly 15 percent) failed to qualify, whereas almost 40 percent of the applications of female married non-breadwinners were rejected (Hermans 1988: 258). The definition of disablement may have further disadvantaged women. It equated the loss of work capacity with earning capacity. Assessments have taken into consideration education and training as well as previous job experience. In the second half of the 1980s, however, the proportion of women among *new* claimants steadily climbed, and in the 1990s around 45 percent have been women (SCP 1995: 177).

The reform of unemployment insurance benefits has a mixed record. On the one hand, there appears to have been considerable improvement in women's likelihood of receiving insurance benefits among the registered unemployed, which reduced differences in women's and men's recipient rates for this type of benefit. On the other hand, looking at unemployment compensation as a whole (insurance and assistance benefits), the picture is not nearly so positive for women. In the early 1990s men receiving compensation exceeded the number of male unemployed, whereas only around 70 percent of unemployed women received compensation (calculated from *Statistical Yearbook* 1994: 106, 132), and the unemployment rate of women was nearly double that of men. The gender gap was as wide as a decade earlier, and as previously the discrepancy stems from difficulties of unemployed married women in claiming benefits. If they fail to qualify for insurance benefits or exhaust them, their chances of receiving compensation under the unemployment assistance scheme (RWW), which takes into account the income of a partner, are smaller.

The success of the pension reform in equalizing entitlement stands out not only compared to the other two Dutch reforms but also in comparison to reforms in the USA and the UK. What lies behind the success of the pension reform? The reform individualized entitlement to the family pension so that each spouse received 50 percent. Critics of this arrangement have argued that it creates inequities between working wives and wives who are homemakers. Both receive the same pension but working wives pay contributions while wives at home do not (Sjerps 1988). It also seems that several Dutch married women shortly after the reform were unaware that they had a pension of their own (Döring et al. 1992: 36). These criticisms aside, the reform individualized entitlement and equalized women's and men's access to old age pensions in the Netherlands. Wives' pensions also radically altered the distribution of income of retired couples. In close to half of the couples where the wife was 65 or older the incomes of the spouses were relatively "equal" (the wife's contribution to the family income was in the range of 45–55 percent) as opposed to only 15 percent of all couples (SCP 1993a: 162).

Two aspects of the Dutch policy legacy came into play as crucial determinants of the outcome. Traditionally, contribution requirements have been waived for persons with no income, without a reduction in benefits, as in the UK. Ironically, this leniency may be related to a deep-seated breadwinner mentality where the head of the household was responsible for contributions. Second, the reform has been possible because national old age insurance (AOW) is truly a universal scheme covering the entire population, unlike the British basic retirement pension which is a pseudo-universal scheme based on labor market status and contributions. Similarly, the Dutch disablement scheme, which also passes itself off as a universal scheme, differs from the old age citizen pensions. In the case of Dutch disability benefits the importance of the policy legacy is illuminated by a comparison with Swedish disability benefits. In the Netherlands a universal program was superimposed upon an employee insurance scheme, and the eligibility requirements of the employee scheme continued to be decisive. To qualify for disability benefits, a minimum income has been required, and implicitly also labor market status since disablement is defined and assessed as the loss of earning power.

Total individualization has been formulated as a goal for the 1990s. The discussion surrounding this aspiration has emphasized gender reconstruction as a necessary component. The dependence of women on men's income and the dependence of men on women's domestic services and care must be replaced by financial independence and "care independence" (SCP 1988a: 382). A dilemma, however, pervades this sort of restructuring of benefits and obligations. Individualization eliminates women's financial dependence upon their husbands, simultaneously individualization without financial independence worsens women's situation.

This raises the question of how realistic assumptions about women's financial independence and men's care independence for the next generation are. The proportion of women with no independent source of income has declined, and by the early 1990s nearly half of all Dutch women had earnings of their own. Defining financial independence as earnings equivalent to the net minimum wage, around 70 percent of women in paid employment met this requirement but only around one-fifth of all married or cohabiting women did so. In other words, although a growing number of women have become economically independent, they only totaled around one-third of all Dutch women, and the vast majority of married women still lacked financial autonomy (SCP 1993a: 168, Maassen van den Brink 1994: 3).

Of course, what is essential here is the work and pay patterns of the generation coming of age in the 1990s. The differences in financial independence between younger female and male workers (under 25 years) are quite small, but the incidence of financial independence was not impressive for either sex – only around 50 percent for the age group of 20–4 years of age. Equally important, income differences between the sexes start to set in around age 30 as men become increasingly financially independent and women increasingly less likely to be so (SCP 1993a: 168).

The principal reform affecting men's role as carer was the introduction of parental leave in the public sector in 1989 and in the private sector in 1991. Parental leave allows both the father and mother to reduce their weekly working hours to twenty during a six-month period. Although leave is paid in the public sector and many parents – 40 percent of fathers – have taken leave,[2] several features of leave in the private sector make it an unattractive option. Leave is unpaid, it does not count toward an occupational pension, and it can lower vacation pay (SCP 1993a: 30–1, 213–14). In the early 1990s Dutch men were only imperceptibly moving toward care independence.

In summary, Dutch women's entitlements to social benefits have undergone far-reaching change since the early 1970s. The reforms of the past decade have substantially reduced the inequalities between women's and men's social benefits and tax allowances. Benefits have been individualized, and women's access to employee insurance schemes has improved because modest thresholds in these schemes were further lowered during the 1980s and the 1990s. The principle of care has increasingly challenged the principle of maintenance in family policy. In the late 1970s the Dutch eliminated tax exemptions for children, and in the early 1980s they redesigned the child allowance system elevating the principle of care as the main basis of entitlement (SZW 1990: 24). The funding of child allowances was transferred to the state in the late 1980s so that child allowances in the Netherlands were similar those in the UK and Sweden. An increasing number of medical benefits have been transferred to the universal health insurance scheme, including services for mothers and infants. Maternity benefits were also improved in 1990 when the duration of paid leave was lengthened to sixteen weeks and coverage through voluntary insurance extended to family workers and the self-employed (SCP 1993a: 213).

In other respects, the male breadwinner model has been less susceptible to change. The 1984 tax reform was not a complete break with the model. A sole earner's allowance was introduced, and any unused portion of the wife's allowance was transferable to the husband. Although entitlement to many social benefits has been individualized, medical benefits provided by the Bismarckian scheme remain familialized through coverage of the breadwinner's partner and children. Likewise a non-working wife's coverage in the national pension schemes indirectly depends upon her husband's contributions. The family minimum continues to shape the construction of several benefits, and a proposed reform of social assistance norms privileges the couple and reduces the benefits of single individuals and sole parents. As long as means tested benefits are not individualized, the negative consequences for married women are twofold. They are ineligible for benefits if their husbands are employed, and if their husbands claim means tested benefits married women may leave employment or not seek work (see Sjerps 1988).

Finally, care tasks have remained in the private sphere – either in the home or through non-profit private providers of services often relying on voluntary unpaid labor (*Statistical Yearbook* 1988: 362–3). Many domestic workers who perform caring tasks are not encompassed by the formal definition of an "employee" so that these carers are not covered by the employee social insurance schemes. This system depends on the work of married women, and it can exist because of the surviving features of the breadwinner model. Despite the interesting innovation of credits for childcare in the new unemployment insurance scheme and the principle of care supplanting the principle of maintenance as a basis of entitlement to child allowances, there are no benefits granted to carers explicitly as compensation for their work, as in the UK and Sweden. Instead policies aid women in their role as carers and instill the notion that care is a womanly obligation. Family services step in when the woman of the house is unable to perform her domestic duties. Currently, informal care or "substitution" is lauded as a remedy to the high costs of medical services. Childcare remains an example of the "maximum private responsibility model." The availability of licensed care is minimal, and very few mothers utilized center based care in the early 1990s (Maassen van den Brink 1994: 45). Dutch successes have been combined with a serious shortcoming of reform efforts. So far the infrastructure policies – adequate day care provision and paid leave for all parents – which are required if total individualization for the next generation is to be a reality have yet to be implemented.

Sweden: individualization and shared family roles

The core of Swedish reforms has consisted of individualization, accompanied by a phasing out of women's entitlements as wives, and gender reconstruction measures promoting shared family roles. Parental benefits have aimed at increasing men's activities as carers, whereas the expansion of public childcare and active labor market policy measures tailored to women's needs have aided them to become earners.

The major "individualization" reform abolished joint taxation of spouses' earnings. Because of the sharp progressivity of taxation rates and the restructuring of tax relief related to family responsibilities, the reform created strong incentives for married women to enter the labor market. Tax allowances which were previously shared by a married couple were individualized. The value of the housewife bonus was substantially reduced,[3] it was allowed to atrophy, and finally abolished in 1991. These measures favored a married couple who changed from a single earner to two earners by reducing the percentage of income tax paid on their combined earnings. Equally important, a couple would continue to gain as the wife increased her earnings to the optimal point where both spouses earned the same income (OECD 1980: 56, Gustafsson 1990: 159).

In income maintenance policies individualization reforms have virtually eliminated entitlements as wives for younger women. The most controversial reforms concerned widow pensions. The ATP widow pensions are gradually being phased out.[4] Survivor benefits in the basic pension system were overhauled for new claimants (from 1990) at the same time as equal entitlement of women and men was introduced. The main thrust of the reform was to design survivor benefits to protect families with young children against loss of income through the death of an earning parent. Survivors heading families with young children (under 12) receive a pension, and child pensions have also been improved. When there are no children or older children, the pension amounts to an adjustment allowance paid for a year.

Individualization has both worsened and improved married women's entitlements. Reforms, such as survivor benefits and the eventual elimination of the ATP widow pension, reduced women's potential benefits. In other instances, individualization has enhanced women's social rights. This is especially true of the tax reform and benefits where a husband's earnings previously disqualified a married woman from entitlement, such as training allowances and study grants.

Gender reconstruction reforms were spurred by the emergence of an ideology of shared roles in the family which challenged the traditional division of labor between husband and wife. The new ideology emerged in the 1960s as a critique of the traditional role of women in the family as well as the advocacy of women's dual roles as mother and earner (Myrdal and Klein 1956). Women's emancipation could not be achieved solely by expanding their roles. Instead simultaneous changes in the roles of men were required. Without such changes women would assume a double work load as earners and carers (Moberg 1961).

The first legislation embodying the new ideology of shared roles was the 1974 Parental Insurance Act. In its conception, parental insurance constituted a radical departure from earlier policies which had identified the principle of care with motherhood. The care principle was extended to the father, and parental benefits replaced maternity benefits. Besides long-term leave, short-term benefits in connection with the birth of a child, care of a sick child, and helping a child start day care or school have been available. Another important feature of parental insurance is flexibility to encourage equal parenting. Parents can divide leave in a variety of ways, and they can utilize it up to the eighth birthday of the child. For example, since 1979 parents of preschool children have been entitled to reduce their working hours (without pay), but they can use the parental allowance to compensate for their loss of earnings. However, until 1986 entitlements of mothers and fathers were differentiated in that a father did not have the right to earnings related benefits unless the mother did. The 1986 reform granted both parents equal and uniform entitlement, and thus included *all* parents.

The rationale behind the reform was to eliminate a barrier to fathers' taking parental leave. Equal parenting is also furthered by the construction of temporary benefits to care for a sick child; the same maximum number of days (sixty days in the mid-1990s) are reserved for each parent.

In spite of both parents' entitlement, as we saw in chapter 4, it is mothers who are the primary caregivers. Slightly over one-quarter of the claimants of the parental leave were fathers, but their share of time caring for a child during its infancy was much smaller. Of the total number of days of regular leave to care for a child around 90 percent were paid to mothers and 10 percent to fathers in the mid-1990s (RFV 1995: 28). On the other hand, most fathers utilized paternity leave in connection with the child's birth. They also more frequently took advantage of the temporary benefit to care for a sick child, and their share of paid days of leave was about one-third in the early 1990s (RFV 1995: 29). On the whole, there has only been a slight narrowing in the father/mother ratio of days of regular leave during the past two decades, but these statistics also mask a steady increase in the time fathers spend in caring for their children because of the lengthening of the period of benefits. To combat the continued reluctance of men to take parental leave, recent legislation has earmarked one month of leave for the father which cannot be transferred to the mother.

Although unsuccessful in achieving an equally shared role of caregiver between mothers and fathers, parental insurance reforms have broken down the division between paid work in the market and unpaid work in the home. Like paid work, benefits are taxable income and count toward the ATP pension. Other benefits and allowances have also strengthened the component of paid care. A care allowance for a handicapped child, originally a pension for the child, allows parents to use it either in paying other persons for care services or as remuneration to the parent caring for the child. In the early 1990s the amount of this care allowance was raised so that the full allowance was the most generous flat rate benefit within the basic pension system. Since 1991 a parent who has cared for a sick or disabled child can receive a special supplement to the basic pension in recompense for not having an ATP pension. A recent reform also introduced short-term cash benefits to care for a close relative, and nearly 30 percent of the claimants were men (RFV 1995: 57, 62, 24).

In many instances provision of care services in the public sector has paved the way for payment for the same services in the home. For example, during the 1960s home helps (*barnvårdinnor*) employed by the local government provided care for a sick child so that the mother could go to work. With this precedent, it was quite natural for parental insurance to pay the parents to care for their sick child. The advent of retrenchment has brought a new dynamic into play. Care in the home by a relative or another person is more economical than institutionalized care or hospitalization. Benefits previously reserved for relatives were recently extended to persons outside the family. From 1995 the cash benefit can be transferred from the parents to any other person who stays home from work to care for a sick child (SCB 1995: 39). The cuts in benefit levels make this arrangement even more economical. Nonetheless this development is very different from the solution in the Netherlands which is "substitution" or unpaid informal care.

The other two policies promoting shared roles, primarily by aiding women to become earners, have been the expansion of childcare and active labor market policy measures. Public day care expanded during the past two decades. From 1970 to 1990 coverage increased from roughly 10 percent to nearly 60 percent of all children aged 1 to 6. In the early 1990s approximately 85 percent of all children whose parents wanted municipal day care had received a place (SCB 1995: 36–7). Previously the availability of full-time care lagged behind places in part-time arrangements, and municipal family day care was more prevalent than childcare centers. Over the decades the balance has shifted toward full-time center based care.

Labor market measures to promote women's employment were placed on the agenda in the early 1970s, and during the decade training and job creation programs were increasingly geared to women. In the early 1960s only 40 percent of the new trainees were women but by the mid-1970s the percentage had risen to 55 percent. Public works projects traditionally focused almost exclusively on construction and infrastructure improvements. In the 1970s service jobs in the public sector took precedence. Besides the creation of permanent jobs, relief works projects providing services absorbed a growing number of women as the decade progressed – from around 10 percent to 40 percent in the late 1970s (Ruggie 1984: 151–4). The combined effect of these policies – together with the rapid expansion of the social service state in the 1970s – was to improve women's opportunities to become earners and their entitlements based on labor market status (table 8.5).

The gendered differentiation in entitlements has changed in four ways over the years, and these changes lack counterparts or are much weaker in the other three countries. Women's access to benefits as earners has steadily increased; whereas in the 1960s most benefits of this type were the prerogative of men. Second, entitlements as workers have been coupled to benefits based on the principle of care, improving women's benefits as carers. This change has been interpreted as evidence of the strength of the work principle and that care policies conform to a citizen worker policy regime where the norm is a mother who works outside the home (Leira 1992, Hobson 1994). The coupling of entitlements based on care and work performance can also be understood as a move toward equating paid and

Table 8.5 *Swedish women's individual entitlements to earnings related benefits, 1970–90 (%)*[a]

	1970	1980	1990
Sickness benefits coverage	59	81	83
Unemployment insurance			
Coverage	44	76	84
Beneficiaries	–	48	72
ATP			
Old age beneficiaries	9	34	60
Disability beneficiaries	21	61	85

Notes:
[a] Coverage for sickness benefits is the percentage of all working age women. Coverage for unemployment insurance is the percentage of female workers. Unemployment insurance beneficiaries are the percentage of registered unemployed women. ATP old age beneficiaries are the percentage of all female old age pensioners. ATP disability beneficiaries are the percentage of all women recipients of basic disability benefits.
Sources: Allmän försäkring 1970: 68, 127, 289, 292, 297, 303, 311, 1980: 107, 270, 291, SOS 1993: 35, 199, 229, SCB 1989b: 70–1, AMS 1980, 1990: table 14, AKU November 1990: 2.

unpaid work or integrating two alternative feminist visions of a women-friendly welfare state – the universal breadwinner model with the caregiver parity model. This coupling differs in principle from maternity benefits which either compensate for illness or unemployment but not for parenting or care work. Third, women's relatively few entitlements as wives have been either abolished or they are being phased out of existence and no longer apply to younger women. Finally, as in the UK and the Netherlands, there has been an expansion of benefits based on the principle of care. These benefits are primarily claimed by women but the novel development is that they are increasingly claimed by men, although still a small minority – between 25 and 30 percent in the 1990s. This development underlines another facet of the importance of coupling entitlements based on the principle of care with those derived from paid work.

What works and what does not

On the basis of this analysis of gender equality reforms in the four countries, we can draw some broad conclusions about what works and what doesn't. Of the reforms to achieve equality between the sexes, the reformulation of laws in gender neutral terms has generally failed to modify outcomes in any significant way or has been to the detriment of women. In the USA because of the construction of spouse benefits, gender neutral reforms have usually extended entitlement to men and have rarely benefited women. In the UK adult dependant allowances and entitlement to assistance benefits were the prerogative of the breadwinner, and gender neutral reforms have meant a formal increase in women's social rights. In actual fact, the legislation has scarcely affected women's and men's utilization rates of these benefits. Few US men are recipients as spouses, fathers, or widowers; and few British women are claimants of adult dependant allowances or assistance benefits received by couples.

Gender neutral reforms have often been cosmetic; the sole change has been to extend formal entitlement to both sexes. The principal flaw of this type of reform is that it does not address the root cause of the gender differentiation in women's and men's entitlements: how the gendered division of labor interacts with social provision. Basic policy constructions have not been altered, and the pivotal position of market work for entitlement to insurance benefits remains central. This construction, together with additional qualifying conditions, awards men social rights as earners and denies many women workers such rights.

Reforms based on the principle of care, with the noticeable exception of the USA, have generally enhanced women's entitlements as mothers and caregivers during the past two decades. These reforms, which entail gender reinforcement, have both positive and negative effects. Such entitlements provide women with new social rights rectifying the imbalance in men's and women's entitlements in systems of social provision where work related benefits are predominant. Reforms introducing benefits attached to the principle of care have also challenged the principle of maintenance, transferring rights which were previously the prerogative of the father to the mother – as in the case of child allowances. By conferring direct rights such reform measures have the potential to supersede a woman's indirect rights via her husband. Entitlements based on the principle of care are also important because they alter notions of deservingness by acknowledging the significance of care to society.

One drawback of a strategy to expand benefits based on the principle of care is that benefit levels have often been lower than benefits based on market work. In the UK benefits related to care are non-contributory, and the contributory principle is held up as a justification for not raising benefits related to care. Swedish benefits, with the exception of when the beneficiary has previous earnings, are also not as generous as work related benefits. As long as there is no parity in the benefits accorded by the caregiver model and work related benefits, a strategy based on the principle of care perpetuates different levels of social provision for women and men. A further disadvantage of this strategy is that it can easily lock women into the role of carer, impeding their entry and full integration into the labor market with its rewards of earnings and higher benefits. Finally, this type of reform improves women's social benefits *vis-à-vis* men's, but it sustains a gendered differentiation in their entitlements.

In contrast to the gender reinforcement approach, gender recognition reforms have generally aimed to improve women's social rights by altering the bases of entitlement. Gender recognition as a strategy aims to strengthen women's social rights as workers. Among the concrete examples of this type of reform are care credits to improve women's ability to claim a pension or other benefits in their own right in work related schemes. Although reforms of this type have been introduced in all four countries, we know very little about their effect, and whether the credits have enabled women to claim benefits they otherwise would not have qualified for. Reforms specifically designed to help women enter the labor market or help them get a good job have a better track record. The chief failing of gender recognition measures is their concentration on women, while gender differentiation in entitlements pertains to both women and men.

Gender reconstruction reforms have been more successful in altering women's entitlements and less effective in producing changes in men's. In the case of Swedish parental insurance, which did seek a fundamental restructuring of women's and men's social rights, fathers have been slow to take leave of longer duration; instead they have utilized short-term benefits. Men's failure to utilize parental benefits is related to employer pressures and career demands, especially in the private sector, and income differences between parents. In families where both parents hold well paid jobs 40–50 percent of the fathers took leave. Generally the higher the mother's earnings, the more likely it is that the father has claimed a parental allowance (SCB 1986: 152). Major changes in utilization rates seem to hinge upon an equalization of women's and men's employment opportunities and earning capacities. The introduction of a "daddy month" in 1995, assigning one month of leave to the father, may induce more fathers to take leave. But without high replacement rates of parental benefits, it is hard to imagine fathers taking more leave than this.

The lack of far-reaching change can be interpreted as the failure of gender neutral legislation, but it should not blind us to the merits of a policy construction which integrates market work and care work in the home and simultaneously grants equal entitlement to women and men. If women become earners, this construction enhances their benefits as caregivers. In this way, it provides an incentive for women to engage in market work. This policy construction also encourages men to become caregivers more than entitlements based solely on the principle of care.

Individualization reforms have tended to be more successful in equalizing access to social benefits than gender neutral measures. As a strategy of reform, individualization has been easier to pursue when the breadwinner model has focused on the family as the unit of benefits and contributions, as in the Dutch case. Applying the approach encounters more difficulties when the breadwinner model centers on the individual as the beneficiary with supplements for family members, as in the USA and the UK. Its application to US and British policies lays bare a potential dilemma of individualization. The strategy requires the elimination of entitlements as wives which is to the detriment of those women who either have only this sort of entitlement or those who have meager benefits as workers. The analyses of the differing outcomes of the Dutch reforms and the Swedish experience suggest the necessity of a particular pre-existent policy construction – entitlement based on citizenship or residence – to ensure equal access of women and men. The Dutch case also illustrates the pitfalls of individualization if it is not combined with provision of adequate day care facilities and labor market measures to assist women in becoming earners – and not merely peripheral workers.

In sum, individualization is not a strategy without potential hazards for women. The Swedish case points to three policies which are prerequisites for its implementation to be more helpful than harmful to women: first, the provision of adequate social benefits whose entitlement is based on citizenship or residence; second, policies to aid women in achieving a substantial measure of financial independence through their own earnings; and, third, a marginalization of means tested programs where the family is the unit of benefits. The importance of this last prerequisite becomes more apparent in the next chapter which examines the impact of retrenchment on women's social rights.

9   Welfare state retrenchment

The past fifteen years have been an era of welfare state retrenchment, and
retrenchment measures have often undercut or blunted the impact of
gender equality reforms. This chapter compares the policy responses in the
four countries since the early 1980s with the purpose of, first, analyzing the
impact of retrenchment and related policy changes on the social rights of
women and, second, elucidating the gender biases in retrenchment strategies – differences in the impact on women and men. More specifically, I
examine core welfare state policies – concentrating on income maintenance
programs – and strategies to divest the state of its welfare functions in this
area. My discussion attempts to specify both the similarities and differences
in retrenchment efforts across the four countries. The differing responses in
the four countries have consequences for women's entitlements, and the
interplay between retrenchment strategies and existing policy constructions
has influenced the gender bias of outcomes.

Before looking at retrenchment efforts in the four countries, it is necessary to clarify what retrenchment entails and how it is analyzed here.
Retrenchment is often equated with cuts in expenditure. A definition focusing on social expenditures is unsatisfactory, however, because spending is
an aggregate measure which conceals important policy changes.[1] An alternative approach has been to conceptualize retrenchment in terms of the
residual and institutional models discussed in chapter 1. One variant of
this approach sees retrenchment as a restructuring towards a residual
model of welfare – as "residualization" (Brown 1988, Pierson 1990,
Sainsbury 1992, Land 1992, Stephens et al. 1995). Residualization implies
enlarging the role of the market in welfare provision, and restricting state
provision to a minimum safety net in cases of market failure and family
breakdowns.[2]

Conceptualizing retrenchment as welfare state restructuring in a
residualist direction has two advantages. It provides specific criteria for
comparing changes across countries. Employing the dimensions of variation in chapter 1 (table 1.1), retrenchment can be further concretized. The
dimensions suggest several types of change that need to be investigated:

changes in coverage, the range of benefits and services, benefit levels, the dominant type of program, and the role of private organizations. Changes in coverage involve tightening eligibility requirements and disentitlement. The range of benefits and services focuses attention on the contraction or elimination of programs and the degree to which the responsibility of social provision has shifted from the state to the market or the family. With respect to benefit levels, the crucial criterion in determining a change of a residualist character is the adequacy of benefits and whether they provide a socially acceptable standard. Finally, a hallmark of the residual model is the importance of means tested programs. Has retrenchment entailed a shift to means tested benefits?

A second advantage of this sort of conceptualization is that it highlights policy moves involving structural changes. An analysis focusing exclusively on spending cuts leads to the unsurprising conclusion that there has been a deterioration of benefits, and in many instances women have suffered more than men. The central issue, however, is whether retrenchment measures embody a fundamental welfare state restructuring that affects women's social rights or whether these measures entail a downsizing with little modification of the distinctive features of welfare states.

Retrenchment in the 1980s and 1990s

The retrenchment process was initially triggered by a common set of difficulties confronting most advanced industrial countries. The stagflation of the 1970s culminated in the second oil shock, producing a serious recession in the early 1980s. Many countries experienced zero economic growth or worse, unprecedented high levels of unemployment for the postwar period, mounting public deficits, and rising government expenditure. Several observers argued that the cause of these problems was the expansion of the welfare state, and they proposed retrenchment as a solution. Demands for retrenchment were also often fueled by neo-liberal and conservative ideologies. Irrespective of ideological convictions, policy makers in our four countries attempted to halt the growth of the public sector and reduce government expenditures as a percentage of the GDP.

Strategies and priorities, however, differed significantly. In 1982 the Swedish Social Democrats returned to power on pledges to reverse the retrenchment measures introduced by the non-socialists, and the party remained in government until the early 1990s. By contrast, parties intent upon rolling back the frontiers of the state came into office between 1979 and 1982 in the other three countries. These governments embarked on a substantial social policy rollback, but the measures they adopted differed with respect to the scope and type of welfare state restructuring.

The USA: disentitlement and reinforcing dual welfare

Welfare state retrenchment was central to Reagan's blueprint for rolling back the state, and it was a major plank in the Republicans' Contract with America in the mid-1990s. The retrenchment measures of the Reagan administration and the Contract with America share important features. Both singled out the "welfare" tier of public provision for the heaviest cuts. Ultimately a strategy of this sort reinforces the existing system of dual welfare, which favors "social security" insurance benefits and treats means tested benefits harshly. The Contract with America renewed and deepened the attack on the welfare tier and entitlements based on need. The proposals of the Contract urged a drastic tightening of eligibility requirements and greater disentitlement. A second characteristic has been a concern about the incentive structure of social programs in relation to the unemployed. Social programs had to be redesigned so that individuals "choose" employment rather than social benefits. This involved proposals for reduced benefits, tightening eligibility requirements, the elimination of programs, work obligations in exchange for assistance benefits, and expanded fiscal welfare. The expansion of fiscal welfare advantages those with earnings, and it has been part of a larger redistributive strategy to substitute tax exemptions and credits for social services and benefits. A third similarity was to propose tax reforms to defund the welfare state. Under Reagan, tax cuts together with a recession and increased military spending created an enormous budget deficit. The president's fiscal strategy was in effect to "pull the revenue plug" (Meyer 1986: 72), and concern about the deficit inhibited new initiatives in the area of social policy during most of the 1980s. A final common point was to advocate the transfer of welfare responsibilities from the central government to the states and a major overhaul of the system of federal grants to the states.

This retrenchment strategy has been more to the detriment of women than men in three respects. First, assaults on entitlements based on need impinge more heavily on women's social rights because of their weaker entitlements based on the market. Second, women bear the brunt of cuts because the recipients of means tested benefits are mainly women. Third, the celebration of the work ethic and earned rights has condoned benefit cuts for those outside the labor force – wives and widows – and for less than perfect workers – the unemployed, the disabled, and persons who exit from the labor market before regular retirement age. A closer examination of the cuts introduced by the Reagan administration clarifies their gender bias and how Reagan's policies foreshadowed the Contract with America.

Cuts in the two tiers of public welfare

Heavy cuts in social spending were among Reagan's top priorities, but the two tiers of public provision fared quite differently with respect to the scope of proposed reductions. Spending on social insurance benefits was to be trimmed by approximately 10 percent. By contrast, assistance programs – such as AFDC, Medicaid, food stamps, and housing assistance – were to be cut by nearly 30 percent. The sharpest cuts – roughly 60 percent – were reserved for special project grants for the delivery of education, health, employment, and social services by state and local governments. The president only got about one half of what he had asked for – cuts totaling somewhat under 10 percent of prior policy levels. With a few exceptions, the pattern of cuts largely corresponded to his recommendations (Bawden and Palmer 1984: 184–7).

Several cuts in the "welfare" tier imposed hardships on women. Among the programs faced with large cuts, and whose clients consisted overwhelmingly of women, were food stamps, Aid to Families with Dependent Children (AFDC), the Work Incentive Program (WIN), and housing assistance. These programs were cut through tightening eligibility requirements and/or reducing federal grants to the states. These measures decreased the number of beneficiaries, and the long-term effect was that at the end of the decade their numbers were roughly the same as in 1980.[3]

Eligibility requirements for food stamps were tightened in terms of allowable income, reducing program participants by one million persons (or around 5 percent of the participants). Similarly, the AFDC conditions of eligibility became more restrictive by setting a ceiling on allowable income and reducing deductions for day care and other work expenses. As a result, around 400,000 AFDC families (about 10 percent of recipients) lost their eligibility, and most of them also became ineligible for Medicaid. An additional 300,000 AFDC families experienced benefit reductions (Stoesz and Karger 1992). By the mid-1980s both the real value of benefits in cash and kind to AFDC recipients had declined by 15 percent compared to a decade earlier, and participation rates had fallen by nearly 20 percent (Reischauer 1989: 14).

Cuts in the "social security" tier affected benefits to the unemployed, the disabled, widows with dependent children, and the future benefits of early retirees. Unemployment benefits reached a smaller portion of the jobless under Reagan than in previous administrations, and the proportion of the unemployed eligible for insurance benefits declined in the 1980s. During the height of the recession in the early 1980s only 45 percent of the unemployed received benefits (Smeeding 1984: 113). For unemployed women who headed households the decline was marked; only one out of six received benefits and the percentage lifted out of poverty fell to around 15 percent (Pearce 1985: 456–7). Terminations of disability insurance (DI) benefits increased dramatically during 1981–2 through more rigorous screening procedures. Approximately 10 percent of the beneficiaries were eliminated from the rolls; nor could they qualify for assistance benefits for the disabled. Judging from social security statistics, women and men fared equally badly (SSB, *Annual Statistical Supplement* 1991: 185).

The social security cuts related to early retirement have special ramifications for women. The Reagan administration proposed to increase the maximum reductions in benefits for early retirement and simultaneously raise the pension age. Starting in the year 2000 an increase in the retirement age from 65 to 67 will be gradually phased in over two decades, and maximum reductions in pensions will also be increased. These changes in the pension age and larger reductions in benefits for early retirement potentially affect women to a greater degree than men in three ways. Women have been more likely than men to take early retirement, which reduces benefits. In the early 1980s, when Congress enacted the changes, 70 percent of the women OASI beneficiaries had reduced benefits for early retirement compared to 55 percent of the men. Second, the maximum reduction of benefits is larger for spouses (wives) than for workers; in the next century the maximum reduction for retired workers will increase from 20 to 30 percent and for spouses from 25 to 35 percent. In the mid-1990s four out of five wives retired early. Third, survivor benefits suffer a double deterioration as a result of the 1983 legislation and the growing trend in early retirement. A widow's benefits are eroded by both her husband's and her own early retirement. The pension of a widow whose husband retires at 62 is reduced to nearly 80 percent of the deceased worker's benefit, whereas she receives 100 percent if he retires at the normal pension age. In the mid-1990s nearly half of the newly awarded male beneficiaries retired at the age of 62 compared with 30 percent in 1980. A widow's pension decreases additionally if she elects to receive benefits earlier than the normal retirement age (SSB, *Annual Statistical Supplement* 1994: 50–4, 211, 262). Finally, the duration of benefits for widowed mothers was shortened by reducing the age of dependent children from 18 to 16. Together with raising the normal pension age, this worsens the problem of the "widow gap."

Grant cuts to promote private sector involvement and for-profit provision

Through reductions in special grants programs for childcare services, employment and training, housing, and social services for the elderly, the Reagan administration sought to promote more private sector involvement in these areas. These programs aided women, and cuts impaired women's access to benefits in kind and services either by reducing availability of public provision or substituting for-profit provision. Most damaging were cuts in employment and training programs and subsidies for childcare that affected women's ability to become earners.

Childcare has been described as the "prototypical illustration of 'privatization' as an explicit policy of the Reagan Administration" (Kamerman and Kahn 1989: 236). Initially the administration cut federal subsidies to day care, reducing their real value by about 25 percent. Subsequently producer subsidies were concentrated to Head Start – an educational program with limited full-time places. In line with the "deregulation" aspirations of the administration, the federal government also relinquished its role of setting minimum standards for federally funded childcare. At the same time, the administration expanded tax expenditures for day care, creating an incentive for parents/consumers to purchase care in the market. In the process, the proportions of revenues allocated to producer subsidies and consumer subsidies for day care were reversed. The largest increase in consumer subsidies occurred through the Dependant Care Tax Credit, which is non-refundable and must be used for tax deduction purposes. Through additional tax expenditures the administration also introduced the possibility of employer sponsored day care and salary reduction plans. Changes also altered the distributional impact of consumer subsidies (Kamerman and Kahn 1989, Hayes et al. 1990). The disregards of AFDC mothers for day care were reduced, while tax credits were increased and day care as a fringe benefit was made more attractive. These tax expenditures and fringe benefits are often not available to the working poor, and they are counterproductive to the goal of moving solo mothers off welfare into work. During the decade center based care became more prevalent, and most of this type of care is for-profit.

The Reagan administration also worked to end government's involvement in employment programs. Besides introducing legislation to increase the responsibility of the private sector for job training, the president wanted to terminate the Work Incentive Program (WIN) which provided job counseling, training, and placement services for welfare recipients. Instead he proposed a mandatory "workfare" scheme for AFDC recipients which would require them to work in return for benefits. Congress rejected the proposal to abolish WIN but appropriated less revenue to the program (Bawden and Palmer 1984: 198, 366–7, Miller 1990: 55). The proposal to make workfare mandatory was amended by Congress so that it became an option for the states. Few mandatory schemes were introduced, but those that were implemented later influenced the Family Support Act of 1988.

The Family Support Act stiffened work obligations by requiring all AFDC recipients, except mothers with children under 3 years old, to participate in job search, training, or work experience programs (previously mothers with children 6 years or older had similar obligations but work registration generally sufficed to meet the requirement). Although ambitious in its scope, appropriations were underdimensioned in relation to the task. Furthermore, to receive federal funding, only a small portion of AFDC mothers needed to be participating in the workfare programs (JOBS) which replaced WIN. Equally problematic, the new legislation failed to improve benefits, which have generally been below the poverty line. However, in line with the administration's shift from benefits to tax expenditures the Family Support Act strengthened incentives for employment in three ways. It increased the maximum amount of tax deductions for day care and other work expenses. Second, it disregarded the earned income tax credit for the working poor with children. Finally, to lessen the effects of the poverty trap, working former recipients could retain Medicaid and food stamps during a transitional period.

Looking back at Reagan's retrenchment strategy, one of its most distinctive features was a concentration on cutbacks in public assistance. Despite high poverty rates the number of recipients was slashed. In effect Reagan's retrenchment efforts strengthened the existing system of dual welfare by shielding "social security" insurance benefits from major cuts. However, since the overwhelming proportion of government outlays for income maintenance goes to insurance benefits, the concentration on assistance programs offered less scope for reducing social expenditures. A similar irony characterized Reagan's efforts to get people to work, at the same time as his administration cut back on employment services, vocational education, and training programs in the early 1980s. The passage of the Family Support Act in 1988 also buttressed the system of dual welfare. The increased obligation to participate in work activities was sweetened by the promise of support services, including childcare services. The proposed expansion of day care in the welfare tier bolstered one aspect of the bifurcated structure of public provision: the targeting of public services to a needy clientele.

The Contract with America

Emerging victorious from the mid-term election of 1994, the Republicans sought to enact the Contract with America, which builds on the Reagan retrenchment legacy. The Contract called for sharp cutbacks in the welfare tier and devolution of responsibility to help the poor to the states. The estimated effects of the welfare bill based on the Contract would make deeper cuts in the rolls of programs in the welfare tier than the Reagan administration did.

The retrenchment recipe of the Contract with America is disentitlement. At present the coverage of US assistance programs is the most limited of the four countries because only certain categories of the poor have entitlement. Nevertheless, entitlement has been a matter of right for all individuals who meet the statutory criteria. The welfare bill proposed to alter radically the statutory criteria of entitlement. The most far-reaching proposal was to abolish AFDC and the school lunch program. Instead cash payments would be made to the states which could use the money in any way they chose to help the poor. In effect, this would erode the only existing basis of uniform entitlements of mother only families. The welfare bill limited the duration of benefits for solo mothers to a two-year spell, and it restricted their entitlement to five years during a lifetime. Mothers who become pregnant while receiving assistance would be disqualified. Additionally legal immigrants would be barred from assistance benefits (legal immigrants have been able to receive benefits after three years of residence). Heavier cuts in Medicaid located in the welfare tier have been proposed compared to those suggested for Medicare in the social security tier. In sum, measures based on the Contract with America perpetuated the gender bias of Reagan's retrenchment strategy.

The UK: sustained erosion of national insurance benefits

Although the Thatcher governments and their successors also dealt severely with unemployment benefits and means tested programs, an overriding policy thrust was to weaken the national insurance scheme – the cornerstone of the Beveridge welfare state – and the state earnings related pension scheme (SERPS). In retrospect the strategy seems to have been to effect an incremental erosion of the national insurance scheme. The main steps were to abolish earnings related supplements, to tax short-term benefits, to change indexation of pensions to base them on prices, to convert the sickness benefit into statutory sick pay (SSP) and later maternity benefits into maternity pay (SMP), and to eliminate the possibility of reduced benefits for reduced contributions. In the 1990s national insurance benefits have been further eroded by making the major disability benefit taxable and reducing the period of payment of unemployment benefits. A frontal attack on SERPS in the mid-1980s failed, but modifications lowered benefits substantially. The state also became less involved in financing, phasing out its contributions to pensions under the National Insurance Act while introducing incentives for private pension schemes in the form of tax expenditures and special introductory bonuses. Overall, contributions were raised (Parry 1990: 142) and benefits were lowered. In other words, insured persons in the state schemes paid more and received less – making it more inviting to opt out.

The number of recipients of national insurance benefits declined as a result of SSP and SMP and through exhaustion of unemployment benefits due to long-term joblessness. As the rolls of recipients of assistance benefits swelled, eligibility criteria were tightened in conjunction with the introduction of income support in 1988. The tightening of eligibility rules reduced the number of recipients of assistance, and in the early 1990s rules were once again tightened.

In summary, the Reagan and Thatcher administrations – and their heirs – shared a concern over welfare dependency, and they adopted similar strategies to remove recipients from the assistance rolls. Both tightened eligibility requirements and expanded fiscal welfare–tax expenditures. A basic dissimilarity in their approaches, however, was that the Reagan administration largely scaled down means tested programs, thus scarcely modifying the existing bifurcated structure of public welfare provision, whereas the Thatcherite project sought to alter the balance between "universal" programs (both contributory and non-contributory) and means tested benefits. Since 1979 when Thatcher entered office, a twin shift has occurred, first, toward privatization of pensions, sickness, and maternity benefits and, second, toward means tested benefits and greater targeting to the "needy." Despite these changes, privatization did not alter the statutory status of benefits, giving British employers less leeway to determine coverage and benefit levels compared to their counterparts in the USA. Nor has central government responsibility for assistance benefits – a typical feature of British social provision – come under attack, as in the USA.

The twin shift to private and means tested benefits shaped the gender bias in Thatcher's retrenchment strategy. The erosion of national insurance benefits has adversely affected both women's and men's social rights. Retrenchment in the UK has not contained the same sort of gender bias as in the USA where earned rights were subjected to less severe cuts which advantaged men. Instead retrenchment measures aimed at debilitating the national insurance scheme – especially those which stiffened contribution requirements – have undercut women's claims to insurance benefits, as documented in chapter 8 (table 8.3) and preserved the preponderance of men among the recipients of insurance benefits. At the same time privatized benefits retained the lower earnings limit, which has barred women from entitlement to benefits, and added new obstacles. The move to private benefits has clearly weakened women's pension rights and entitlement to maternity benefits. Simultaneously the expansion of occupational and fiscal welfare associated with private benefits tends to favor men, especially those with assets, whereas the growing importance of means tested programs strengthens the importance of family relationships in determining entitlements.

The privatization of benefits

One aspect of Thatcher's and Major's efforts to restructure the British welfare state was to make former national insurance benefits, such as sickness and maternity benefits, a responsibility of employers and to marketize supplementary or occupational pensions. Statutory sick pay (SSP) is one of several examples of the sustained incrementalism in the Tories' retrenchment strategy.[4] In 1983 SSP replaced sickness benefits for employees. The government's original proposal called for a total transfer, but employers and insurance companies balked. Initially the state remained responsible for funding, while administration and payment of benefits were transferred to employers for the first eight weeks of illness. In the mid-1980s the period of payment of SSP was lengthened to six months – the full duration of sickness benefits in the national insurance scheme. Employers became responsible for part of the cost in 1991, and by the mid-1990s all but smaller employers bore the full cost of SSP. The next likely step is to transfer the costs of industrial injury benefits to employers (DNISR 1994: 131–2).

For beneficiaries the effects of these changes constituted an erosion in benefits. Unlike national insurance sickness benefits, SSP was taxable and provided no supplements for family members. Two features of the reforms affected women. First, the retention of the lower earnings limit has excluded nearly 20 percent of the female labor force during the past decade. On the other hand, the employee's past contribution record no longer determined eligibility, which could help women in temporary and part-time work (Lonsdale and Byrne 1988: 145). Second, the process of shifting costs to employers operated against women workers with low earnings. Changes introduced in 1990 and 1991 altered the range of earnings in qualifying for the higher rate so that nearly five million employees – mainly women – were no longer eligible for the higher rate (Cm 931, Lister 1992: 35).

Maternity benefits were reformed along similar lines during the latter part of the 1980s when statutory maternity pay (SMP) was introduced, and the maternity grant was abolished. The reform reduced coverage and lowered benefits of working mothers and mothers in general, despite the fact that more mothers were in employment. At the end of the 1980s slightly over 40 percent of *all* mothers received some type of maternity pay and around 20 percent of all mothers received the higher rate (90 percent of earnings during six weeks) (calculated from McRae 1991: 85). These recipient rates contrast with those in the early 1980s when nearly all mothers received the maternity grant, and the national insurance benefit – the maternity allowance – was paid to nearly 50 percent of all mothers and the earnings related supplement (ERS) to slightly under 30 percent. Even among working mothers coverage receded both with respect to benefits in general and benefits paid at a higher rate. Although 80 percent of women who worked during their pregnancy received some form of maternity benefits only 65 percent received SMP and approximately 40 percent the higher rate (McRae 1991: 86, 91, 110). In 1980 around 90 percent of working mothers received the maternity allowance and over 50 percent received the ERS (see table 4.2). Nor was the higher rate of SMP as lucrative as the ERS. The latter was paid for eighteen weeks, whereas the duration of payment of the higher rate of SMP is much shorter, and the lower rate is paid for the remainder of the period. In 1990 the lower rate was less than 20 percent of the average earnings of a female full-time worker (EOC 1991: 25).

A more dramatic move toward privatization occurred as part of the attack on the state earnings related pension scheme. The Social Security Act of 1986 made a second tier pension compulsory for workers whose earnings are above the lower limit for national insurance contributions. They can choose between the state pension, an employers' pension, an appropriate personal pension, or some combination of these. The reform allowed individuals to contract out of SERPS or the guaranteed employers' pension. Simultaneously the future benefits of SERPS were downgraded and indirectly also those of employers' pensions which are required to provide benefits corresponding to SERPS. The weakening of state and employers' pensions made personal pensions more attractive. With the introduction of the appropriate personal pension system, the government launched a major campaign stressing tax incentives and special introductory bonuses. The number of individuals covered by SERPS decreased from over 12 million in 1986 to 7.5 million in 1990. Conversely, the new system covered 4 million individuals, who were overwhelmingly men (nearly 3 million) (Davies and Ward 1992: 17, 29).

The downgrading of SERPS entailed negative consequences for women's benefits both as workers and wives. The most important changes were that benefits were to be calculated on the basis of average lifetime earnings instead of earnings from the twenty best years, and the replacement rate was reduced from 25 to 20 percent of final earnings. This formula not only lowers benefits but it also can act as a disincentive for part-time employment among women, especially in combination with pension credits for home responsibilities. A stipulation for receiving credits is the absence of earnings above the lower limit for contributions. The second negative change was that widows' pensions were cut in half – from 100 to 50 percent of their deceased husbands' benefit. Despite these changes, SERPS retained two positive features for women. A mother can receive credit for caring for children; second, pension benefits are guaranteed. Personal pensions do not guarantee benefits, and they do not give credits for being out of the labor market due to caring for children. However, the Social Security Act of 1989 made all paid maternity leave pensionable from 1993. Persons covered by SERPS are disadvantaged, however, since contributions are not tax deductible, as they are for employers' and personal pensions (Groves 1991).

The full force of these changes in the pension system for women will first be felt in the next century as SERPS matures. Bryn Davies and Sue Ward have estimated the effects of benefits based on lifetime earnings for women with intermittent work histories. Their estimates indicate SERPS benefits amounting to only between 5 to 8 percent of final earnings compared to benefits between 15 and 20 percent of final earnings for women working full time during their entire lives (Davies and Ward 1992: 48, 54).

The shift to means tested benefits

A second facet of Thatcher's retrenchment efforts, and continued by Major, has been a shift to means tested benefits and greater targeting. When Thatcher left office, spending on means tested programs as a proportion of the social security budget had grown from 16 percent in 1979/80 to 25 percent (calculated from the *Annual Abstract of Statistics* 1991: 48; cf. Hill 1990: 79), and during Major's governments its share continued to expand, amounting to nearly 35 percent in the mid-1990s (DNISR 1994: 139). The number of claimants of means tested benefits and persons provided for has also risen. Since 1980 the number of claimants of the major assistance benefit has nearly doubled. In the 1990s more than one-tenth of the population claimed Income Support and over 15 percent of the population were reliant on this program, and nearly one-quarter of the population received some sort of means tested benefit (Hills 1993: 41).

Greater targeting to help the worst off has been a principal argument to legitimize a conversion of benefits to means tested programs. Intensified targeting among recipients of means tested benefits has occurred, and in the process erosion of the national guarantee of assistance and disentitlement ensued. The 1988 reform substituting income support for supplementary benefit entailed greater targeting among recipients of means tested benefits rather than a shift in resources to the worst off groups (Berthoud 1987). The changeover reduced the number of claimants by half a million and the number of persons provided for fell by nearly 1 million (calculated from DSS 1989: 247, 368). The rolls of recipients were cut by raising the minimum age of claimants to 18 and lowering the number of permissible hours of employment of claimants to twenty-four hours a week. A peculiarity of public assistance in the UK is the exclusion of persons in full-time employment. The income support reform restored the former sex composition of recipients of public assistance: as in 1980 women once again substantially outnumbered men among the adults provided for by income support (Sainsbury 1993a: 94). In the early 1990s the government deployed the same tactic so that full employment for the purposes of claiming assistance was lowered from twenty-four to sixteen hours a week.

The shift to means tested benefits away from insurance benefits for the unemployed has been quite massive. Fewer of the unemployed received insurance benefits, and the number of the jobless receiving assistance benefits had increased nearly fourfold by the 1990s (DSS 1994: 149). This trend of increasing reliance on means tested benefits was further reinforced by the introduction of the Job Seeker's Allowance in the mid-1990s. The duration of flat rate contributory benefits was reduced from one year to six months so that the unemployed had to turn to means tested benefits after a shorter period without work (DNISR 1994: 131, EOB 1995: 7). In particular, this shift has penalized married women because they often fail to qualify for means tested benefits. In the early 1990s unemployed married women were much less likely to be claimants of income support or combined insurance benefits and income support than men and other women. The availability for work test was made more rigorous in the late 1980s, and several conditions made women more vulnerable to disqualification and withdrawal of benefits. These conditions may further discourage women from claiming benefits. Among the most important changes was that the claimant had to be available and accept full-time work. Nor could the claimant refuse a job after thirteen weeks on the grounds of the type of work, rate of pay, or traveling distance (Callender 1992: 136–8).

Along with the unemployed, solo mothers have become more reliant on means tested benefits. In the early 1990s 70 percent of lone parents relied on social assistance (Lister 1994c: 213), and the poverty rate of solo mothers has increased. The government's strategy in the 1990s appears to have been an attempt to change the income package of solo mothers from full reliance on assistance to a combination of earnings, means tested benefits, and maintenance payments (cf. Lister 1992). The main vehicle for this strategy has been Family Credit, an income tested program to aid families with low earnings, which replaced family income supplement in the late 1980s. Several features of Family Credit advantage solo mothers and attenuate the poverty trap. Solo mothers received the same benefits as two parent families; and child benefit, which is taken into account in determining the rate of assistance, does not count as income in the family credit scheme. Although over 40 percent of all families receiving family credit were headed by solo mothers in the mid-1990s (DSS 1994: 9), the program has not altered the employment patterns of solo mothers. Nor has it completely eliminated the unemployment trap. Gradually, recipients of family credit have become automatically eligible for several of the same benefits that followed from assistance. This development creates major disincentives to increasing earnings above the threshold for family credit, and together with the low number of minimum working hours (sixteen), it has the makings of an underemployment trap in low paid part-time jobs.

The shift to means tested benefits has also been accompanied by a strengthening of family responsibilities in determining benefits. The cohabitation rule, modified as the "living together as husband and wife rule," applies to means tested programs in assessing economic resources so that both formal and informal families are the unit of benefit. In the mid-1980s the full employment rule excluding persons from assistance was extended to partners (Lister 1992: 42). The most extreme case of elevating family relationships in determining women's social rights has been the Child Support Act of 1991. This made it obligatory for lone parents receiving means tested benefits (or if their current partner received these benefits) to apply for child maintenance from the absent parent. Mothers who fail to comply or refuse to disclose the identity of the father are penalized through benefit reductions (Lister 1994c, Land 1994b). Because the collected maintenance is deducted from their means tested benefits, mothers and their children on income support are no better off economically, while mothers receiving Family Credit can keep a small portion (£15 a week in the mid-1990s).

The twin shift to "private" and means tested benefits involves three major contradictions. Although one of the government's main social policy goals of the 1980s was that the social security system should help the needy (Barr and Coulter 1991: 277), the fiscal welfare associated with private benefits advantages the well off, functioning as "upside-down benefits" or "reverse targeting" (Sinfield 1993: 41–4). In the early 1990s tax relief for all non-state pensions totaled £9.3 billion compared with £7.5 billion spent on means tested benefits for the elderly (DNISR 1994: 134). A further contradiction in the Thatcherite project has been the emphasis on altering the incentive structure so that people will seek work rather than depend on benefits, while several features of means tested benefits are counterproductive in getting people into employment. The government has failed to eliminate the unemployment and poverty traps which are aggravated by linking eligibility to a series of benefits – income maintenance, housing benefits, council tax benefits, and certain medical and dental benefits. The thrust of the government's policy has meant that increasingly more people as recipients of means tested benefits have found themselves in this situation, and the poverty rate has doubled (Glennerster 1991: 170, Fritzell 1992: 26).

Finally, retrenchment has weakened the remaining vestiges of the male breadwinner model in the national insurance scheme, while the shift to occupational pensions and means tested benefits restores its influence. Several supplements based on the maintenance responsibilities of the family provider have been abolished, and women's entitlements derived from their family status as dependants deteriorated through major cuts in widow's benefits in the late 1980s. Simultaneously the weakening of the national insurance scheme and SERPS makes it more difficult for women to improve their entitlements as workers. The receipt of occupational pension benefits reflects an even stronger gendered differentiation in entitlements than that of national insurance benefits, and social provision through means tested benefits familializes entitlements.

The Netherlands: retrenchment tempered by solidarity and equivalence

In several respects, Dutch retrenchment efforts differed from those in the USA and Britain. The Dutch strategy in the 1980s focused on the reduction of benefit levels (both flat rate and earnings related programs) and shifting claimants to minimum benefits rather than reducing the number of beneficiaries. At the same time reforms individualizing benefits, increased entitlements. Thus the ability of the Dutch to stabilize expenditures on transfers as a proportion of the GDP entailed a reduction in real transfers per beneficiary which exceeded the increase in beneficiaries during the 1980s (OECD 1991a: 45).

The growing number of beneficiaries led to a further deterioration in the support ratio (the ratio of persons in the workforce to beneficiaries), causing worries about the financial viability of the social security system. This deterioration prompted a reorientation in strategy around 1990. In a major statement *Een werkend perspectief* (Jobs in the Future), the government gave priority to reducing the number of beneficiaries and getting people into paid employment.

An additional contrast was a Dutch preference for across the board reductions, whereas the British have constantly whittled away at benefits through a multitude of small cuts. Dutch policy makers directed their attention first to national insurance benefits and minimum benefits, which comprised the bulk of all benefits, and subsequently to employee insurance schemes providing earnings related benefits. Although the Dutch tightened eligibility requirements, this did not result in total disentitlement as in the USA because of the social minimum. Nor were assistance benefits initially singled out for the harsh treatment typical in the USA and the UK. When minimum benefits were cut, the worst off groups were compensated by annual lump-sum cash payments (1981–7), and supplements topped up earnings related benefits which fell below the social minimum. From the mid-1980s, however, campaigns to detect and reduce fraud in assistance programs have recurred (Cox 1994: 185–6, SCP 1995: 181–6).

Several of these differences appear related to societal values and the principles of solidarity and equivalence which are central to Dutch social provision. The principle of solidarity stipulates that the burden of contributions is to be shared by all insured persons according to their ability to pay – and benefits providing a flat rate minimum are to be available to all. This principle militates against exclusion from minimum benefits and falling below the social minimum. The principle of equivalence, which undergirds the employee insurance schemes, requires that benefits correspond to contributions. This principle was important in shaping the 1987 reform of unemployment benefits, which diverged from Reagan's and Thatcher's policies, and the disability benefits reform of the early 1990s.

The effects of these two principles on retrenchment efforts have had different consequences for women and men – and accordingly the gender bias of Dutch retrenchment. The principle of solidarity has aided both sexes in retaining a socially acceptable standard through minimum benefits. However, when minimum benefits are means tested the recipient is often the head of the household, and when this is not the case married and cohabiting women are usually ineligible because of their partner's earnings. The influence of the principle of equivalence in structuring unemployment and disability benefits reforms, as we shall see, has favored men with long contribution records.

Cuts and reforms

The newly installed center right government failed to upgrade national insurance benefits and subsequently cut minimum benefits and the minimum wage by 3 percent in 1984. More important because of its long-term effects, the minimum wage was frozen, and the link between it and the wage index was severed. As a result, minimum benefits were no longer indexed to wage trends in the private sector, but benefits were frozen since they were still tied to the minimum wage (SCP 1986: 92–3). For the rest of the decade the minimum wage remained frozen, increases in benefits were modest, and the gap between benefits and the average wage widened.

There is evidence that these policy moves had a stronger negative impact on women. Examining the annual lump sum grants paid to households managing entirely on a minimum income, we find that women were overrepresented (SCP 1986: 95). During the 1980s the poverty rate of solo mothers increased from 6 percent to 12 percent (Mitchell 1991: 68; Förster 1994: 199). Toward the end of the decade women were also more likely to head households with a disposable income below the social minimum compared to men (11 percent as against 6 percent in 1987) (SCP 1991: 137). The freezing of the minimum wage was also more detrimental to women than to men. Although only a small portion of the workforce are minimum wage earners, nearly two-thirds of them are women.

The fact that the social minimum continued to revolve around the family as norm has influenced retrenchment efforts and has heightened the importance of a partner's income. Women receiving assistance benefits have been subject to more controls as authorities sought to uncover "fraud" among single individuals and solo mothers claiming benefits while living with a partner. To cut costs new rules required divorced women to claim alimony in order to qualify for assistance (Holtmaat 1992: 347), a policy resembling and predating the British Child Support Act. The National Assistance Act scheduled to come into effect in January 1996 extends the work test to all partners and stiffens the work test of mothers who must be available for work unless they have a child under 6. The concern about a partner's earnings also resulted in introducing a means test in the "citizen" pension scheme (DNISR 1994: 107). Since the late 1980s the allowance for a spouse who is not entitled to a pension (younger than 65) has been means tested.

Turning to changes in the employee insurance schemes, an across the board cut was phased in between 1984 and 1986. The replacement rate was lowered from 80 percent to 70 percent of the daily wage in the case of sickness, unemployment, and disability benefits.[5] Subsequent efforts to cut earnings related benefits have concentrated on reforming unemployment and disablement insurance whose costs exceed those in most countries. (Each category of benefit absorbed between 4 and 6 percent of the GDP in the mid-1980s.) The 1987 reform of unemployment insurance, bringing short-term and extended benefits under one scheme, succeeded in putting a brake on costs. The new scheme introduced a complex scale of duration of benefits (six months to five years) based on age and years of employment. It lengthened the work test for extended benefits to three out of the last five years before unemployment, whereas previously the work test had been the same for short- and long-term benefits: twenty-six weeks during the year prior to unemployment. For older workers meeting the stiffer work test, the duration of earnings related benefits was increased from two to five years. It also continued to guarantee benefits for older workers until retirement, and the age for benefits until retirement was revised downwards.

The favorable outcome for older workers is best understood by the principle of equivalence. Older employees who have paid contributions during their entire working lives deserve decent benefits. At the same time this favorable treatment of older workers worked to the disadvantage of women. On the eve of the 1987 reform the labor market participation rate of older women (aged 55–65) was a mere 11 percent compared to nearly 45 percent for men in same age group. Unsurprisingly the sharpest disparity in the proportion of women and men collecting benefits was among older workers (SVR 1994: 34, 182), and only older workers could receive benefits for the maximum duration.[6]

In the early 1990s disability benefits were reformed, borrowing features of the 1987 unemployment insurance reform. The employment history as reflected in the age of the claimant determined both the duration of payment of a benefit of 70 percent of former earnings and the level of the follow up benefit. The new method of calculating disability benefits automatically excluded younger workers (32 and under) from the standard earnings related benefit, but they were guaranteed the social minimum. Older workers (59–64) could receive an earnings related benefit until they were eligible for an old age pension. The exclusion of younger workers disqualified one-third of the beneficiaries from regular benefits, but it took a higher toll of female beneficiaries – 20 percent compared to 10 percent of the male beneficiaries (calculated from SVR 1994: 128).

To sum up, the principles of solidarity and equivalence have had a moderating influence on retrenchment reforms in the Netherlands so that the outcome was quite different from measures introduced in the USA and the UK. In certain respects, however, both principles operated to the disadvantage of women. The principle of equivalence has favored older workers, while the female labor force is primarily composed of younger workers. Favorable treatment of older workers in earnings related schemes also works against women because the differentials in men's and women's wages and earnings increase with age (SCP 1993a: 142, 153). The principle of solidarity has safeguarded the social minimum as a right of Dutch citizens and residents but as benefits have been cut the social minimum has become more important, and it is based upon family responsibilities. The shift to means tested minimum benefits has been a negative aspect of the Dutch retrenchment process for women because this type of benefit disqualifies many married women, and it contains a powerful disincentive to engage in paid work. The generous Dutch social minimum has created an enormous threshold before a partner's earnings pay off. A married woman has to earn an annual income of 25,000 guilders before a single cent is added to net family income (Gustafsson and Bruyn-Hundt 1991: 36).

Windows of opportunity

The reorientation in the government's retrenchment strategy in 1990 – its emphasis on changing the unfavorable support ratio by getting people into employment – led to a major reversal in childcare policies. The government eliminated tax deductions for childcare costs, and the Childcare Incentive Act earmarked funds corresponding to the amount of earlier tax expenditures for the development of childcare centers. The Act was originally to provide childcare subsidies during 1990–3, producing an estimated twofold increase in full-time subsidized places in childcare centers, but it has been extended to 1997. It is too early to assess the effects of this policy change, but a doubling of places represents a modest increase in coverage from 2 to 4 percent (OECD 1990: 131, SCP 1993a: 209–11, Gustafsson 1994). Nonetheless it was a move from a "private" solution based on fiscal welfare toward greater public responsibility in funding childcare services – entailing a shift from consumer subsidies to producer subsidies – which was totally the opposite of policies in the USA.

Health insurance has also been reformed, and as a byproduct of the reforms women's individual rights to medical benefits have been strengthened. The goal of the reform, as formulated in the late 1980s, was "a regulated competitive market for health insurance" (Schneider et al. 1992, SCP 1990). The original reform plans envisioned substantial competition through marketization to achieve effectiveness and cost control. This was to be attained through the introduction of a basic insurance compulsory for all residents. Compulsory and voluntary insurance would no longer be determined by income but by the type of medical service. The basic insurance would provide a package of health and hospital services corresponding to most services covered by the Health Insurance Act (ZFW) and the Exceptional Medical Costs Act (AWBZ). No merger of the two types of insurance has occurred. Instead more services are to be assigned to the compulsory scheme (AWBZ). The transfer of medical benefits affects women's social rights because under AWBZ benefits are individual entitlements, whereas under ZFW married women have not been insured in their own right but as family members.

The retrenchment balance sheet for Dutch women is mixed, and it illustrates that the welfare state crisis can offer windows of opportunity. Negatively, the cuts in minimum benefits, the preferential treatment of older workers, and increased means testing undermined women's social rights. But the concurrent introduction of reforms to individualize women's social rights – not merely remove supplements for family members as in the UK – gave Dutch women new entitlements. The 1990 reorientation in retrenchment strategy emphasizing getting people into work has had contradictory consequences. On the one hand, this emphasis has created a favorable climate to establish eligibility requirements in employee insurance schemes that accommodate women's working patterns. It also resulted in a change in childcare policies from tax exemptions toward provision of care facilities. On the other hand, it strengthened the rationale for introducing work obligations for mothers with young children. Similarly, health insurance reforms helped to individualize medical benefits, at the same time as rising medical care costs have increased the pressure for "substitution" which relies on unpaid care in the home.

Sweden: the third way and its collapse

The Swedish program to contain costs in the 1980s diverged significantly from the retrenchment strategies pursued in the other three countries. Cost containment measures were embedded in a larger program for economic recovery. In one respect, however, there was a similarity between how the Dutch and Swedes dealt with cuts, which reflects the influence of the principle of solidarity. In both countries governments introduced across the board cuts combined with measures to compensate vulnerable groups. Cutbacks were characterized by efforts to distribute the negative effects across the entire population. In addition reforms which enhanced social entitlements were implemented. Despite these similarities, differences stand out in retrenchment efforts in the Netherlands and Sweden.

The first wave of retrenchment measures in Sweden was introduced by the non-socialist government from 1980 onwards.[7] When the Social Democrats returned to power in 1982, they reversed most of these measures and launched a program for economic recovery – The Third Way (Sainsbury 1991). The main thrust of their policy was to curb public sector spending. The government sought to stabilize social expenditures through a period of no new reforms and attempts to eliminate or reduce automatic increases. Second, new resources were pumped into the active labor market policy to stimulate jobs in construction, to create special work programs for young people, and to expand job training. Third, the government devalued the Swedish crown by 16 percent. The devaluation decreased the real value of wages and benefits; in effect it was an across the board cut for the entire population. By avoiding or postponing compensation for the 1982 devaluation, its negative effects were commonly shared. Simultaneously measures were introduced to cushion vulnerable groups: pensioners, families with children, students, and the unemployed. Once the economy revived, non-indexed benefits were upgraded and benefit levels restored.

Although this cost containment program does not seem very remarkable, especially in comparison to the retrenchment efforts of neo-liberal governments, the outcome in Sweden was similar to the other countries – a stabilization of social spending as a percentage of GDP in the 1980s. Simultaneously, the government transformed a central government budget deficit of 13 percent of GDP in 1983 to a modest surplus at the end of the decade, and the rate of unemployment was reduced to 1.6 percent. These promising developments in the economy encouraged the Social Democrats to introduce new reforms in the latter part of the decade. Among the reforms were better sickness benefits and unemployment benefits, especially for part-time workers, and the continued expansion of public day care and parental benefits. Swedish women's social entitlements generally improved during the 1980s (figure 4.1 and table 8.5), whereas in the other countries retrenchment undermined women's benefits during the decade.

Retrenchment efforts gained new momentum in the 1990s as the economy worsened, and unemployment began to rise. An initial target for cuts was sickness benefits followed by unemployment insurance. Payment of the first two weeks of sickness compensation was transferred to employers, the replacement rates for sickness and unemployment benefits were lowered from 90 to 80 percent of earnings, and employee contributions were introduced. By the mid-1990s retrenchment measures encompassed the entire cash transfer system. Because Sweden has approximated the institutional model of social policy, cuts have affected all citizens and residents in their everyday lives. Although the major reductions have been across the board cuts, lower benefits affect women's and men's standard of living differently. Benefits have generally contributed a larger portion of women's income packages compared to men's so that reductions often have a more substantial impact on women's livelihood. Taking an extreme example, transfers accounted for 50 percent of the disposable income of solo mothers in 1990, and for those with two or more children or preschool children, they amounted to around 60 percent (Jansson and Sandqvist 1993: 22–3). The effects of cuts are also more far-reaching when transfers constitute the sole source of income and provide minimum benefits. While insurance benefits comprise the single source of income for both sexes, men rarely have benefits which only afford a minimum income. However, unlike the USA and the UK, disentitlement has not been an integral part of retrenchment, and in contrast to the UK and the Netherlands, Swedish policy makers have shunned means tested programs. For the most part, gender bias has pertained to benefit levels – not disqualification from benefits or altering the bases of entitlement.

In the mid-1990s the Social Democrats returned to office, and they gave top priority to reducing the budget deficit, which had climbed to 13 percent of GNP in 1993. To consolidate central government finances they proposed spending cuts and revenue increases, amounting to approximately 60 billion crowns during the following four years (SAP 1994: 14). Given this amount, no aspect of the transfer system was spared, and the government presented a tough program of cuts and tax increases. The 1995–6 budget statement estimated a decrease in the disposable incomes of households because of cuts in transfers by 3 percent and increases in direct taxes – primarily social insurance premiums and lower tax allowances – of 10.5 percent (R&D 1995/15: 3).

The Social Democrats' program to consolidate state finances hit women very hard. Although it was designed so that the wealthiest paid a larger share than others, the government's budget estimates noted that cuts in disposable income were deepest for the lowest income groups and households with children (SB 1995: 70–4). In justifying the program, the government emphasized the necessity to cut cash transfers to households in order to maintain high quality public services (SB 1995: 68–9). More specific proposals were a further reduction of the replacement rates of earnings related benefits to 75 percent, including parental benefits, a 16 percent cut in child allowances, and the elimination of larger allowances for families with several children (three or more). Nor did proposed reforms of advanced maintenance allowances and pensions bode well for women.

In April 1995 an inquiry commission, appointed by the non-socialist government, recommended that advanced maintenance allowances should not be paid to children whose parents had high incomes. The most controversial proposal, and in total opposition to individualization, was that half of the income of a current partner should be taken into account in determining eligibility and the allowance amount. The commission fixed the ceiling at such a high annual income (over 300,000 crowns) that only 0.1 percent of solo parents would be disqualified and less than 5 percent would receive reduced allowances based on their own earnings. However, the proposed measures potentially affected as many as one-third of mothers through their partner's income (SOU 1995: 375–97). The Social Democratic government did not follow the commission's recommendation. It chose to strengthen revenues by enlarging the support obligations of fathers whose share in the funding of advanced maintenance allowances had successively declined. In the 1990s the payments of non-custodial parents had dropped to around one-third of the expenditure on the allowances.

A major overhaul of the pension system has been on the policy agenda since the mid-1980s, and a reform backed by all the parties is scheduled for adoption by parliament. The reform does not alter the double-decker character of the pension system. The basic pension is to be raised substantially. As a step in harmonizing Swedish social policy with the EU the conditions of entitlement were changed from citizenship to residence for a period of forty years. This change and its possible repercussions have not received much attention. Currently nearly all elderly persons in Sweden receive a basic pension but the exclusionary effects of forty years of residence during one's adult life may lower the recipient rate, making the ATP the main source of pension income – a development which could be disastrous for women.

More debate and investigation has centered on the elimination of two features of the earnings related pension, which have aided many women: benefits based on the fifteen best years of earnings and a work history of only thirty years to qualify for a full pension. Instead the reform proposes to calculate benefits on lifetime earnings, and to strengthen pension rights based on parenting in two ways. Besides the existing arrangement of parental benefits counting toward the state earnings related pension, the previous earnings of the caregiver would be topped up to 75 percent of the average income and they would be granted one basic amount irrespective of employment or earnings (Ståhlberg 1995: 15–18). Married couples would also have the option to combine and split their income counting toward the ATP pension.

In summary, the main retrenchment measures in the 1990s to date have been a myriad of cuts affecting virtually all benefits and allowances. The most extensive cuts have been the successive lowering of the replacement rates of unemployment insurance, sickness benefits, and parental allowances from 90 to 75 percent of earnings. These reductions represented deeper cuts than those undertaken by the neo-liberal governments in the other three countries. In this respect, Swedish policy makers appear more resolute in their efforts to trim the welfare state, intimating a move in a residualist direction. On the other hand, several features of Swedish strategy lend themselves to another interpretation. Writing in the late 1980s Ramesh Mishra argued that Swedish strategy and policies during that decade could be described as "welfare state maintenance" (1990: 2). In the mid-1990s the strategy appeared to be a downsizing to maintain four aspects of Swedish social provision which constitute its distinctiveness, and which are crucial to women's social rights: universal public services, basic security reflected in "citizen" benefits, income security provided by earnings related benefits, and minimal reliance on means tested benefits. The contours of this strategy emerge most clearly in those choices that differ from the retrenchment efforts in the other countries. Although the Social Democratic government initiated massive cuts in the cash transfer system, priority has been assigned to preserving equal access to high quality public services. The Social Democrats have chosen not to introduce means tested benefits. For example, they decided to cut universal child allowances rather than make them means tested. Downsizing is also evident in the government's choice of across the board reductions in earnings related benefits. A final indication of a strategy to maintain the welfare state is that Swedish governments have substantially increased the funding of social provision. Cuts in transfers have been combined with the introduction of *pro rata* fees on earnings of insured persons to bolster the finances of unemployment and sickness insurance, along with the ATP pension system.

Conclusion

Retrenchment efforts across nations reveal a number of commonalities and similar outcomes. The similarities have caused speculations about a convergence in welfare state policies. They have become more residualist, and European welfare state policies increasingly resemble those of the USA (e.g. Haveman et al. 1986, Brown 1988). The prevalence of cutbacks and their negative consequences for beneficiaries have also fostered the idea that it makes little difference what choices governments make.

The preceding analysis points to more variation in the choices of policy makers than suggested by the convergence thesis, and I have argued that retrenchment strategies and the existing policy constructions have influenced the impact on women's and men's entitlements. Cuts in benefits have significant consequences, but more important are structural changes which alter the basis of entitlements, such as shifts to market provision and means testing, or the lack of policies to eliminate inequalities in women's and men's social rights.

Instead of convergence, four distinct patterns emerge from a comparison of the policies of the countries since 1980. Looking at US policies the lack of change both with respect to the breadwinner model and the residual model is striking. In 1980 US policies most closely approximated the residual model. Means tested programs were more prominent in social provision, major statutory programs were lacking, and private provision through employer sponsored benefits was more prevalent. Despite the twin shift to private and means tested benefits in the UK, the USA continued to be the nearest fit of the residual model in the mid-1990s because of the incomplete nature of its welfare state and its poorer record in alleviating poverty. Retrenchment measures strengthened dual welfare. Efforts were made to downsize the existing bifurcated welfare state.

Three features of US retrenchment intensified the residualist aspects of social provision and deepened the inequalities in women's and men's entitlements. The retrenchment strategy of the Reagan administrations and the Contract with America concentrated on reducing the number of people eligible for benefits, and the majority of those removed from the rolls or slated for future disentitlement have been women. Second, during the Reagan years the private sector became even more important in social provision than it had been. Fiscal welfare increased, for-profit services expanded, and private welfare expenditures rose, accounting for roughly 40 percent of social spending in 1990 (Kerns 1992: 59). Coverage in the third tier of welfare stagnated in the 1980s, and women's coverage lags behind men's in all occupational categories. The expansion of fiscal welfare as the main economic support to families with children has blocked the introduction of benefits based on the principle of care, such as child allowances or care allowances. For most women, motherly tasks are rewarded primarily through entitlements as wives. Third, benefits in the welfare tier were meager, and they have deteriorated since the mid-1970s. Simultaneously the poverty rate, which was the highest of the four countries in 1980, also increased, and the gender poverty gap was widest in the late 1980s. The sex segregation of the two tiers of public provision and the differing rates of effectiveness in removing beneficiaries from poverty have contributed to the feminization of poverty. Welfare benefits lift a smaller percentage of recipients out of poverty compared to social security benefits. Within the social security tier the continued influence of the breadwinner model on women's benefits and the disparity between women's and men's coverage in the third tier of occupational welfare increase the risk of poverty among older women. The bifurcation of social policy not only aggravates women's poverty, it has also impeded the development of comprehensive employment and childcare policies. As long as these policies remain in the welfare tier, it is unlikely that they will generate broad popular support or provide the foundation to build toward the individual model of social policy.

Changes in British social provision have been the most dramatic since 1980 through the twin shift to "private" and means tested benefits and policies have moved in a residualist direction closer to those of the USA. In this respect, retrenchment in the UK represents a restructuring of income maintenance policies and conforms with the convergence thesis. Both occupational and personal pensions increased in importance, and during the 1980s private pension payments inched ahead of public pensions (Barr and Coulter 1991: 294). The extent of the shift to means tested benefits is apparent in the increase in expenditures on this type of benefit as a proportion of social security spending, which virtually doubled, and the growing proportion of the population receiving means tested benefits. This development contrasts with the USA where the share of households receiving means tested benefits has been relatively stable since 1980.

The twin shift has eroded national insurance benefits. The simultaneous restructuring of the economy through flexibilization poses a double hindrance to women's entitlements as workers. Many are likely to qualify for neither insurance benefits nor occupational benefits. Even more than the national insurance scheme, occupational benefits and means tested benefits reflect the influence of the breadwinner model in making the husband the beneficiary and leaving married women without individual entitlement. This erosion in entitlements heightens the importance of benefits based on the principle of care for women's individual rights, which may lead to a more pronounced gendered dualism in women's and men's entitlements.

Dutch social provision is at odds with the convergence thesis because changes toward the institutional model have offset moves in a residualist direction. In certain respects Dutch policies have entailed a restructuring toward both the institutional and individual models of social policy. Coverage of the Dutch population was extended through the individualization of entitlement to benefits during the 1980s and 1990s. Efforts to marketize health insurance may ironically lead to the conversion of the dual insurance system into a single scheme covering the entire population and the demise of the Health Insurance Act (ZFW), which is currently the most familialized scheme. Child allowances, earlier based on the insurance model with the father as beneficiary, are now universal benefits awarded to the mother. Women's increased labor market participation, which grew more rapidly in the 1980s than in the other three countries, enlarged their entitlements to benefits in the employee insurance scheme because qualifying conditions posed low hurdles.[8] While individualization reforms have accorded women social rights and equalized entitlements within marriage, few policies have been put in place to alter the gendered division of women as caregivers and men as earners.

The main residualization was the growing importance of means tested benefits as both recipients and expenditures rose, but this trend was reversed in the 1990s (SVR 1994: 14). The introduction of new means tested measures since the mid-1980s apparently has not produced a marked increase in the number of assistance beneficiaries, but the inability of many married women to claim these benefits may be a dampening factor. In short, since 1980 there has been a simultaneous shift toward universal and means tested benefits which affected women's entitlements in contradictory ways – "citizen" benefits enhance their social rights while means tested benefits have undermined them. The performance of these two types of benefit in alleviating women's poverty in the 1980s was also strikingly different. Elderly women receiving universal pensions scarcely experienced poverty, whereas the poverty rate of solo mothers whose prime source of income was often assistance benefits rose during the decade and in the late 1980s they had a higher poverty rate than the rest of the population.

The key features of Swedish social provision, despite cutbacks, still approximated the institutional model in the mid-1990s. Entitlement to universal benefits based on citizenship or residence has not been altered.

Provision of day care has expanded since 1980, with the aim of making childcare services a public good and coverage universal for preschool children. The goal has not been accomplished but coverage corresponded more closely to demand than fifteen years ago. The non-socialists' efforts to privatize services in the care sector yielded modest results. At the end of their term in office (1991–4) the number of private employees in the care sector was a mere 6 percent (R&D 1995 (22/23): 16; Ds 1995: 25). Coverage of the population expanded primarily through women's increased entitlements as workers, which in contrast to the Netherlands encompassed the vast majority of working age women. The cuts in Swedish insurance benefits have been the most sweeping, but benefit levels remain high in relation to the other three countries. Lastly, means tested benefits continued to play a negligible role. High unemployment rates in the early 1990s did not produce a major increase in utilization of assistance benefits, and no means tested benefits were introduced.[9] So far the current downsizing of the Swedish welfare state has not entailed a restructuring in a residualist direction.

Cuts in benefits impose hardships on women, especially women with low incomes, and lower replacement rates can also reinforce mothers' utilization of parental benefits. Nevertheless, a downsizing strategy which maintains the basic features of Swedish social provision upholds women's social rights. As argued throughout this book, entitlements based on citizenship or residence are pivotal to the individual model of social policy by eliminating social rights mediated through family relationships. Means tested benefits jeopardize individual entitlement and financial independence by creating disincentives for paid employment. Even more important to women's entitlements is the social service state. Public services have aided women as consumers, as workers, and as mothers, and public responsibility for childcare has facilitated combining employment and motherhood. Nearly all women are employed, providing them with both an independent income through earnings and access to work related social benefits. The coupling of benefits derived from labor market status and care has eroded the distinction between paid and unpaid work in social provision, and it may offer the key to ending a gendered differentiation in entitlements where women receive benefits solely as caregivers and men solely as earners.

Notes

INTRODUCTION

1 Examples of model recipients whose assumed characteristics may not be very representative are the married production worker whose wife is a homemaker or the female worker employed in manufacturing industry.

1 MAINSTREAM WELFARE STATE VARIATIONS

1 Another criticism of Esping-Andersen's analysis, which also may be a source of the anomalies, has to do with problems of reliability and validity. One example is his scores measuring decommodification through unemployment insurance where the Netherlands tops the list while the US, the UK, and Sweden are very similar, though the scores of the US and the UK are slightly higher. The scores are calculated on the basis of formal program characteristics, such as benefit levels, work tests, and duration of benefits, rather than the compensation actually paid to the unemployed in each country. Using this sort of measure, which is arguably better, alters the rank order as follows: Sweden, the UK, and the USA.

2 At the same time one must be aware of two drawbacks of spending as an indicator of welfare state effort. First, differences in demographic composition of populations (the proportion of elderly or children) can affect the size of spending "automatically". Second, social spending as a percentage of GDP can be misleading as an indicator of welfare commitment over time. In this instance, differences in the growth of the GDP are not taken into account. For example, in the 1970s through the early 1980s social expenditures as a percentage of the GDP increased rapidly in Sweden and Denmark, while the increase in Norway was sluggish, yet real growth in social expenditures in Norway was greater than in Sweden or Denmark (Johansen 1986).

3 Of the OECD countries only Spain had a lower employment/population ratio in 1980 than the Netherlands.

4 In cross-national comparisons of density of union membership Sweden generally ranks at the top, whereas the Netherlands is at the lower end of the scale. In the early 1980s between 80 and 85 percent of Swedish employees were organized in unions, but in the Netherlands the figure was only around 40 percent (Wallerstein 1989: 482; cf. Korpi 1983: 31) and had fallen to about 30 percent toward the end of the decade (SYN 1988: 146).

5 A reorganization reform transformed the Labor Councils into regional offices of the Social Insurance Bank in 1988. The corporatist nature of the councils was

retained in the representative composition of the regional offices at the same time as it was modified. The board of the offices consisted of representatives of employees, employers, and government appointed representatives with preference given to womens' and pensioners' organizations (SZW 1990: 8–10). In the 1990s the corporatist administration of benefits has come under fire, and the Industrial Boards are scheduled for reform (SCP 1995).

6 Although voluntarism has declined over the years, it is still important in services, such as home helps and day care.

7 For one of the clearest statements on citizenship as participation in politics and the sharing of social goods, see Nils Karleby's discussion on the "problem of taking part" (Karleby 1926: 87–102).

8 Earnings related supplements (ERS) were available in the case of unemployment and sickness benefits, and widow's pensions from 1966 to 1982, and a state superannuation scheme (SERPS) providing earnings related benefits to supplement the flat rate pension was being phased in.

3 THE MALE BREADWINNER MODEL AND WOMEN'S ENTITLEMENTS AS WIVES

1 Dutch family law, liberalized in 1971, introduced no fault divorce on the grounds of "lasting dislocation" (Kooy 1977).

2 Correspondence from Riki Holtmaat, 20 March 1995.

3 Beveridge's recommendation for the qualifying age for a widow's pension was more in line with that recently adopted in the USA. He proposed that it be set at 60 (Groves 1983: 45–6).

4 The 1913 Swedish old age insurance scheme was to be fully phased in by the 1950s. Compulsory insurance was combined with a means tested supplement, which in practice served as a meager pension for the needy elderly until the 1946 reform (Elmér 1960).

5 Widow's pensions were first introduced in 1919 in the Netherlands, in 1925 in the UK, and mothers' pensions for needy widowed mothers at the state level in the USA during 1911–30 in forty-four states.

6 Statistics on women's labor market participation rates vary depending on the source. OECD statistics provide one picture, with the highest rates in Sweden followed by the USA, the UK, and no figures for the Netherlands (OECD 1982: 33). National census data furnish a very different picture of higher participation rates of British women compared to US and Swedish women. Part of the difference is explained by dissimilar definitions of the economically active population which comprises everyone above the age of 15, while in the UK the economically active have been defined as persons below pension age, and the retirement age for women is 60.

4 WOMEN'S ENTITLEMENTS AS MOTHERS AND CAREGIVERS

1 David Ellwood (1988) has estimated that to be better off than a non-working AFDC mother, a mother with two children would need a full-time job paying US$5 per hour during the mid-1980s. The minimum wage was then US$3.35.

2 The measures of the economic resources of single parent families in relation to two parent families are based on data from the Swedish income distribution surveys (HINK). It needs to be pointed out that the picture presented here of the well-being of mother only families relative to two parent families differs substantially from the results of analyses using "profile" or "model" families (Heclo and Cockburn 1974, Heidenheimer et al. 1975: 211, Adams and Winston 1980, Kamerman and Kahn 1983). Calculations using "profile" families typically suggest that solo mothers who are employed have a higher disposable income than two parent families with a single earner. In the real world this is seldom the case.

3 The differences in the estimates of mothers receiving maternity benefits in the USA is due to dissimilar focuses of the surveys. The lower estimate from the *1990 National Child Care Survey* pertains to leave after the birth of the youngest child, and the higher estimate from the Current Population Report refers to leave in connection with the birth of the first child.

4 To qualify for maternity benefits, part-time employees in the Netherlands had to work at least fourteen hours a week or two days a week and earn at least 40 percent of the minimum wage.

5 To be eligible for maternity pay in the UK a woman had to have two years of continuous service with the same employer and have worked at least sixteen hours a week or five years of continuous employment and worked at least eight hours a week.

5 WOMEN'S EMPLOYMENT AND ENTITLEMENTS AS WORKERS

1 Older statistics have generally underestimated women's economic activity in a variety of ways, and contemporary figures overstate female labor market participation so that the picture of change may be exaggerated. Earlier statistics did not always count family workers and persons working a limited number of hours as economically active. Conversely present-day labor market participation rates tend to inflate women's involvement in paid work. Current participation rates in some countries are based on fewer hours of work compared to the past, and unemployed women or those absent from work are included in the labor force (cf. Nyberg 1991, de Vroom and Blomsma 1991: 97).

2 For an interesting analysis of time spent in paid work based on the working age population instead of the labor force, see Jonung and Persson (1993).

3 The spouse benefit is 50 percent of the insured worker's benefit. Because the benefit calculation weights lower earnings more heavily, a wife must earn approximately 30 percent – rather than 50 percent – of her husband's earnings (Iams 1993: 31) to qualify for benefits based entirely as a worker.

4 In the early 1980s the contribution rates levied against earnings up to the lower limit were higher than upon earnings between the lower and upper income limits, and the employers' rate was nearly double that paid by employees (DHSS 1981: 227).

5 In 1980 the average gross and net weekly earnings of female part-time workers were a mere £6 and £2 above the contributions threshold respectively and their gross earnings were £2.50 above the income tax threshold (Hakim 1989: 498; Martin and Roberts 1984: 43).

6 The work test for Dutch unemployment benefits was 130 days (twenty-six weeks or six months) during the previous twelve month period. The Unemployment Insurance Act generally assumed a full working week of five days, but employees working a shorter work week had to work a minimum of sixty-five days (SZW 1982: 40–1). In effect these rules imposed a longer qualification period (thirty-two weeks or roughly eight months) for the employee who barely met the minimum requirements of the insurance definition compared to the regular full-time worker. After the 1987 reform the requirement for short-term benefits did not specify days or hours, only the number of weeks, and for extended benefits the requirement was a minimum of eight hours per week for three years out of five (SZW 1990: 50–1). In the mid-1990s the requirement was at least fifty-two days per year (SZW 1995).

7 The work test for ATP disability benefits consisted of minimum earnings during two of the four previous years or during three years for a longer period in the past.

8 To qualify for unemployment insurance benefits, the Swedish worker had to be employed five months out of the previous year and to have worked at least ten days and at least seventy hours per month.

6 ACCESS TO BENEFITS AND THE STRATIFYING EFFECTS OF BASES OF ENTITLEMENT

1 Married women were neither regarded nor recorded as recipients of the old age pension in official statistics. In 1980 these "invisible recipients" – wives of married men receiving family pensions – accounted for nearly half of the female beneficiaries (*Statistical Yearbook* 1984: 358).

2 Schemes to protect US workers from loss of income because of short-term illness consist of self-insurance, group insurance plans, and paid sick leave provided through labor management negotiations, employer sponsored fringe benefits, or mandatory social insurance protection in a few states.

3 In 1965 Swedish housewives as insured individuals entitled to cash benefits numbered over one million; in 1980 their numbers had fallen to 350,000 and in the latter part of the decade to under 100,000 (*Allmän försäkring* 1980: 35, RFV 1989: 15). Since 1986 the possibility of insuring spouses at home has been eliminated. But spouses already insured remained covered as long as there is no change in their income and they do not take out voluntary sickness insurance.

4 Available statistics make no distinction between the two Dutch disability insurance schemes.

5 Prior to the 1980 equal rights legislation the eligibility of Dutch married women in the national disability insurance scheme was restricted. The equal rights legislation came into force retroactively from 1 January 1979.

6 The UK differs from the other three countries and most OECD countries where women's unemployment rates are generally higher than men's.

7 In a era of increased global migration this basis of entitlement may have greater potential for stratification among citizens and non-citizens as well as among denizens and newcomers irrespective of their citizenship.

7 BENEFIT INEQUALITIES AND REDISTRIBUTIVE OUTCOMES

1 A replication of table 7.1 using the latest available data (1993) reveals slightly higher proportions of women beneficiaries but the same basic pattern (DSS 1994: 187, 193, 243).

2 The benefit formula of the state earnings related pension scheme (SERPS) is less disadvantageous for women, but the female/male differential has widened over the years. Women's benefits relative to men's fell from 0.77 in the mid-1980s to 0.63 in the early 1990s (calculated from DSS 1994: 122–3).

3 Sickness benefits in the Netherlands show the largest gender benefit gap in available statistics. On average women's benefits have been approximately 55 percent of men's over the years (calculated from SVR 1994: 72).

4 Kirsten Scheiwe's analysis of German pensions reveals that the average benefits of women were only 40 percent of those of men in the old *Länder*.

5 Over-estimations of poverty among single individuals may occur as the result of the Swedish definition of family. Young adults with an income but living with their parents are counted as separate families.

8 GENDER EQUALITY REFORMS AND THEIR IMPACT

1 Not all gender neutral reforms have extended rights to British women. In equalizing the pension ages of women and men, the government finally opted for raising the retirement age of women from 60 to 65. This change is scheduled to be phased in over a ten-year period during the second decade of the 21st century (DNISR 1994: 132).

2 The large percentage of fathers among public sector employees who take parental leave reflects the male dominance of the Dutch civil service – nearly three-quarters of civil servants are men.

3 In the 1970s the Swedish spouse allowance amounted to 5 percent of the average earnings of a production worker, and total tax relief for the couple was around 10 percent. This contrasted with the other countries where the "housewife bonus" ranged between 10 and 15 percent, and standard deductions for a couple totaled between 30 and 35 percent of the average earnings of a production worker (calculated from OECD 1977).

4 The abolition of the ATP widow pension affects women born after 1945. The rationale for the change was that these women will have an ATP pension in their own right as workers.

9 WELFARE STATE RETRENCHMENT

1 Looking at the social expenditures of the four countries as a percentage of the GDP, it is virtually impossible to detect the effects of policy changes since spending was nearly the same in 1980 and 1990 (OECD 1994b: 59–60).

2 For another variant, inspired by the residual and institutional models, which conceives of retrenchment as a deinstitutionalizing process, see Mishra 1990: 18–19, 34.

3 The programs whose beneficiaries were held in check were AFDC, food stamps, and disability insurance and Medicaid until 1987 (SSB 1991: 305, 307, 185, 272).

4 For a description of the sustained cuts of unemployment benefits during the 1980s, see Atkinson and Micklewright (1989).

5 The cut in the replacement rate in the Dutch employee insurance schemes, however, did not apply to maternity benefits whose replacement rate remained at 100 percent of earnings. A possible explanation of this generosity is that a cut in maternity benefits would not have yielded major savings compared to other benefits. In the mid-1980s only 20 percent of all mothers received maternity benefits under the employee insurance scheme, and their duration was relatively short (12 weeks) (DHSS 1988b).

6 In 1995 the Dutch reversed the preferential treatment of older workers by introducing a uniform duration for extended unemployment benefits for all employees who met a stiffer work test (four out of five years). One aspect of the work test, however, took women's employment patterns into account: employment during a year was a minimum of *fifty-two days* of paid work (SZW 1995).

7 The retrenchment measures introduced by the Swedish non-socialist government in the early 1980s included reductions of benefits, a change in the principles of indexation lowering benefit levels, tightening of eligibility criteria, and a proposal to reintroduce two waiting days for sickness benefits (Olsson 1990: 225).

8 The extension of Dutch entitlements also runs counter to the mainstream discussion on retrenchment which has highlighted the contraction of social entitlements, often in contrast to the era of welfare state expansion (e.g. Stephens et al. 1995). This picture of rollback and stagnation in entitlements is based on analysis which has failed to distinguish between women's and men's social rights.

9 The proportion of the Swedish population receiving social assistance did increase from around 6 percent in the late 1980s – a period of economic boom – to 8 percent in 1994 when unemployment was high. But only 8 percent of recipient households – or 0.8 percent of all households – received benefits during the entire year (SOS 1995: 10, 32, 58).

References

Abel-Smith, Brian (1983) "Sex equality and social security," in Jane Lewis (ed.), *Women's Welfare, Women's Rights*. London: Croom Helm.

Abrahamson, Peter E. (1991) "Welfare and poverty in the Europe of the 1990s: social progress or social dumping?," *International Journal of Health Services*, 21, 237–64.

Abramovitz, Mimi (1988) *Regulating the Lives of Women: Social Welfare Policy from Colonial Times to the Present*. Boston: South End Press.

Abukhanfusa, Kerstin (1987) *Piskan och moroten. Om könens tilldelning av skyldigheter och rättigheter*. Stockholm: Carlssons.

Adams, Carolyn Teich and Winston, Kathryn Teich (1980) *Mothers at Work: Public Policies in the United States, Sweden and China*. New York: Longman.

AKU (Various years) *Arbetskraftsundersökningnen. Råtabeller*. Stockholm: Central Bureau of Statistics.

Allardt, Erik (1986) "The civic conception of the welfare state in Scandinavia," in Richard Rose and Rei Shiratori (eds.), *The Welfare State East and West*. New York: Oxford University Press.

Allmän försäkring (Selected years) Stockholm: National Social Insurance Board.

AMS [National Labor Market Board) (1980) *Meddelande från Statistiksektionen*. Stockholm: National Labor Market Board.

(1981) *De erkända arbetslöshetskassornas verksamhet och Det kontanta arbets-marknadsstödet år 1980*. Stockholm: National Labor Market Board.

(1990) *Rapport från Utredningsenheten 1990: 12*. Stockholm: National Labor Market Board.

Annual Abstract of Statistics (Various years) London: HMSO.

Ashford, Douglas (1986) *The Emergence of Welfare States*. Oxford: Blackwell.

Atkinson, A. B. (1989) *Poverty and Social Security*. New York: Harvester Wheatsheaf.

Atkinson, Tony and Micklewright, John (1989) "Turning the screw: benefits for the unemployed 1979–1988," in Andrew Dilnot and Ian Walker (eds.), *The Economics of Social Security*. Oxford: Oxford University Press.

Baldock, Cora V. and Cass, Bettina (eds.) (1983) *Women, Social Welfare and the State in Australia*. Sydney: George Allen and Unwin.

Baldwin, Sally and Falkingham, Jane (eds.) (1994) *Social Security and Social Change: New Challenges to the Beveridge Model*. New York: Harvester Wheatsheaf.

Barr, Nicholas and Coulter, Fiona (1990) "Social security: solution or problem?," in John Hills (ed.), *The State of Welfare*. Oxford: Oxford University Press.

Bawden, D. Lee and Palmer, John L. (1984) "Social policy, challenging the welfare state," in John L. Palmer and Isabel V. Sawhill (eds.), *The Reagan Record*. Cambridge: Ballinger.

Bergmann, Barbara (1986) *The Economic Emergence of Women*. New York: Basic Books.

Berkowitz, Monroe, Johnson, William J. and Murphy, Edward H. (1976) *Public Policy Toward Disability*. New York: Praeger Publishers.

Berthoud, Richard (1987) "New means tests for old: the Fowler plan for social security," in Maria Brenton and Clare Ungerson (eds.), *The Year Book of Social Policy 1986–1987*. London: Longman.

Bock, Gisela and Thane, Pat (eds.) (1991) *Maternity and Gender Policies: Women and the Rise of the European Welfare States, 1880s–1950s*. London: Routledge.

Bolderson, Helen (1988) "Comparing social policies: some problems of method and the case of social security in Australia, Britain and the USA," *Journal of Social Policy*, 17, 267–88.

Borchorst, Anette (1994) "Welfare state regimes, women's interests and the EC," in Diane Sainsbury (ed.), *Gendering Welfare States*. London: Sage.

Borchorst, Anette and Siim, Birte (1984) *Kvinder og velfærdstaten. Mellam moderskab og lønarbejde i 100 år*. Aalborg: Aalborg University Press.

(1987) "Women and the advanced welfare state – a new kind of patriarchal power?," in Anne Showstack Sassoon (ed.), *Women and the State*. London: Hutchinson.

Bradshaw, Jonathan and Millar, Jane (1991) *Lone Parent Families in the UK*. London: HMSO.

Bradshaw, Jonathan, Ditch, John, Holmes, Hilary and Whiteford, Peter (1993) *Support for Children. A Comparison of Arrangements in Fifteen Countries*. London: HMSO.

Brenton, Maria (1982) "Changing relationships in Dutch social services," *Journal of Social Policy*, 11, 59–80.

Brocas, Anne-Marie, Cailloux, Anne-Marie and Oget, Virginia (1990) *Women and Social Security: Progress Toward Equality of Treatment*. Geneva: International Labor Office.

Brown, Joan and Small, Stephen (1985) *Maternity Benefits*. London: The Public Policy Institute.

Brown, Michael K. (1988) "Remaking the welfare state: a comparative perspective," in Michael K. Brown (ed.), *Remaking the Welfare State: Retrenchment and Social Policy in America and Europe*. Philadelphia: Temple University Press.

Bruegel, Irene (1983) "Women's employment, legislation and the labour market," in Jane Lewis (ed.), *Women's Welfare, Women's Rights*. London: Croom Helm.

Bryson, Lois (1992) *The State and Welfare: Who Benefits?*, London: Macmillan.

Burtless, Gary (1986) "Public spending for the poor: trends, prospects and economic limits," in Sheldon H. Danziger and Daniel H. Weinberg (eds.), *Fighting Poverty*. Cambridge: Harvard University Press.

Bussemaker, Jet (1991) "Equality, autonomy and feminist politics," in Elizabeth Meehan and Selma Sevenhuijsen (eds.), *Equality Politics and Gender*. London: Sage.

Bussemaker, Jet and van Kersbergen, Kees (1994) "Gender and welfare states: some theoretical reflections," in Diane Sainsbury (ed.), *Gendering Welfare States.* London: Sage.

Callender, Claire (1987) "Redundancy, unemployment and poverty," in Caroline Glendinning and Jane Millar (eds.), *Women and Poverty in Britain.* Brighton: Wheatsheaf.

(1992) "Redundancy, unemployment and poverty," in Caroline Glendinning and Jane Millar (eds.), *Women and Poverty in Britain, the 1990s.* New York: Harvester Wheatsheaf.

Casper, Lynne M., McLanahan, Sara and Garfinkel, Irwin (1994) "The gender–poverty gap: what we can learn from other countries," *American Sociological Review,* 59, 594–605.

Castles, Francis G. (1978) *The Social Democratic Image of Society.* London: Routledge and Kegan Paul.

Castles, Francis G. and Mitchell, Deborah (1990) *Three Worlds of Welfare Capitalism or Four?,* Public Policy Discussion Paper No 21. Canberra: Australian National University.

(1992) "Identifying welfare state regimes: the links between politics, instruments and outcomes," *Governance,* 5, 1–26.

(1993) "Worlds of welfare and families of nations," in Francis G. Castles (ed.), *Families of Nations: Patterns of Public Policy in Western Democracies.* Aldershot: Dartmouth.

CBS [Central Bureau of Statistics] (1976) *Echtscheidingen in Nederland 1900–1974.* 's-Gravenhage: Staatsuitgeverij.

(1985) *Arbeidskrachtentelling 1981.* Part 1. 's-Gravenhage: Staatsuitgeverij/cbs-publikaties.

(1993) *Statistiek van de algemene bijstand 1990–1991.* 's-Gravenhage: sdu/uitgeverij/cbs-publikaties.

Chamberlayne, Prue (1993) "Women and the state: changes in roles and rights in France, West Germany, Italy and Britain, 1970–1990," in Jane Lewis (ed.), *Women and Social Policies in Europe: Work, Family, and the State.* Aldershot: Edward Elgar.

Cm 931. *Statutory Sick Pay Regulations 1990.* London: HMSO.

Cohen, Bronwen and Clarke, Karen (1986) *Childcare and Equal Opportunities.* London: HMSO.

Cohen, Bronwen and Fraser, Neil (1991) *Childcare in a Modern Welfare System.* London: Institute of Public Policy Research.

Cox, Robert H. (1993) *The Development of the Dutch Welfare State: From Workers' Insurance to Universal Entitlement.* Pittsburgh: University of Pittsburgh Press.

CPR (Current Population Reports) (1982) Series P-60, No. 131. *Characteristics of Households and Persons Receiving Selected Noncash Benefits 1980.* Washington, DC: US Bureau of the Census.

(1983a) Special Studies Series P-23, No. 129. *Child Care Arrangements of Working Mothers.* Washington, DC: US Bureau of the Census.

(1983b) Series P-60, No. 138. *Characteristics of the Population Below the Poverty Level 1981.* Washington, DC: US Bureau of the Census.

(1990) Special Studies Series P-23, No. 165. *Work and Family Patterns of American Women.* Washington, DC: US Bureau of the Census.

Daily, Lorna M. and Turner, John A. (1992) "Private pension coverage in nine countries," *Monthly Labor Review*, 115 (5), 40–3.

Daniel, W. W. (1980) *Maternity Rights: The Experience of Women*. London: Policy Studies Institute.

Davidson, Alexander (1989) *Two Models of Welfare: The Origins and Development of the Welfare State in Sweden and New Zealand, 1888–1988*. Stockholm: Almqvist and Wiksell International.

Davies, Bryn and Ward, Sue (1992) *Women and Personal Pensions*. London: Equal Opportunities Commission, HMSO.

de Kam, Flip, Pommer, Evert, Weisbeek, Joop and Wiebrens, Caspar (1988) "Economic crisis and its aftermath: the reform of social security in the Netherlands, 1984–1986," in Jean-Pierre Jallade (ed.), *The Crisis of Redistribution in European Welfare States*. Stoke-on-Trent: Trentham Books.

de Vroom, Bert and Blomsma, Martin (1991) "The Netherlands: an extreme case," in Martin Kohli, Martin Rein, Anne-Marie Guillemard, and Herman van Gunsteren (eds.), *Time for Retirement: Comparative Studies of Early Exit from the Labor Force*. Cambridge: Cambridge University Press.

DHSS (Department of Health and Social Security) (Various years) *Social Security Statistics*. London: HMSO.

   (1988) *Tables of Social Benefit Systems in the European Communities*. London: Department of Health and Social Security, International Relations Division.

Dilnot, Andrew (1989) "Not her own income: the reform of the taxation of marriage," in Maria Brenton and Clare Ungerson (eds.), *Social Policy Review 1988–9*. Harlow: Longman.

DNISR (Danish National Institute of Social Research) (1994) *Recent Trends in Cash Benefits in Europe*. Social Security in Europe, 4. Copenhagen: The Danish National Institute of Social Research.

Dominelli, Lena (1991) *Women Across Continents: Feminist Comparative Social Policy*. New York: Harvester Wheatsheaf.

DSS (Department of Social Security) (Various years) *Social Security Statistics*. London: HMSO.

   (1992) *Households below Average Income: A Statistical Analysis 1979–1988/89*. London: Department of Social Security.

Döring, Diether, Hauser, Richard, Rolf, Gabriele and Tibitanzl (1992) "Old age security of women in the twelve EC-countries: to what extent are Beveridge's two main principles of universality and guaranteed minimum fulfilled?," paper presented at the conference "Social Security 50 Years after Beveridge," University of York, September 27–30.

Ds (1995: 25) *Vad blev av de enskilda alternativen?* Stockholm: Ministry of Finance.

Duvall, Henrietta J., Goudreau, Karen W. and Marsh, Robert E. (1982) "Aid to families with dependent children: characteristics of recipients in 1979," *Social Security Bulletin*, 45 (4), 3–9, 19.

Eduards, Maud (1988) "Att studera politik ur ett könsperspektiv," *Statsvetenskaplig tidskrift*, 91 (3), 207–21.

   (1990) "Att studera och värdera välfärd," *Kvinnovetenskaplig tidskrift*, 11 (2), 3–12.

EG (*Employment Gazette*) (1990) "Women in the labour market, results from the 1989 Labour Force survey," *Employment Gazette*, 98, 619–43.

Ellwood, David T. (1988) *Poor Support: Poverty in the American Family*. New York: Basic Books.

Elmér, Åke (1958, 1963, 1971, 1975) *Svensk socialpolitik*. Lund: Gleerup/ Liber Läromedel.

(1960) *Folkpensioneringen i Sverige*. Lund: Gleerup.

Elvander, Nils (1972) *Svensk skattepolitik 1945–1970*. Stockholm: Rabén and Sjögren.

Emanuel, Han, Halberstadt, Victor and Petersen, Carel (1984) "Disability policy in the Netherlands," in Robert H. Haveman, Victor Halberstadt and Richard V. Burkhauser (eds.), *Public Policy toward Disabled Workers*. Ithaca: Cornell University Press.

EOC (Equal Opportunities Commission) (1988) *Women and Men in Britain 1987*. Equal Opportunities Commission. London: HMSO.

(1991) *Women and Men in Britain 1991*. Equal Opportunities Commission. London: HMSO.

Ergas, Yasmine (1990) "Child-care policies in comparative perspective," in *Lone-Parent Families*. Paris: OECD.

Esping-Andersen, Gøsta (1990) *The Three Worlds of Welfare Capitalism*. Cambridge: Polity Press.

Esping-Andersen, Gøsta and Korpi, Walter (1987) "From poor relief to institutional welfare states," in Robert Erikson, Erik Jørgen Hansen, Stein Ringen and Hannu Uusitalo (eds.), *The Scandinavian Model*. Armonk: Sharpe.

EOB (Equal Opportunities Bulletin) (1995) *Bulletin on Women and Employment in the EU*, No. 6. Brussels: Equal Opportunities Unit, European Commission.

Eurostat (1988) *Labour Force Survey: 1988 Results*. Luxemburg: Office for Official Publications of the European Communities.

FES (Family Expenditure Survey) (1984) *Family Spending: A Report on the Family Expenditure Survey 1983*. London: HMSO.

(1991) *Family Spending: A Report on the Family Expenditure Survey 1990*. London: HMSO.

Flora, Peter (ed.) (1986a, 1987) *Growth to Limits* Vols. 1–2, 4. Berlin: De Gruyter.

(1986b) "Introduction," in *Growth to Limits*. Vol. 1. Berlin: De Gruyter.

Förster, Michael (1994) "The effects of net transfers on low incomes among non-elderly families," *OECD Economic Studies*, 22, 181–221.

Fraser, Nancy (1989) *Unruly Practices: Power, Discourse and Gender in Contemporary Social Theory*. Minneapolis: University of Minnesota Press.

(1994) "After the family wage: gender equity and the welfare state," paper presented at the Crossing Borders conference, Stockholm, 27–29 May.

Fritzell, Johan (1992) "Ojämlikets- och fattigdomsutveckling under 1980-talet. Sverige i internationell belysning," *SOU 1992: 19, Bilaga 8 till LU 92*. Stockholm: Ministry of Finance.

Fuchs, Victor R. (1988) *Women's Quest for Economic Equality*. Cambridge: Harvard University Press.

Furniss, Norman and Tilton, Timothy (1977) *The Case for the Welfare State*. Bloomington: Indiana University Press.

Garfinkel, Irwin and McLanahan, Sara S. (1986) *Single Mothers and Their Children: A New American Dilemma*. Washington, DC: The Urban Institute Press.

Gelb, Joyce and Palley, Marian Lief (1987) *Women and Public Policies*, 2nd edn. Princeton: Princeton University Press.

GHS (General Household Survey) (Various years) *General Household Survey*. London: HMSO.

Ginn, Jay and Arber, Sara (1991) "Gender, class and income inequalities in later life," *British Journal of Sociology*, 42 (3), 369–96.

(1993) "Pension penalties: the gendered division of occupational welfare," *Work, Employment and Society*, 7 (1), 47–70.

Ginsburg, Norman (1992) *Divisions of Welfare*. London: Sage.

Glazer, Nathan (1986) "Welfare and 'Welfare' in America," in Richard Rose and Rei Shiratori (eds.), *The Welfare State East and West*. New York: Oxford University Press.

Glendinning, Caroline and Millar, Jane (eds.) (1987) *Women and Poverty in Britain*. Brighton: Wheatsheaf.

(1992) *Women and Poverty in Britain: The 1990s*. New York: Harvester Wheatsheaf.

Glennerster, Howard (1991) "The radical right and the future of the welfare state," in Howard Glennerster and James Midgley (eds.), *The Radical Right and the Welfare State*. Hemel Hempstead: Harvester Wheatsheaf.

Gordon, Linda (1990) "The new feminist scholarship on the welfare state," in Linda Gordon (ed.), *Women, the State and Welfare*. Madison: University of Wisconsin Press.

Gordon, Margaret S. (1988) *Social Security Policies in Industrialized Countries*. Cambridge: Cambridge University Press.

Griffiths, John (1986) "What do Dutch lawyers actually do in divorce cases?," *Law and Society Review*, 20, 135–75.

Groves, Dulcie (1983) "Members and survivors: women and retirement legislation," in Jane Lewis (ed.), *Women's Welfare, Women's Rights*. London: Croom Helm.

(1991) "Women and financial provision for old age," in Mavis Maclean and Dulcie Groves (eds.), *Women's Issues and Social Policy*. London: Routledge.

Groves, Harold M. (1963) *Federal Tax Treatment of the Family*. Washington, DC: The Brookings Institution.

(1969) "Taxing the family unit," *National Tax Journal*, 22, 109–20.

Gunnarsson, Evy (1990) "Kvinnors fattigdom i valfärdsstaten," *Kvinnovetenskaplig tidskrift*, 11 (2), 28–36.

Gustafsson, Siv (1990) "Labor force participation and earnings of lone parents: a Swedish case study including comparisons with Germany," in *Lone-Parent Families*. Paris: OECD.

(1994) "Childcare and types of welfare states," in Diane Sainsbury (ed.), *Gendering Welfare States*. London: Sage.

Gustafsson, S. S. and Bruyn-Hundt, M. (1991) "Incentives for women to work: a comparison between the Netherlands, Sweden and West Germany," *Journal of Economic Studies* 18, 30–65.

Gustafsson, Siv and Jacobsson, Roger (1985) "Trends in female labor force participation in Sweden," *The Journal of Labor Economics*, 3 (1), S256–74.

Gustafsson, Siv and Stafford, Frank (1993) "Three regimes of childcare," paper presented at the ECPR workshop on Welfare States and Gender, Leiden.

Hadenius, Axel (1987) "Välfärdspolitikens dimensioner," in *Festskrift till professor skytteanus Carl Arvid Hessler*, Acta Universitatis Upsaliensis, No. 103.

Hakim, Catherine (1989) "Workforce restructuring, social insurance coverage and the black economy," *Journal of Social Policy*, 18, 471–503.

  (1993) "The myth of rising female employment," *Work, Employment and Society*, 7, 97–120.

Hartog, Joop and Theeuwes, Jules (1985) "The emergence of the working wife in Holland," *Journal of Labor Economics*, 3 (1), S235–55.

Hauser, Richard and Fischer, Ingo (1990) "Economic well-being among one-parent families," in Timothy M. Smeeding, Michael O'Higgins and Lee Rainwater (eds.), *Poverty, Inequality and Income Distribution in Comparative Perspective*. New York: Harvester Wheatsheaf.

Haveman, Robert, Wolfe, Barbara and Halberstadt, Victor (1986) "The European welfare state in transition," in John L. Palmer (ed.), *Perspectives on the Reagan Years*. Washington, DC: The Urban Institute Press.

Hayes, Cheryl D., Palmer, John D. and Zaslow, Martha J. (1990) *Who Cares for America's Children?* Washington, DC: The Urban Institute Press.

Hayghe, Howard V. (1993) "Working wives' contributions to family incomes," *Monthly Labor Review*, 116 (8), 39–43.

Heckscher, Gunnar (1984) *The Welfare State and Beyond: Success and Problems in Scandinavia*. Minneapolis: University of Minnesota Press.

Heclo, Hugh (1974) *Modern Social Politics in Britain and Sweden*. New Haven: Yale University Press.

Heclo, Hugh and Cockburn, Christine (1974) "Income maintenance for one-parent families in other countries." Appendix 3 of the *Finer Report on One-parent Families*, Cmnd 5429. London: HMSO.

Hedström, Peter and Ringen, Stein (1990) "Age and income in contemporary society," in Timothy M. Smeeding, Michael O'Higgins and Lee Rainwater (eds.), *Poverty, Inequality and Income Distribution in Comparative Perspective*. New York: Harvester Wheatsheaf.

Heidenheimer, Arnold J. (1982) "Education and social security entitlements in Europe and America," in Peter Flora and Arnold J. Heidenheimer (eds.), *The Development of the Welfare States in Europe and America*. New Brunswick: Transaction Publishers.

Heidenheimer, Arnold, Heclo, Hugh and Adams, Carolyn Teich (1975, 1983) *Comparative Public Policy*. New York: St Martin's Press.

Hermans, Pieter C. (1988) "Differentials in outcomes of the application of Dutch disability insurance legislation to women and men," *International Social Security Review*, 41, 249–60.

Hernes, Helga (1984) "Women and the welfare state: the transition from private to public dependence," in Harriet Holter (ed.), *Patriarchy in a Welfare Society*. Oslo: Universitetsforlag.

  (1987) *Welfare State and Women Power*. Oslo: Norwegian University Press.

HEW (Department of Health, Education, and Welfare) (1979) *Social Security and the Changing Roles of Men and Women*. Washington, DC: Department of Health, Education, and Welfare.

Hill, Michael (1990) *Social Security Policy in Britain*. Aldershot: Edward Elgar.

Hills, John (1993) *The Future of Welfare: A Guide to the Debate*. London: Joseph Rowntree Foundation.

HMSO (1991) *Occupational Pension Schemes 1987, Eighth Survey by the Government Actuary*. London: HMSO.

Hobson, Barbara (1991) "Decommodification in gender terms: an analysis of Esping-Andersen's social policy regimes and women's social citizenship," paper presented at the Conference on Gender, Citizenship, and Social Policy, New Orleans, Louisiana, 31 October 1991.

——— (1994) "Solo mothers, social policy regimes and the logics of gender," in Diane Sainsbury (ed.), *Gendering Welfare States*. London: Sage.

Holtmaat, Riki (1992) *Met zorg een recht? Een analys van het politiek-juridisch vertoog over bijstandswet*. Zwolle: Tjeenk-Willink.

Hupe, Peter L. (1993) "Beyond pillarization: the (post) welfare state in the Netherlands," *European Journal of Political Research*, 23 (4) Annual Review 1993, 359–86.

Hutton, Sandra (1994) "Men's and women's incomes: evidence from survey data," *Journal of Social Policy*, 23, 21–40.

Hutton, Sandra and Whiteford, Peter (1994) "Gender and retirement incomes: a comparative analysis," in Sally Baldwin and Jane Falkingham (eds.), *Social Security and Social Change: New Challenges to the Beveridge Model*. New York: Harvester Wheatsheaf.

Iams, Howard M. (1993) "Earnings of couples: a cohort analysis," *Social Security Bulletin*, 56 (3), 22–32.

Irick, Christine (1986) "An overview of OASDI revenue, expenditures, and beneficiaries, 1974–85," *Social Security Bulletin*, 49 (6), 21–8.

ISSR (*International Social Security Review*) (1970) "Social security in the Netherlands," *International Social Security Review*, 23, 3–61.

James, Estelle (1987) "The nonprofit sector in comparative perspective," in Walter W. Powell (ed.), *The Nonprofit Sector: A Research Handbook*. New Haven: Yale University Press.

Janoski, Thomas (1990) *The Political Economy of Unemployment*. Berkeley: University of California Press.

Jansson, Kjell and Sandqvist, Agneta (1993) "Inkomstfördelning under 1980-talet," *SOU 1992: 19, Bilaga 19 till Långtidsutredningen 1992*. Stockholm: Ministry of Finance.

Johannesson, Jan and Schmid, Gunther (1980) "The development of labor market policy in Sweden and Germany: competing or convergent models to combat unemployment?," *European Journal of Political Research*, 8, 387–406.

Johansen, Lars Nørby (1986) "Welfare state regression in Scandinavia?," in Else Øyen (ed.), *Comparing Welfare States and their Futures*. Aldershot: Gower.

Jones, Catherine (1985) *Patterns of Social Policy*. London: Tavistock.

Jonung, Christina and Persson, Inga (1993) "Women and market work: the misleading tale of participation rates in international comparisons," *Work, Employment and Society*, 7, 259–74.

Kahn, Alfred J. and Kamerman, Sheila (1983) *Income Transfers for Families with Children*. Philadelphia: Temple University Press.

Kaim-Caudle, P. R. (1973) *Comparative Social Policy and Social Security*. London: Martin Robertson.

Kamerman, Sheila B. (1984) "Women, children and poverty: public policies and female-headed families in industrial countries," *Signs*, 10, 249–71.

Kamerman, Sheila B. and Kahn, Alfred J. (1988) "Social policy and children in the United States and Europe," in John L. Palmer, Timothy Smeeding, Barbara Boyle Torrey (eds.), *The Vulnerable*. Washington, DC: The Urban Institute Press.

(1989) "Child care and privatization under Reagan," in Sheila B. Kamerman and Alfred J. Kahn (eds.), *Privatization and the Welfare State*. Princeton: Princeton University Press.

(1991) "A US policy challenge," in Sheila B. Kamerman and Alfred J. Kahn (eds.), *Child Care, Parental Leave, and the Under 3s: Policy Innovation in Europe*. New York: Auburn House.

Kamerman, Sheila B., Kahn, Alfred J. and Kingston, Paul (1983) *Maternity Policies and Working Women*. New York: Columbia University Press.

Kangas, Olli and Palme, Joakim (1989) "Public and private pensions: the Scandinavian countries in a comparative perspective," *Meddelande 3/1989*. Stockholm: Swedish Institute for Social Research.

Karleby, Nils (1926) *Socialismen inför verkligheten*. Stockholm: Tiden.

Katzenstein, Peter J. (1985) *Small States in World Markets*. Ithaca, NY: Cornell University Press.

Kerns, Wilmer L. (1992) "Private social welfare expenditures, 1972–90," *Social Security Bulletin*, 55 (3), 59–66.

Kindlund, Sören (1988) "Sweden," in Alfred J. Kahn and Sheila B. Kamerman (eds.), *Child Support: From Debt Collection to Social Policy*. Newbury Park: Sage.

Knijn, Trudie (1994) "Fish without bikes: revision of the Dutch welfare state and its consequences for the (in)dependence of single mothers," *Social Politics: International Studies in Gender, State and Society*, 1, 83–105.

Koesoebjono, S. (1983) "Costs of maternity leave in the Netherlands, 1977: an exploratory study," *Population and Family in the Low Countries* III. Voorburg/Brussels: Netherlands Interuniversity Demographic Institute.

Kohl, Jurgen (1982) "Trends and problems in postwar public expenditures in Western Europe and North America," in Peter Flora and Arnold Heidenheimer (eds.), *The Development of Welfare States in Europe and America*. New Brunswick: Transaction Books.

Kolberg, Jon Eivind (1991) "The gender dimension of the welfare state," in Jon Eivind Kolberg (ed.), *The Welfare State as Employer*. Armonk: Sharpe.

Kommunernas finanser 1981 (1983) Stockholm: National Central Bureau of Statistics.

Kool, C. (1983) "Een indicatie voor kosten van de voorgestelde verloven voor werknemers," Bijlage 2. *Zorg en Beroepsarbeid*, Advies 83/19, Emancipatieraad.

Kooy, Gerrit (1977) "The Netherlands," in Robert Chester (ed.), *Divorce in Europe*. Leiden: Martinus Nijhoff Social Science Division.

Korpi, Walter (1980) "Social policy and distributional conflict in the capitalist democracies: a preliminary comparative framework," *West European Politics*, 3, 296–316.

(1983) *The Democratic Class Struggle*. London: Routledge and Kegan Paul.

Korpi, Walter and Palme, Joakim (1993) "Socialpolitik, kris och reformer: Sverige i internationell belysning," *SOU 1993: 16 Nya villkor för ekonomi och politik, Bilaga 17*. Stockholm: Ministry of Finance.

(1994) "The strategy of equality and the paradox of redistribution," unpublished paper. Stockholm: Swedish Institute for Social Research.

(Forthcoming) *Social Citizenship: A Century of Social Policy Development in the Western World*.

Koven, Seth and Michel, Sonya (1990) "Womanly duties: maternalist politics and the origins of welfare states in France, Germany, Great Britain and the United States," *American Historical Review*, 95, 1073–108.

(eds.) (1993) *Mothers of a New World*. London: Routledge.

Kramer, Ralph M. (1981) *Voluntary Agencies in the Welfare State*. Berkeley: University of California Press.

Kuhnle, Stein and Selle, Per (1989) "Integrated dependence or separate autonomy? Relations between government and voluntary organizations in Norway," paper presented at the ECPR workshop on Needs, Contributions and Welfare, Paris.

Land, Hilary (1985) "Who still cares for the family? Recent developments in income maintenance, taxation and family law," in Clare Ungerson (ed.), *Women and Social Policy: A Reader*. London: Macmillan.

(1992) "Whatever happened to the social wage?," in Caroline Glendinning and Jane Millar (eds.), *Women and Poverty in Britain the 1990s*. New York: Harvester Wheatsheaf.

(1994a) "The demise of the male breadwinner: in practice but not in theory: a challenge for social security systems," in Sally Baldwin and Jane Falkingham (eds.), *Social Security and Social Change: New Challenges to the Beveridge Model*. New York: Harvester Wheatsheaf.

(1994b) "Reversing 'the inadvertent nationalization of fatherhood': the British Child Support Act 1991 and its consequences for men, women and children," *International Social Security Review*, 46 (4), 91–100.

(1995) "Social security policies from the perspective of gender inequalities," *European Institute of Social Security Yearbook* (forthcoming).

Land, Hilary and Parker, Roy (1978) "United Kingdom," in Sheila B. Kamerman and Alfred J. Kahn (eds.), *Family Policy: Government and Families in Fourteen Countries*. New York: Columbia University Press.

Langan, Mary and Ostner, Ilona (1991) "Gender and welfare," in Graham Room (ed.), *Towards a European Welfare State?* Bristol: SAUS Publications.

Leader, Shelah Gilbert (1983) "Fiscal policy and family structure," in Irene Diamond (ed.), *Families, Politics and Public Policy*. New York: Longman.

Leira, Arnlaug (1989) *Models of Motherhood*, Report 89/7. Oslo: Institute of Social Research.

(1992) *Welfare States and Working Mothers: The Scandinavian Experience*. Cambridge: Cambridge University Press.

Lewis, Jane (1980) *The Politics of Motherhood: Child and Maternal Welfare in England 1900–1939.* London: Croom Helm.

(1992a) "Gender and the development of welfare regimes," *Journal of European Social Policy*, 2 (3), 159–73.

(1992b) *Women in Britain since 1945.* Oxford: Blackwell.

(1993) "Introduction: women, work, family and social policies in Europe," in Jane Lewis (ed.), *Women and Social Policies in Europe*: *Work, Family and the State.* Aldershot: Edward Elgar.

(ed.) (1983) *Women's Welfare, Women's Rights.* London: Croom Helm.

Lewis, Jane and Ostner, Ilona (1991) "Gender and the evolution of European social policies," paper presented at the CES Workshop on Emergent Supranational Social Policy: The EC's Social Dimension in Comparative Perspective, Center for European Studies, Harvard University.

(1994) *Gender and the Evolution of European Social Policies*, Working Paper No. 4/94, Centre for Social Policy Research, University of Bremen.

(1995) "Gender and the evolution of European social policy," in Stephan Leibfried and Paul Pierson (eds.), *European Social Policy: Between Fragmentation and Integration.* Washington, DC: Brookings Institution.

Lewis, Jane and Piachaud, David (1987) "Women and poverty in the twentieth century," in Caroline Glendinning and Jane Millar (eds.), *Women and Poverty in Britain.* Brighton: Wheatsheaf.

Lingg, Barbara A. (1985) "Women social security beneficiaries aged 62 or older, 1960–83," *Social Security Bulletin*, 48 (2), 27–31.

(1990) "Women beneficiaries aged 62 or older, 1960–88," *Social Security Bulletin*, 53 (7), 2–12.

Lister, Ruth (1992) *Women's Economic Dependency and Social Security.* Manchester: Equal Opportunities Commission.

(1994a) "'She has other duties' – women, citzenship and social security," in Sally Baldwin and Jane Falkingham (eds.), *Social Security and Social Change: New Challenges to the Beveridge Model.* New York: Harvester Wheatsheaf.

(1994b) "Dilemmas in engendering citizenship," paper presented at the Crossing Borders conference, Stockholm, 27–9 May.

(1994c) "The Child Support Act: shifting family obligations in the United Kingdom," *Social Politics: International Studies in Gender, State and Society*, 1 (2), 211–22.

Lonsdale, Susan (1990) *Women and Disability.* London: Macmillan.

Lonsdale, Susan and Byrne, Dominic (1988) "Social security: from state insurance to private uncertainty," in Maria Brenton and Clare Ungerson (eds.), *The Year Book of Social Policy 1987–88.* London: Longman.

Lonsdale, Susan and Seddon, Jennifer (1994) "The growth of disability benefits: an international comparison," in Sally Baldwin and Jane Falkingham (eds.), *Social Security and Social Change: New Challenges to the Beveridge Model.* New York: Harvester Wheatsheaf.

Lopata, Helena Znaniecka and Brehm, Henry P. (1986) *Widows and Dependent Wives: From Social Problem to Federal Program.* New York: Praeger.

Lundqvist, Lennart (1992) *Dislodging the Welfare State? Housing and Privatization in Four European Countries.* Delft: Delft University Press.

Lybeck, Johan A. (1984) *Hur stor är den offentliga sektorn?* Malmö: LiberFörlag.

Maassen van den Brink, Henriëtte (1994) *Female Labor Supply, Child Care and Marital Conflict.* Amsterdam: Amsterdam University Press.

MacLennan, Emma and Weitzel, Renate (1984) "Labour market policy in four countries: are women adequately represented?," in Gunther Schmid and Renate Weitzel (eds.), *Sex Discrimination and Equal Opportunity.* Aldershot: Gower.

Maier, Friederike (1991) "Part-time work, social security protections and labor law: an international comparison," *Policy and Politics*, 19 (1), 1–11.

    (1992) *The Regulation of Part-Time Work: A Comparative Study of Six EC Countries*, WZB Discussion Paper. Berlin: Wissenschaftszentrum Berlin.

Mallan, Lucy B. (1975) "Young widows and their children: a comparative report," *Social Security Bulletin*, 38 (5), 3–21.

Marklund, Staffan and Svallfors, Stefan (1987) *Dual Welfare: Segmentation and Work Enforcement in the Swedish Welfare System*, Research Reports from the Department of Sociology, University of Umeå, No 94.

Marshall, T.H. (1950) *Citizenship and Social Class and Other Essays.* Cambridge: Cambridge University Press.

Martin, Jean and Roberts, Ceridwen (1984) *Women and Employment.* The Report of the 1980 DE/OPCS Women and Employment Survey. London: HMSO.

Martin, Jean, Meltzer, Howard and Elliott, David (1988) *The Prevalence of Disability among Adults.* OPCS Surveys of Disability in Great Britain, Report 1. London: HMSO.

Maxfield, Linda Drazga (1985) "Income of new retired workers by age at first benefit receipt: findings from the new beneficiary survey," *Social Security Bulletin*, 48 (7), 7–26.

Maxfield, Linda Drazga and Reno, Virginia P. (1985) "Distribution of income sources of recent retirees: findings from the new beneficiary survey," *Social Security Bulletin*, 48 (1), 7–13.

McRae, Susan (1991) *Maternity Rights in Britain.* London: Policy Studies Institute.

Mellor, Earl F. and Haugen, Steven E. (1986) "Hourly paid workers: who they are and what they earn," *Monthly Labor Review*, 109 (2), 20–6.

Mellor, Earl F. and Stamas, George D. (1982) "Usual weekly earnings: another look at intergroup differences and basic trends," *Monthly Labor Review*, 105 (4), 15–24.

Meyer, Jack A. (1986) "Social programs and social policy," in John L. Palmer (ed.), *Perspectives on the Reagan Years.* Washington, DC: The Urban Institute Press.

Micklewright, John (1989) "The strange case of British earnings-related unemployment benefit," *Journal of Social Policy*, 18, 527–48.

Millar, Jane (1987) "Lone mothers," in Caroline Glendinning and Jane Millar (eds.), *Women and Poverty in Britain.* Brighton: Wheatsheaf.

    (1989) *Poverty and the Lone-Parent Family: the Challenge to Social Policy.* Aldershot: Avebury.

Miller, Dorothy C. (1990) *Women and Social Welfare.* New York: Praeger.

Mishra, Ramesh (1977) *Society and Social Policy.* London: Macmillan.

    (1984) *The Welfare State in Crisis.* Brighton: Wheatsheaf.

    (1990) *The Welfare State in Capitalist Society.* New York: Harvester Wheatsheaf.

Mitchell, Deborah (1991) *Income Transfers in Ten Welfare States.* Aldershot: Avebury.

Moberg, Eva (1961) "Kvinnans villkorliga frigivning," in Hans Hederberg (ed.), *Unga liberaler*. Stockholm: Almqvist and Wiksell.

Mott, Frank L. (ed.) (1982) *The Employment Revolution: Young American Women in the 1970s.* Cambridge: The MIT Press.

Myrdal, Alva and Klein, Viola (1956) *Women's Two Roles*. London: Routledge and Kegan Paul.

Nardone, Thomas (1986) "Part-time workers: who are they?," *Monthly Labor Review*, 109 (2), 13–19.

Nasenius, Jan and Veit-Wilson, John (1985) "Social policy in a cold climate: Sweden in the eighties," in Catherine Jones and Maria Brenton (eds.), *The Year Book of Social Policy in Britain 1984–5*. London: Routledge and Kegan Paul.

NCCS (National Child Care Survey) (1991) Hofferth, Sandra L., Brayfield, April, Deich, Sharon and Holcomb, Pamela, *The National Child Care Survey, 1990*. Washington, DC: The Urban Institute Press.

Nelson, Barbara J. (1984) "Women's poverty and women's citizenship: some political consequences of economic marginality," *Signs*, 10, 209–31.

(1990) "The origins of the two-channel welfare state: workmen's compensation and mothers' aid," in Linda Gordon (ed.), *Women, the State, and Welfare*. Madison: University of Wisconsin Press.

Newton, Margaret W. (1988) "Women and pension coverage," in Sara E. Rix (ed.), *The American Woman 1988–89: A Status Report*. New York: W. W. Norton.

Nyberg, Anita (1991) "Vad mätar statistiken?," *Mannen som norm i statistiken?* Stockholm: Delegationen för jämställdhetsforskning.

O'Connor, Julia S. (1993) "Gender, class, and citizenship in the comparative analysis of welfare state regimes: theoretical and methodological issues," *British Journal of Sociology*, 44 (3), 501–18.

O'Higgins, Michael (1988) "The allocation of public resources to children and the elderly in OECD countries," in John L. Palmer et al., *The Vulnerable*. Washington DC: Urban Institute.

O'Neill, June (1985) "The trend in the male–female wage gap in the United States," *Journal of Labor Economics*, 3 (1), S91–116.

OECD (Organization for Economic Co-operation and Development) (1977) *The Treatment of Family Units in OECD Member Countries under Tax and Transfer Systems*. Paris: OECD.

(1980) *The Tax/Benefit Position of Selected Income Groups in OECD Member Countries*. Paris: OECD.

(1982) *Economic Outlook. Historical Statistics 1960–1980*. Paris: OECD.

(1983) *Employment Outlook*. Paris: OECD.

(1984a) *Employment Outlook*. Paris: OECD.

(1984b) *The Tax/Benefit Position of Production Workers 1979–1983*. Paris: OECD.

(1985a) *Social Expenditure 1960–1990*. Paris: OECD.

(1985b) *Measuring Health Care, 1960–1985*. Paris: OECD.

(1987) *Employment Outlook*. Paris: OECD.

(1988) *Employment Outlook*. Paris: OECD.

(1989) *Economic Survey of the Netherlands 1988/1989*. Paris: OECD.

(1990a) *Employment Outlook*. Paris: OECD.

(1990b) *The Tax/Benefit Position of Production Workers 1986–1989*. Paris: OECD.

(1991a) *Economic Survey of the Netherlands 1991/1992*. Paris: OECD.

(1991b) *Employment Outlook*. Paris: OECD.

(1991c) *Economic Outlook. Historical Statistics 1960–1989*. Paris: OECD.

(1992a) *The Tax/Benefit Position of Production Workers 1988–1991*. Paris. OECD.

(1992b) *Labour Force Statistics 1970–1990*. Paris: OECD.

(1994a) *Employment Outlook*. Paris: OECD.

(1994b) *New Orientations for Social Policy*. Social Policy Studies, No. 12. Paris: OECD.

Oldman, Oliver and Temple, Ralph (1960) "Comparative analysis of the taxation of married persons," *Stanford Law Review*, 12, 585–605.

Olsson, Sven (1986) "Sweden," in Peter Flora (ed.), *Growth to Limits*. Vol. 1. Berlin: De Gruyter.

(1987) "Sweden," in Peter Flora (ed.), *Growth to Limits*. Vol. 4. Berlin: De Gruyter.

(1990) *Social Policy and Welfare State in Sweden*. Lund: Arkiv.

Orloff, Ann Shola (1991) "Gender in early US social policy," *Journal of Policy History*, 3, 249–81.

(1993) "Gender and the social rights of citizenship: the comparative analysis of gender relations and welfare states," *American Sociological Review*, 58, 303–28.

(1994) "Restructuring welfare: gender, work and inequality in Australia, Canada, the United Kingdom and the United States," paper presented at the Crossing Borders Conference, Stockholm, 27–29 May.

Orshansky, Mollie (1968) "The shape of poverty in 1966," *Social Security Bulletin*, 31 (3), 3–32.

Palme, Joakim (1990a) "Models of old-age pensions," in Alan Ware and Robert E. Goodin (eds.), *Needs and Welfare*. London: Sage.

(1990b) *Pension Rights in Welfare Capitalism, The Development of Old-Age pensions in 18 OECD Countries 1930 to 1985,* Swedish Institute for Social Research, 14. Stockholm.

Palmer, John L. and Sawhill, Isabel V. (eds.) (1984) *The Reagan Record*. Cambridge: Ballinger.

Parry, Richard (1986) "United Kingdom," in Peter Flora, *Growth to Limits*. Vol. 2. Berlin: De Gruyter.

(1987) "United Kingdom," in Peter Flora, *Growth to Limits*. Vol. 4. Berlin: De Gruyter.

(1990) "Needs, services and political success under the British Conservatives," in Alan Ware and Robert E. Goodin (eds.), *Needs and Welfare*. London: Sage.

Pateman, Carole (1988) "The patriarchal welfare state," in Amy Gutmann (ed.), *Democracy and the Welfare State*. Princeton: Princeton University Press.

(1992) "Equality, difference, subordination: the politics of motherhood and women's citizenship," in Gisela Bock and Susan James (eds.), *Beyond Equality and Difference*. London: Routledge.

Pattison, David and Harrington, David E. (1993) "Proposals to modify the taxation of social security benefits: options and distributional effects," *Social Security Bulletin*, 56 (2), 3–21.

Pearce, Diana M. (1985) "Toil and trouble: women workers and unemployment compensation," *Signs*, 10, 439–59.

Peattie, Lisa and Rein, Martin (1983) *Women's Claims: A Study in Political Economy*. Oxford: Oxford University Press.

Pechman, Joseph A., Aaron, Henry J. and Taussig, Michael K. (1968) *Social Security: Perspectives for Reform*. Washington, DC: The Brookings Institution.

Perman, Lauri and Stevens, Beth (1989) "Industrial segregation and the gender distribution of fringe benefits," *Gender and Society*, 3, 388–404.

Persson, Inga (1993) *Svenska kvinnor möter Europa*, Bilaga 16 till Långtidsutredningen 1992. Stockholm: Ministry of Finance.

Pichault, Camille (1984) *Day-Care Facilities and Services for Children under the Age of Three in the European Community*. Commission of the European Communities.

Pierson, Christopher (1991) *Beyond the Welfare State?* Cambridge: Polity.

Pierson, Paul (1990) "Taking the jewel from Labor's crown? Thatcher's assault on the British welfare state," paper presented at the Seventh International Conference of Europeanists, Washington, DC, 23–5 March.

Plantenga, Janneke and van Velzen, Susan (1993) *Wage Determination and Sex Segregation in Employment: The Case of the Netherlands*, Working Paper of the European Commission Network of Experts on the Situation of Women in the Labour Market. Manchester: UMIST.

(1994) "Flexibilization of working life: the case of part-time work in the Netherlands," paper presented at the Crossing Borders conference, Stockholm, 27–9 May.

Polinsky, Ella (1969) "The position of women in the social security system," *Social Security Bulletin*, 32 (7), 3–33.

Pott-Buter, Hettie A. (1993) *Facts and Fairy Tales about Female Labor, Family and Fertility: A Seven Country Comparison*. Amsterdam: Amsterdam University Press.

Price, Daniel N. (1985) "Unemployment insurance, then and now, 1935–1985," *Social Security Bulletin*, 48 (10), 22–32.

Qvist, Gunnar (1975) "Landsorganisationen i Sverige och kvinnorna på arbetsmarknaden (1898–1973)," in Eva Karlsson (ed.), *Kvinnor i arbetarrörelsen. Hågkomster och intervjuer*. Stockholm: Prisma.

R&D (1995) Various issues. *Från riksdag och departement*. Stockholm: Riksdagens förvaltningskontor.

Rainwater, Lee (1979) "Mothers' contributions to the family money economy in Europe and the United States," *Journal of Family History*, 4, 198–211.

Rainwater, Lee, Rein, Martin and Schwartz, Joseph (1986) *Income Packaging in the Welfare State*. Oxford: Clarendon Press.

Randall, Vicky (1982) *Women and Politics*. London: Macmillan.

Reischauer, Robert D. (1989) "The welfare reform legislation: directions for the future," in Phoebe H. Cottingham and David T. Ellwood (eds.), *Welfare Policy for the 1990s*. Cambridge: Harvard University Press.

RFV [National Social Insurance Board] (Various years) Social Insurance Statistics. *Facts*. Stockholm: National Social Insurance Board.

Richardson, Ann (1984) *Widows Benefits*. London: Policy Studies Institute.

Robinson, Olive (1988) "The changing labor market: growth of part-time employment and labor market segmentation in Britain," in Sylvia Walby (ed.), *Gender Segregation at Work*. Milton Keynes: Open University Press.

Roebroek, Joop M. (1989) "Netherlands," in John Dixon and Robert P. Scheurell (eds.), *Social Welfare in Developed Market Countries*. London: Routledge.

(1993) *The Imprisoned State*. Tilburg University, Department of Social Security Studies.

Roebroek, Joop and Berben, Theo (1987) "Netherlands," in Peter Flora, *Growth to Limits*. Vol. 4. Berlin: De Gruyter.

Rubery, Jill and Tarling, Roger (1988) "Women's employment in declining Britain," in Jill Rubery (ed.), *Women and Recession*. London: Routledge and Kegan Paul.

Ruggie, Mary (1984) *The State and Working Women*. Princeton: Princeton University Press.

Sainsbury, Diane (1988) "The Scandinavian model and women's interests: the issues of universalism and corporatism," *Scandinavian Political Studies*, 11, 337–46.

(1991) "Swedish social democracy in transition: the party's record in the 1980s and the challenge of the 1990s," *West European Politics*, 14 (3), 31–57.

(1992) "Welfare state retrenchment and restructuring: policy choices in the US, the UK, the Netherlands and Sweden during the 1980s," paper presented at the American Political Science Association Annual Meeting in Chicago, 3–6 September.

(1993a) "Dual welfare and sex segregation of access to social benefits," *Journal of Social Policy*, 22, 69–98.

(1993b) "The Swedish social democrats and the legacy of continuous reform: asset or dilemma?," *West European Politics*, 16 (1), 39–61.

(ed.) (1994) *Gendering Welfare States*. London: Sage.

SAP (1994) Election Manifesto adopted by the Swedish Social Democratic Party Board, 19 August.

Sassoon, Anne Showstack (ed.) (1987) *Women and the State*. London: Hutchinson.

SB (1995) *The Swedish Budget 1995/96*. Stockholm: Ministry of Finance.

SCB [Central Bureau of Statistics] (1973) *Arbetsmarknadsstatisktisk årsbok 1973*. Stockholm: Central Bureau of Statistics.

(1980) *Barnomsorgsundersökning 1980*. Statistiska meddelanden. S 1980: 20. Stockholm: Central Bureau of Statistics.

(1981) *Socialvården 1980*. Stockholm: Central Bureau of Statistics.

(1983a) *Barnomsorgsundersökning 1983*. Statistiska meddelanden. S 1983: 12. Stockholm: Central Bureau of Statistics.

(1983b) *Socialvard 1981*. Stockholm: Central Bureau of Statistics.

(1985) *Pensionärer*, Levnadsförhållanden, Rapport 43. Stockholm: Central Bureau of Statistics.

(1986) *Kvinno- och mans vär(l)den. Fakta om jämställdheten i Sverige 1986*. Stockholm: Central Bureau of Statistics.

(1989a) *Barnomsorgsundersökningen 1989*. Statistiska meddelanden, S 11 SM 8901 Stockholm: Central Bureau of Statistics.

(1989b) *Arbetsmarknaden i siffror 1970–1988*. Stockholm: Central Bureau of Statistics.

(1989c) *Inkomstfördelningen 1987 för individer och familjer – tabellsammanställning*. Statistiska meddelanden, Be 20 SM 8902. Stockholm: Central Bureau of Statistics.

(1991) *Barnomsorgsundersökning 1991*. Statistiska meddelanden, S 11 SM 9101. Stockholm: Central Bureau of Statistics.

(1993a) *Inkomstfördelningsundersökningen 1991*. Statistiska meddelandena BE 21 SM9301. Stockholm: Central Bureau of Statistics.

(1993b) *Pensionärer 1980–1989*. Levnadsförhållanden, Rapport 81. Stockholm: Central Bureau of Statistics.

(1995) *Women and Men in Sweden, Facts and Figures 1995*. Stockholm: Central Bureau of Statistics.

Schiewe, Kirsten (1994) "German pension insurance, gendered times and stratification," in Diane Sainsbury (ed.), *Gendering Welfare States*. London: Sage.

Schmidt, Manfred G. (1993) "Gendered labour force participation," in Francis G. Castles (ed.), *Families of Nations: Patterns of Public Policy in Western Democracies*. Aldershot: Dartmouth.

Schmitter, Phillip C. (1981) "Interest intermediation and regime governability in contemporary Western Europe and North America," in Suzanne Berger (ed.), *Organizing Interests in Western Europe*. Cambridge: Cambridge University Press.

Schneider, Markus, et al. (1992) *Health Care in the EC Member States*, special issue of *Health Policy*, 20.

SCP [Social and Cultural Planning Office] (1985) *Women on the Move*. Rijswijk: The Netherlands Social and Cultural Planning Office.

(1986) *Social and Cultural Report 1986*. Rijswijk: The Netherlands Social and Cultural Planning Office.

(1988a) *Social and Cultural Report 1988*. Rijswijk: The Netherlands Social and Cultural Planning Office.

(1988b) van Delft, Mariolein and Niphuis-Nell, Marry with Oudijk, Corrine, *Eenoudergezinnen: ontstaan, leefsituatie en voorzieningengebruik*. Rijswijk: The Netherlands Social and Cultural Planning Office.

(1991) *Social and Cultural Report 1990*. Rijswijk: The Netherlands Social and Cultural Planning Office.

(1993a) Hooghiemstra, B. T. J. and Niphuis-Nell, M. *Social atlas von vrouw*. Rijswijk: The Netherlands Social and Cultural Planning Office.

(1993b) *Social and Cultural Report 1992*. Rijswijk: The Netherlands Social and Cultural Planning Office.

(1995) *Social and Cultural Report 1994*. Rijswijk: The Netherlands Social and Cultural Planning Office.

Shaver, Sheila and Bradshaw, Jonathan (1993) *The Recognition of Wifely Labour by Welfare States*, Discussion paper No. 44, Social Policy Research Centre, The University of New South Wales.

Siaroff, Alan (1994) "Work, welfare and gender equality: a new typology," in Diane Sainsbury (ed.) *Gendering Welfare States*. London: Sage.

Siim, Birte (1987) "A comparative perspective on the organization of care work in Denmark and Britain," paper presented at the ECPR workshop on Women and Democratic Citizenship, Amsterdam.

(1988) "Towards a feminist rethinking of the welfare state," in Kathleen B. Jones and Anna G. Jónasdóttir (eds.), *The Political Interests of Gender*. London: Sage.

Sinfield, A. (1993) "Reverse targeting and upside-down benefits," in A. Sinfield (ed.), *Poverty, Inequality and Justice*, Department of Social Policy and Social Work, University of Edinburgh.

SIT (1968) *Report of the Task Force on Social Insurance and Taxes to the Citizens' Advisory Council on the Status of Women*. Washington, DC: US Government Printing Office.

Sjerps, Ina (1988) "Indirect discrimination in social security in the Netherlands: demands of the Dutch women's movement," in Mary Buckley and Malcolm Anderson (eds.), *Women, Equality and Europe*. London: Macmillan.

Skocpol, Theda (1992) *Protecting Soldiers and Mothers: The Political Origins of Social Policy in the United States*. Cambridge: The Belknap Press of Harvard University Press.

Smeeding, Timothy M. (1984) "Is the safety net still intact?," in D. Lee Bawden (ed.), *The Social Contract Revisited*. Washington, DC: The Urban Institute Press.

Smeeding, Timothy, Torrey, Barbara Boyle, and Rein, Martin (1988) "Patterns of income and poverty: the economic status of children and the elderly in eight countries," in John L. Palmer, Timothy Smeeding and Barbara Boyle Torrey (eds.), *The Vulnerable*. Washington DC: Urban Institute.

Smeeding, Timothy M., Rainwater, Lee, Rein, Martin, Hauser, Richard and Schaber, Gaston (1990) "Income poverty in seven countries: initial estimates from the LIS database," in Timothy M. Smeeding, Michael O'Higgins and Lee Rainwater (eds.), *Poverty, Inequality and Income Distribution in Comparative Perspective*. New York: Harvester Wheatsheaf.

Smith, Joan (1984) "The paradox of women's poverty: wage-earning women and economic transformation," *Signs*, 10 (2), 291–310.

Smith, Ralph E. (1979) (ed.) *The Subtle Revolution: Women at Work*. Washington, DC: The Urban Institute Press.

Social Security Handbook (1966) Washington, DC: Social Security Administration.

Social Trends (various years). London: HMSO.

Söderström, Lars (1988) "The redistributive effects of social protection in Sweden," in Jean-Pierre Jallade (ed.), *The Crisis of Redistribution in European Welfare States*. Stoke-on-Trent: Trentham Books.

Sørensen, Annemette and McLanahan, Sara (1987) "Married women's economic dependency, 1940–1980," *American Journal of Sociology*, 93, 659–87.

SOS (1953) *Folkpensioneringen m.m. åren 1939–1950*. Stockholm: Central Bureau of Statistics.

(1964) *Folkpensioneringen m.m. åren 1951–1962*. Stockholm: Central Bureau of Statistics.

(1993) *Socialförsäkring 1989 och 1990* (SOS). Stockholm: National Social Insurance Board.

(1995) *Socialbidrag 1994*, Statistik – socialtjänst 1995: 6. Stockholm: National Board of Health and Welfare.

SOU (1964: 25) *Nytt skattesystem*. Stockholm: Ministry of Finance.

(1995: 26) *Underhållsbidrag och bidragförskott, Del A*. Stockholm: Ministry of Social Affairs.

SSB (various years) *Social Security Bulletin*. Washington, DC: US Department of Health and Human Services.

(Various years) *Social Security Bulletin, Annual Statistical Supplement*. Washington, DC: US Department of Health and Human Services.

(1985) "Women and social security," *Social Security Bulletin*, 48 (2), 17–26.

Ståhlberg, Ann-Charlotte (1988) "Lifetime redistribution of social insurance in Sweden," *Meddelande 3/1988*. Stockholm: Swedish Institute for Social Research.

(1993) *Våra pensionssystem*. Stockholm: SNS Förlag.

(1994) "Kvinnors ATP och avtalspensioner," *SOU 1994: 20, Reformerat pensionsystem, Bilaga B*. Stockholm: Ministry of Social Affairs.

(1995) "The Swedish pension system: past, present and future," in Edward Brunsdon and Margaret May (eds.), *Swedish Welfare: Policy and Provision*. No place of publication: Social Policy Association.

Statistical Abstract of the United States (Various Years) Washington, DC: Bureau of the Census.

Statistical Yearbook of the Netherlands (Various years) 's-Gravenhage: Staatsuitgeverij / Central Bureau of Statistics.

Statistisch jaarboek (1992) 's-Gravenhage: Central Bureau of Statistics.

Statistisch zakboek (1984, 1988) 's-Gravenhage: Central Bureau of Statistics.

Statistisk årsbok (Various years) Stockholm: Central Bureau of Statistics.

Stephens, John D., Huber, Evelyne and Ray, Leonard (1995) "The welfare state in hard times," paper presented at the conference on the "Politics and Political Economy of Contemporary Capitalism," Humboldt University and WZB, Berlin, 26–7 May.

Steuerle, C. Eugene and Bakija, Jon M. (1994) *Retooling Social Security for the 21st Century. Right and Wrong Approaches to Reform*. Washington, DC: The Urban Institute Press.

Stevens, Beth (1988) "Blurring the boundaries: how the federal government has influenced welfare benefits in the private sector," in Margaret Weir, Ann Shola Orloff and Theda Skocpol (eds.), *The Politics of Social Policy in the United States*. Princeton: Princeton University Press.

Stoesz, David and Karger, Howard (1992) *Reconstructing the American Welfare State*. Lanham: Rowman and Littlefield.

SVR [Social Insurance Council] (1994) *Kroniek van de sociale verzekeringen*. Zoetermeer: Social Insurance Council.

SZW [Ministry of Social Affairs and Employment] (1982. 1990) *Social Security in the Netherlands*. The Hague: Ministry of Social Affairs and Employment.

(1995) Info. A Short Survey of Social Security in the Netherlands. The Hague: Ministry of Social Affairs and Employment. (Information sheet).

Therborn, Göran (1989) "'Pillarization' and 'popular movements': two variants of welfare state capitalism: the Netherlands and Sweden," in Francis G. Castles (ed.), *The Comparative History of Public Policy*. Cambridge: Polity Press.

Therborn, Göran and Roebroek, Joop (1986) "The irreversible welfare state," *International Journal of Health Services*, 16, 319–38.

Thompson, Gayle B. (1980) "Economic status of late middle-aged widows," in Nancy Datan and Nancy Lohmann (eds.), *Transitions of Aging*. New York: Academic Press.

Tilly, Chris (1991) "Continuing growth of part-time employment," *Monthly Labor Review*, 114, 10–18.

Tingsten, Herbert (1973) *The Swedish Social Democrats*. Totowa, NJ: Bedminster Press.

Titmuss, Richard (1974) *Social Policy*. London: George Allen and Unwin.

Ungerson, Clare.(ed.) (1985) *Women and Social Policy: A Reader*. London: Macmillan.

UN (United Nations) (1959) *Tax Legislation Applicable to Women*. United Nations Economic and Social Council, Commission on the Status of Women. (UN Doc. No. E/CN.6/344).

USDL (Various years) *Employment and Earnings*. Washington, DC: US Department of Labor, Bureau of Statistics.

(1994) *1993 Handbook on Women Workers: Trends and Issues*. Washington, DC: US Department of Labor, Women's Bureau.

Uusitalo, Hannu (1984) "Comparative research on the determinants of welfare states," *European Journal of Political Research*, 12, 403–22.

van Amelsvoort, A. A. M. (1984) "The Netherlands: minimum wage and unemployment policies," in Robert Walker, Roger Lawson and Peter Townsend (eds.), *Responses to Poverty: Lessons from Europe*. London: Heinemann Educational Books.

van der Burg, Brigitte, Plantenga, Janneke and van Velzen, Susan (1992) *Occupational Segregation in the Netherlands*, External report commissioned by and presented to the European Commission. Utrecht: Economic Institute/CIAV.

Walker, Alan (1987) "The poor relation: poverty among old women," in Caroline Glendinning and Jane Millar (eds.), *Women and Poverty in Britain*. Brighton: Wheatsheaf.

Wallerstein, Michael (1989) "Union organization in advanced industrial democracies," *American Political Science Review*, 83, 481–501.

Webb, Steven (1994) "Social insurance and poverty alleviation," in Sally Baldwin and Jane Falkingham (eds.), *Social Security and Social Change: New Challenges to the Beveridge Model*. New York: Harvester Wheatsheaf.

Wennemo, Irene (1994) *Sharing the Costs of Children: Studies in the Development of Family Support in the OECD Countries*, Swedish Institute for Social Research, 25. Stockholm.

Wiebrens, Casper (1988) "The Netherlands," in Alfred J. Kahn and Sheila B. Kamerman (eds.), *Child Support: From Debt Collection to Social Policy*. Newbury Park: Sage.

Wilensky, Harold (1975) *The Welfare State and Equality*. Berkeley: University of California Press.

(1976) *The New Corporatism, Centralization, and the Welfare State*. Beverley Hills: Sage Professional Papers.

(1982) "Leftism, catholicism and democratic corporatism: the role of parties in recent welfare state development," in P. Flora and H. Heidenheimer (eds.), *The Development of Welfare States in Europe and North America*. New Brunswick, NJ: Transaction Books.

Wilensky, Harold and Lebeaux, Charles N. (1958) *Industrial Society and Social Welfare*. New York: The Free Press.

Wilkinson, Margaret (1982) "The discriminatory system of personal taxation," *Journal of Social Policy*, 11, 307–34.

Wilson, Elizabeth (1977) *Women and the Welfare State*. London: Tavistock.

Woods, John R. (1988) "Retirement-age women and pensions: findings from the new beneficiary survey," *Social Security Bulletin*, 51 (12), 5–16.

(1989) "Pension coverage among private wage and salary workers: preliminary findings from the 1988 Survey of Employee Benefits," *Social Security Bulletin*, 52 (10), 2–19.

(1993) "Pension vesting and preretirement lump sums among full-time private sector employees," *Social Security Bulletin*, 56 (3), 3–21.

Zarf, Wolfgang (1986) "Development, structure and prospects of the German social state," in Richard Rose and Rei Shiratori (eds.), *The Welfare State East and West*. New York: Oxford University Press.

Index